ABIGAIL ADAMS

Witness to a Revolution

Books by Natalie S. Bober

A Restless Spirit
The Story of Robert Frost

Breaking Tradition
The Story of Louise Nevelson

Thomas Jefferson
Man on a Mountain

Abigail Adams
Witness to a Revolution

ABIGAIL ADAMS
Witness to a Revolution

Natalie S. Bober

Aladdin Paperbacks

PHOTO CREDITS: Massachusetts Historical Society, title page, 2, 5, 6 (lower), 13, 32, 40, 43, 72, 112, 131, 141, 174, 175; L. H. Bober, 6 (upper), 7, 8, 25 (lower), 26, 45, 110, 159, 207; Boston Medical Library in the Francis A. Countway Library of Medicine, Boston, 12; National Park Service, Adams National Historical Site, 25 (upper), 57, 91, 148, 149, 156, 184, 189, 196, 206, 220; Colonial Williamsburg Foundation, 27; Museum of Fine Arts, Boston, 36 (City of Boston), 46 (Bequest of Winslow Warren), 58 (Gift of Joseph W., William B., and Edward H. R. Revere), 132, 183 (Bequest of Charles Francis Adams); Washington-Custis-Lee Collection, Washington and Lee University, 63; National Archives, 76, 79, 172; Boston Athenaeum, 77; Private Collector, 93 (Photograph, Child's Gallery, Boston); Metropolitan Museum of Art, 100, 178; Massachusetts Art Commission, 103; Harvard University Portrait Collection, Harvard University, 126 (Bequest of Ward Nicholas Boylston); Yale University Art Gallery, 138; New York State Historical Association, Cooperstown, 144; NYPL Picture Collection, 159; National Gallery of Art, Washington, 195; Library of Congress, 199; White House Historical Association, 200

———

First Aladdin Paperbacks edition February 1998.

Text copyright © 1995 by Natalie S. Bober

Aladdin Paperbacks
An imprint of Simon & Schuster Children's Publishing Division
1230 Avenue of the Americas
New York, NY 10020

Designed by Anne Scatto/PIXEL PRESS
The text for this book was set in Caslon Old Face
Printed and bound in the United States of America

12 14 16 18 20 19 17 15 13 11

The Library of Congress has cataloged the hardcover edition as follows:
Bober, Natalie
Abigail Adams: witness to a revolution / by Natalie S. Bober.
p.   cm
Includes bibliographical references (p. 239) and index.
ISBN 0-689-81916-1 ISBN 978-0-689-81916-2
1. Adams, Abigail, 1744-1818—Juvenile literature. 2. Presidents' spouses—
United States—Biography—Juvenile literature. 3. Women—Biography.
[1. Adams, Abigail, 1744-1818. 2. First ladies]. I. Title
E322.1.A38B63   1994
973.4'4'092—dc20
[B]
94-19259
CIP
AC

FRONTISPIECE: *Weymouth Parsonage*

For My Dearest Friend,

Our Children,

and Theirs

Contents

Contents

Foreword

Abigail Adams is often referred to as the wife of one president and the mother of another. Rarely is she described as a woman in her own right. But it just may be, as later members of the Adams family claimed, that it was John Adams's choice of Abigail Smith for his wife that was a major factor in launching him on his memorable career. And it is certain that it was Abigail's early—and continuing—influence that made it possible for her oldest son, John Quincy Adams, to become our sixth president.

Indeed, her primary focus and concerns were in her role as wife and mother. But Abigail Adams's life deserves exploration for more than this. She lives in history because of her extraordinary letters to her family and to her friends.

More than two thousand letters survive as a written legacy to us because family members recognized their importance and ignored her pleas to burn them. Abigail's letters are her biography, and it is through them that we come to understand her unique character as well as her remarkable intellect, her sense of humor, her independent spirit, and her flair for the English language. It is the spontaneity of her expression that opens a wide window for us on a crucial period in our nation's history, and brings Abigail Adams and her time to life.

I have attempted to tell her story through these letters, in the hope that readers will be able to get inside her head and her heart, to see and feel and think as she did, to experience with her the heartache, the loneliness, the joys.

Witness to the divided loyalties of the colonists and to the gathering storm of the revolutionary war, even the actual Battle of Bunker Hill and its devastating toll of lives, she was able to give a poignant report of the American Revolution and to document the times—and the people—who played a vital role in the birth of our nation.

As she artlessly mingled the momentous with the intimate—the hostilities in Boston with the need for pins from Philadelphia because none were to be had in Massachusetts; the state of the crops on their farm with the labor pains she was at that moment experiencing; sharp comments on politicians with the chatter of her children—she documented what it was like to live at a time when education was not available to young women, and when pregnancy and childbirth meant the fear of death, as did inoculation against smallpox and many of the common diseases of childhood. Women were called upon to make life-and-death decisions for their children, to educate their daughters, and to run their farms when their husbands were away for months, or sometimes years, at a time. Yet they had, at best, second-class legal and political status.

Faced with the unfamiliar task of providing financially for her children while her husband was in Europe for over four years, Abigail used her imagination and discovered talents she hadn't realized she possessed to accomplish her goal. John's unique talent, she believed, was essential for the survival of the nation, so she accepted his abandonment of family life as his patriotic duty. Her resulting situation became, for her, simply the patriotic sacrifice that she, as a woman, could make for her country.

She did the best job she could, but when she was overwhelmed, she wasn't above telling her husband, "I want you for my Protector." Often on lonely nights, in the silence of the cold, dark house, she used her pen as her emotional outlet, pouring out her fears as well as her passionate love for him.

Eighteenth-century women had a view of their role in society that was very different from what we have today. Uppermost in women's minds was the very fact of their feminine identity. Femininity consisted of delicacy, modesty, softness. This was central to their self-concept. It shaped their lives.

Abigail Adams must be viewed as a woman of her times, and in her own context. She spoke out strongly for education for women and for legal status equal to that of men, but she valued the domestic role as the greatest in her life. For her, a woman who spoke with wisdom was not "inconsistent" with one who "cheerfully" tended to her household.

We must be careful not to judge Abigail in terms of today. We must not look at the eighteenth century through a lens ground in the 1990s. That

Abigail achieved the fullest equality permitted by her society is a remarkable tribute to her understanding of the possibilities as well as the limits of her place as a woman in a man's world.

Abigail Adams had a strong sense of the different roles of the sexes in a marriage, but she had an equally strong belief in marriage as a partnership. Her story must, of necessity, deal with her extraordinary relationship with her husband, a husband driven by a need for fame and a profound anxiety for his future, who was her "partner," her lover, her "Dearest Friend" for over fifty-four years of marriage.

Acknowledgments

To research and write a life requires that we explore many avenues. As the biographer searches for documents that give texture to a life, and strives to find the details that give the past a pulse, she needs the cooperation of many people.

As I journeyed back to the eighteenth century in my quest for Abigail Adams, those dedicated librarians and curators whom I met along the way made my task easier and more enjoyable.

I thank particularly Hope Paterson, who graciously opened the Weymouth Parsonage for us, allowed my husband the freedom to photograph, and spoke lovingly of the young Abigail who had grown up there.

David F. Kratz, Agnes Smith, and Jean Dumas, at the Adams National Historic Site, generously shared information, anecdotes and photographs that brought Abigail Adams and her family to life for me. It was Agnes Smith who showed me Abigail's carefully preserved gown which proved conclusively that she was petite.

Celeste Walker, editor of *The Adams Papers*, granted me permission to quote extensively from the letters; and Anne M. Decker painstakingly sought out and verified citations for me.

Virginia H. Smith, Reference Librarian at the Massachusetts Historical Society, kindly checked all citations in letters held by the society. Chris Steele, Curator of Photographs there, made available the society's collection. Judith Michelman, at Harvard University Press, granted permission to quote from the published sources.

Thomas Knoles, Curator of Manuscripts at the American Antiquarian Society, allowed me to read—and quote from—the actual letters of

Abigail to her sister Mary, letters that opened wide a window on a particular time in her life. And at the New York Historical Society, I saw letters in Abigail's own hand written to her uncle Cotton Tufts, that made her request for a "sley for to go to market in winter" all the more poignant.

To the many unsung curators to whom I appealed for photographs and the permission to reproduce them, I offer my thanks. I must particularly mention Susan Greendyke Lachevre, who went to great trouble to have a fine photo made for me of the mural in the Boston State House.

I acknowledge a debt, also, to biographers past and present who have probed the lives of members of the Adams family, and to the many fine chroniclers of the time in which Abigail Adams lived. Their books helped me to understand the forces that shaped her life, and what it meant to be a woman in the eighteenth century.

The librarians at the White Plains Library were most helpful in locating and obtaining a wealth of hard-to-find books. Their efforts spared me untold hours of travel and search.

Jennifer Horowitz offered invaluable help with the mammoth tasks of reference notes and photo searches, making a tedious job more pleasant.

My friend and editor these many years, Marcia Marshall, once again offered encouragement, wisdom, and the astute editorial eye that made this a better book. My son-in-law, Paul Polivy, patiently helped me discover the many new wonders of the computer.

My young friend Jesse Ehrich Freedman read an early draft of the manuscript and made fine suggestions for pictures.

My three granddaughters, Jody and Melanie Lukens-Bober, and Joelle Bober Polivy, have reached the ages where each can read and critique my writing from her own perspective. For their many thoughtful suggestions, and for the joy of sharing, I thank them.

To my son Stephen, who knew before I did that I would write a biography of Abigail Adams, who helped me hone my storytelling skills and, most important, kept me firmly rooted in the eighteenth century, my gratitude and my love.

As always, my husband Larry's patience and understanding seemed inexhaustible. His critical reading of the manuscript at every stage along the way, his extraordinary photographs, and his willingness to undertake any task that would allow me the freedom to write doubles the joy. He makes it all possible. He has ever been, as John was to Abigail, my dearest friend.

Chronology

1744: *November 11*	Abigail Smith born at Weymouth, Mass.
1759:	Abigail Smith meets John Adams.
1760: *March 25*	George III becomes king of England. Writs of Assistance reintroduced.
1761:	John Adams begins courtship of Abigail Smith.
1764: *October 25*	Abigail Smith marries John Adams.
1765: *January*	Stamp Act passed by Parliament.
July 14	Abigail Adams (Nabby) born.
1766:	Stamp Act repealed.
1767: *June 15–July 2*	Townsend Acts passed in Parliament.
July 11	John Quincy Adams born.
1768: *December 28*	Susanna Adams born.
1770: *February 4*	Susanna Adams dies.
March 5	Boston Massacre occurs.
May 29	Charles Adams born.
1772: *September 15*	Thomas Boylston Adams born.
1773: *May 10*	Tea Act passed.
Summer	Abigail begins correspondence and friendship with Mercy Otis Warren.
December 16	Boston Tea Party.

1774:	*March 31*	Parliament passes Boston Port Act in retaliation for Boston Tea Party—to be enacted June 1.
	June	John is elected a delegate to the First Continental Congress.
	September 5	First Continental Congress assembles in Philadelphia.
1775:	*April 19*	Battle of Lexington and Concord begins revolutionary war.
	June 17	Battle of Bunker Hill takes place.
	June 22	Second Continental Congress meets.
	October 1	Abigail's mother, Elizabeth Smith, dies.
1776:	*March 17*	Boston is liberated.
	March 31	Abigail writes letter to John asking him to "Remember the Ladies."
	June	Abigail takes her family to Boston to be inoculated against smallpox.
	July 4	Colonies sign Declaration of Independence.
1777:	*July 11*	Abigail gives birth to stillborn baby, whom she names Elizabeth.
1778:	*February*	John and John Quincy sail for Europe.
	Summer	Abigail's two-year-old niece Louisa Smith comes to live with her.
1779:	*August*	John and John Quincy return from France. John begins work on Massachusetts Constitution.
	October	John is unanimously elected minister plenipotentiary to France.
	November 15	John, John Quincy, and Charles sail to Europe.
1781:	*July*	John Quincy leaves for St. Petersburg, Russia.
	October 19	General Cornwallis surrenders at Yorktown.
1782:	*January*	Charles arrives home from Europe.
	April	John achieves Dutch recognition of American independence.
1783:	*September*	Abigail's father, Reverend William Smith, dies.

⌒ Chronology ⌒

1784:	*June 20*	Abigail and Nabby sail for Europe.
	July 21	Abigail and Nabby enter London.
	July 30	Abigail and Nabby are reunited with John Quincy.
	August 7	Abigail and Nabby are reunited with John after almost five years.
	August 8	The family sets out for Paris. Abigail begins friendship with Thomas Jefferson.
1785:	*February*	John Adams is appointed first American ambassador to the Court of St. James.
	May 12	John Quincy sails home from France.
1785–1787:		The Adamses reside in London.
1786:	*June 12*	Nabby Adams marries Col. William S. Smith.
	November	Shays's Rebellion takes place in Massachusetts.
1787:	*April*	Nabby gives birth to a son and Abigail becomes a grandmother.
	Summer	John Quincy graduates from Harvard. Constitutional Convention meets.
1788:	*April 20*	The Adamses sail for home.
	June 17	John and Abigail arrive in Boston to hero's welcome.
1789:	*April 12*	John Adams is notified officially that he has been elected vice-president.
	April 30	George Washington is inaugurated as first president of the United States.
	July 14	The French Revolution begins.
1791:		A two-party system emerges: Federalists and Republicans.
1792:	*February*	Braintree is renamed Quincy in honor of Abigail's grandfather, John Quincy.
	December	George Washington and John Adams are reelected.
1794:	*May*	John Quincy is appointed minister to the Netherlands. His brother Thomas accompanies him as his secretary.
1795:	*August*	Charles marries Sally Smith, sister of Col. William Smith.

⌒ Chronology ⌒

1797:	*February 8*	John Adams elected second president of the United States. Abigail becomes "First Lady." Thomas Jefferson becomes vice-president.
	April	John's mother, Susanna Boylston Adams, dies.
	July 26	John Quincy marries Louisa Catherine Johnson in London.
1798:	*June 18–July 14*	Alien and Sedition Acts passed.
1799:	*December 14*	George Washington dies.
1800:		Washington, D.C. becomes nation's capital.
	November 30	Charles Adams dies.
1801:	*February 17*	Congress elects Thomas Jefferson president of the United States. The Adamses return to Quincy.
	September 4	John Quincy, Louisa, and their five-month-old son George return from Europe.
1805:	*Summer*	Thomas marries Ann (Nancy) Harrod.
1809:		John Quincy is named ambassador to Russia by newly elected president James Madison.
1811:	*Summer*	Nabby discovers cancerous tumor in her breast.
	October	Nabby has a mastectomy in her parents' home.
	October 16	Mary's husband, Richard Cranch, dies.
	October 17	Abigail's sister, Mary Cranch, dies.
1812:		War with England breaks out.
1813:		Nabby Adams Smith dies of cancer.
1814:	*December 24*	John Quincy signs Treaty of Ghent, ending war with England.
1815:	*April 10*	Abigail's sister, Elizabeth Shaw Peabody, dies suddenly.
1817:	*August 6*	John Quincy and his family return to America. John Quincy is named secretary of state by President James Monroe.
1818:	*October 28*	Abigail Adams dies.

The Quincy-Smith Family

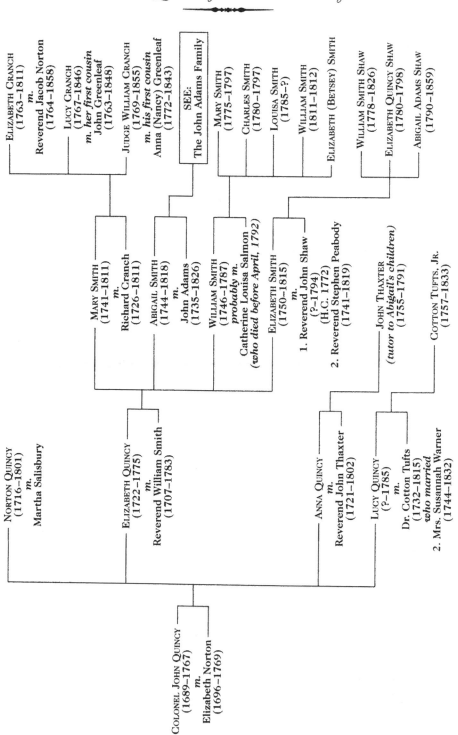

The John Adams Family

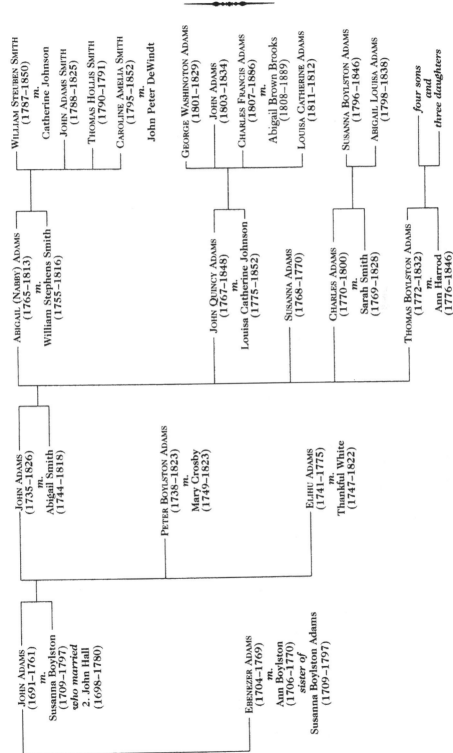

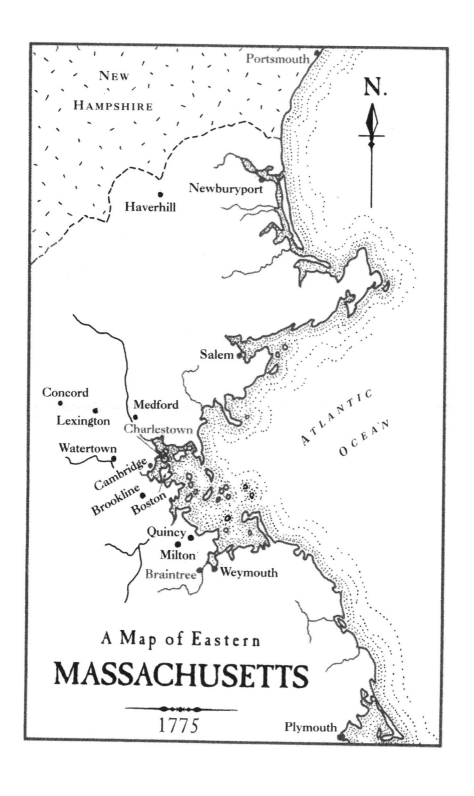

N.

NEW HAMPSHIRE

Portsmouth

Haverhill

Newburyport

Salem

Concord

Medford

Lexington

Charlestown

Watertown

Cambridge

Brookline

Boston

Quincy

Milton

Braintree

Weymouth

ATLANTIC OCEAN

A Map of Eastern

MASSACHUSETTS

1775

Plymouth

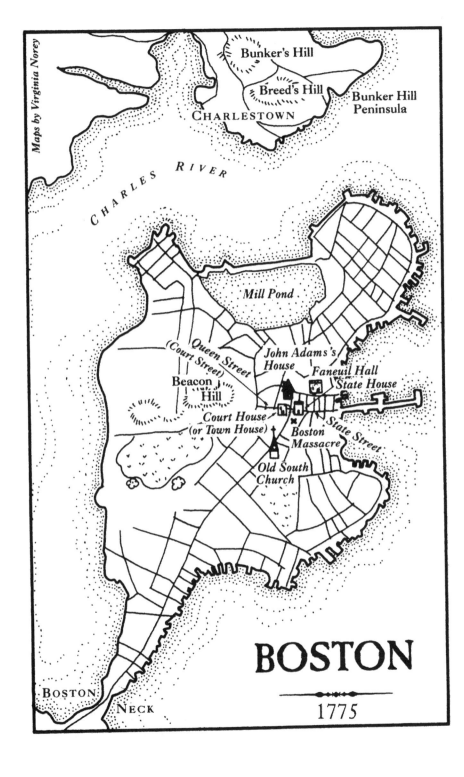

Maps by Virginia Norey

Bunker's Hill

Breed's Hill

Bunker Hill
Peninsula

CHARLESTOWN

CHARLES RIVER

Mill Pond

Queen Street
(Court Street)

John Adams's
House

Faneuil Hall
State House

Beacon
Hill

Court House
(or Town House)

Boston
Massacre

State Street

Old South
Church

BOSTON

BOSTON
NECK

1775

"Is there a dearer name than FRIEND? Think of it for me."

AA TO JA, OCTOBER 25, 1782

ABIGAIL ADAMS

Witness to a Revolution

Mount Wollaston, the estate of Abigail's maternal grandmother.
Watercolor by Eliza Susan Quincy, a young relative of Abigail's, in 1822.

~ CHAPTER I ~
"a very incorrect writer"

Abigail watched as her grandmother poured tea from the graceful porcelain teapot. How she loved to be in this great house, called Mount Wollaston, situated high on a hill in the town of Braintree, and looking out on a vast expanse of ocean. She had a precious bond with this grandmother who seemed to the young girl to transform everything she touched from the ordinary to the special. Abigail sensed that Elizabeth Quincy was proud of her granddaughter's quick mind. She never complained about her being too bookish, as Abigail's mother often did.

Abby was a small, frail child—with fair skin, dark hair, and wide, penetrating black eyes—who dearly loved to read. But she had a stubborn streak that dismayed her mother. Grandmother Quincy said she found Abby's high spirits refreshing, even if she was sometimes hard to manage. "Wild colts make the best horses," Abigail had heard her say to her mother.[1]

Elizabeth Quincy had a lively and cheerful disposition, and was always bubbling with the latest news, gossip, and practical suggestions for peaceful living. Abigail thought Grandmother must surely be a very wise lady.

Abigail also loved tall, white-haired Grandfather Quincy, and treasured the time she could spend with him in his great library. It ran the full length of the house and overlooked Boston Bay. There were wonderful books there. She would be able to read them when she was a little bit older, he promised.

In fact, it didn't really bother her that she was often plagued by illness and unable to play outdoors with her two sisters. Whatever disease was about Abby seemed to catch, and more seriously than Mary and Betsy. But if she could recuperate at Mount Wollaston she didn't mind so much. She knew Grandmother would read stories to her or spin her own wonderful tales.

3

One of Abby's favorites was about their ancestor who had traveled from Normandy with William the Conqueror to help rescue Great Britain in 1066. And it delighted her to learn that a Quincy had been one of the signers of the Magna Carta.* Grandfather even showed her the parchment document attesting to this. Abigail thought Grandmother Quincy was a wonderful teacher. She liked the way she mixed instruction and amusement, and she hoped she could grow up to be just like her.

Abigail Smith had been born on November 11, 1744,† to Elizabeth Quincy Smith and William Smith, in the little seaport town of Weymouth, Massachusetts, ten miles south of Boston. The road to Boston from Weymouth was little more than an ancient Indian path that led north through the neighboring town of Braintree, with dangerous crossings at the brooks and rivers along the way. People traveled on foot or by horse or chaise, a sort of chair on wheels pulled by a horse.

Weymouth had been the first community established in the Massachusetts Bay Colony, an offshoot of the original New England settlement at Plymouth. Now, with a population of about two thousand, it was a beautiful rural town with an abundance of trees, rising hills, and clear running streams. The smell of salt water was always in the air, for Weymouth faced the sea.

The people of Weymouth were mostly farmers, quiet people who valued tradition and were deeply religious. Religion was an ingrained part of their existence, but not a subject for discussion. It was personal and private. Abigail's father was their minister.

Parson Smith was a warmhearted, patient, and gentle man, beloved by his parishioners. He was part of a small minority of ministers at that time who had a college degree. William Smith had attended Harvard College in Cambridge, near Boston, and his love of books was legendary. He passed this love on to his three daughters.

The Weymouth Parsonage, where Mary, Abigail, Betsy, and their brother William were growing up, was a large, rambling house, a mixture of old and new. As their family expanded, and the Smiths outgrew the original tiny house, they built an L-shaped larger addition. The house sat

---

* The great charter of English political and civil liberties granted by King John at Runnymede on June 15, 1215.

† When the Julian calendar was replaced by the Gregorian in 1752, a correction of eleven days was made, and Abigail's birthday became November 22.

Parsonage in Weymouth where Abigail Smith was born. It was later the setting for her courtship by John Adams. Ink and watercolor drawing. Artist unknown.

on the crest of a low hill, with a fine view of the surrounding farmlands and, in the distance, Weymouth's deeply indented coastline.

Inside, the house had an air of warmth and hospitality. Members of Parson Smith's congregation were always welcome, as were many young people, who were encouraged to browse through the books in his fine library. There was frequently a lively and literate group of relatives and friends gathered around his fireside.

Often the three sisters—Mary, fourteen, Abigail, ten, and Betsy, just five—would huddle at the edge of the room, out of the fire's light, listening to their parents and guests discussing the public questions of the times. Nine-year-old Billy was not interested. It was the year 1755, and the French and Indian War, that final contest for control of the North American continent between Great Britain and France, had recently begun. The girls were eager gatherers of all the news. They particularly enjoyed hearing talk of the bravery of a tall, ambitious young man named George Washington. The governor of Virginia had placed him in command of a group of militiamen, citizen soldiers, to fight the French in the Ohio Valley. These overheard conversations inspired Mary and Abigail to read the foreign news and the debates of the British Parliament in the newspapers that arrived each week. Mrs. Smith seemed unaware of her daughters' interest.

Their father did encourage their love of books, and taught them to read and write. But their mother would not hear of their going to school, despite

The parlor of the Weymouth Parsonage
～

pleas to be allowed to attend the local Dame school.* She feared for their health, particularly Abigail's. It was not unusual then for parents to be concerned about the health of their children, for the rate of infant mortality was high in the eighteenth century. Diphtheria, smallpox, whooping cough, and measles were great killers. In 1751 eleven children had died of diphtheria in Weymouth in one week.

Elizabeth Smith was the perfect minister's wife, providing work for poor neighbors and caring for the sick. She refused to meddle in any petty quarrels in the parish, and treated everyone with equal kindness. She taught her daughters to do the same. And she taught them the importance of family affection and compassion. "We should never wait to be requested to do a kind office, an act of love," she told them. Abby often accompanied her when she visited the sick or brought food or firewood to a needy family.

The girls learned from her to accept whatever life brought them. And they learned that marriage and motherhood were the chief functions of every adult female. Despite the fact that there were servants in the household, the girls

* Dame schools, popular at this time, were so called because they were taught by women, or dames.

Abigail's father, the Reverend William Smith, graduated from Harvard College in 1725. He told Abigail that her fine mind was a priceless gift from God. By Daniel Munro Wilson, from "The Chappel of Ease," based on a lost portrait by John Singleton Copley.
～

were taught to help with domestic chores. Mrs. Smith was preparing her daughters for the woman's role decreed by tradition. Yet they grew to be fun-loving girls who were often conspirators against their mother's overprotectiveness. And they were always good friends.

Abby loved best the times that she sat with her father in the warmth of the crackling fire, his large, warm, dark eyes, so much like her own, shining down at her as he read to her from the works of Shakespeare, Dryden, or Pope. When she begged him to convince her mother to allow her to go to school, he gently reminded her of the three great libraries in their family: his, Grandfather Quincy's, and Uncle Isaac Smith's. She could make use of all of them, he told her. He encouraged her to enrich and cultivate her fine, inquisitive mind, explaining that it was a priceless gift from God.

The library at Weymouth Parsonage

～

Parson Smith urged his daughters to speak harshly of no one, to stress the "handsome" aspects of an individual, and then to switch the conversation to "Things rather than Persons."[2] Although he was a minister, he often labored in the fields, planting corn and potatoes, sowing barley, gathering hay, and tending his sheep. Now that his middle daughter had turned ten, he gave her a lamb of her own as a pet. Abby was delighted, and from then on she would watch over their flock of sheep "like an old Devon sheepman." She loved to help her father at lambing time, in spite of her mother's objections that a young lady belonged in the parlor, not in the barn. Abigail thought she could be in both places and still be a lady.

She saw nothing wrong with shelling peas with her own hands for a dinner to be served on a table set with fine linen and silver. Years later she told a granddaughter that she liked being "wild and giddy," and enjoyed it when a neighbor warned her that she would make either a very bad or a very good woman.[3] Mary, on the other hand, was the quiet child, often tending her younger siblings while her mother cared for the community. Years later Abigail remembered that "a thread would govern one, a cable would be necessary for the other."[4] Betsy was the romantic in the family. Growing up with two older sisters who provided her with opportunities for learning from them and their friends, she developed a keen mind, an appealing personality, and a strong will.

As Abigail grew to be a teenager, she was given permission to visit at her aunt Elizabeth and uncle Isaac Smith's home in Boston. Isaac Smith was a wealthy merchant and shipowner. It was in his handsome house that Abigail finally found friends outside her immediate family circle. Here, without her parents or siblings, she began to feel a sense of independence. Her aunt Elizabeth allowed her more freedom than did her mother, all the while communicating to Abigail that she was a favored niece. Her cousin Isaac, Jr., five years younger than she but already preparing for Harvard, shared books and ideas with her. She became friendly with several girls who were about her own age, and she met numerous young men, although none appealed to her.

Abigail found life in Boston very different from life in Weymouth or Braintree. Boston was larger (it was New England's largest town), noisier, dirtier, and more crowded. But it provided constant entertainment—and it was always exciting. The pace of life was faster, too, and the style of living more formal. Almost completely surrounded by the sea, Boston was one of the busiest ports in the British Empire. Its wealth came from overseas trade, and everyone was dependent on the success or failure of its fine ships.

Abigail and her friends loved to browse in the shops to see the latest fashions just arrived from London, or get lost in the maze of narrow, crooked streets paved with cobblestones that had been brought there as ballast on the ships. Sometimes Uncle Isaac took them into his dimly lit

The kitchen in the Weymouth Parsonage

∽

warehouse, where the smells of coffee and wine from Madeira mingled with those of sugar and spices from the West Indies and tea from the Far East.

Often the girls would wander down to the harbor to watch the ships coming in, their tall masts and white sails silhouetted against the bright blue New England sky, with the British Union Jack billowing in the breeze. As a special treat, Uncle Isaac occasionally arranged for them to be taken in a dinghy to one of his ships anchored in the harbor. They loved to peer out the portholes from its dark cabin at the gently rolling tide. They couldn't know then that the tide of Boston Harbor would soon rock the British Empire.

When she returned to Weymouth from Boston, Abigail maintained a "literary correspondence" with her new friends. The young people considered these exchanges of letters an opportunity to improve their minds and polish their writing styles. Abigail had no friends her own age with whom she could talk in the tiny town of Weymouth, so she particularly loved this chance to express her thoughts in letters. It seemed to lessen her sense of isolation while she pursued her solitary studies in literature, history, and religion in her father's library. For she was intent on getting an education, in spite of her mother's feelings on the subject.

Abigail's keen mind, and her ability to express ideas poetically, shine through all her letters. But she was painfully aware that her letters lacked polish. Her writing, she knew, bore the scar of her mother's unwillingness to allow her to have a formal education. She worried about her handwriting, her spelling, and her "pointing" (punctuation), and apologized to her friends for being a "very incorrect writer." She hoped she wouldn't be thought stupid.[5]

While she and her friends liked to consider their correspondence "literary," they were also simply pursuing friendship. The girls shared confidences and discussed their interests. They indulged in flights of imagination by adopting classical pen names in the manner of the times. Abigail became Diana, Roman goddess of the moon.

In the eighteenth century letter writing was a literary art. Abigail thought the novelist Samuel Richardson was the greatest teacher of this art. She loved his books, and read them avidly. *Pamela* and *Clarissa Harlowe* had been published when she was a little girl, and now, just as she was entering her teens, Richardson's seven-volume series, *Sir Charles Grandison*, began to appear. She read them all, eagerly awaiting each new one.

In his stories Richardson dealt with questions that were on the minds of many literate and sensitive young women of the eighteenth century:

personal identity, duty to family and society, sexuality, marriage, and the role of the educated woman. He wrote his novels as a series of letters designed to teach his readers the art of letter writing as well as the art of living. The goal of female education, he said, was to prepare young women to be better wives and mothers.

All the characters in Richardson's books were concerned with questions of conscience. His hero, Sir Charles Grandison, was a "perfect" character, a man of virtue and honor. He became for Abigail the ideal man, the standard by which she would judge all men for the rest of her life. From him she learned that marriage to the right man, one who would respect her accomplishments, could provide her with the sheltered environment necessary to protect her virtue and realize her full potential. Abigail and her sisters understood that their future depended on choosing the right mates, for in marriage they lost their legal identity and were completely dependent on their husbands.

But it seemed to Abigail that she never would find the right man. As she neared her seventeenth birthday, she responded to a letter from a cousin who had just been married:

> You bid me tell *one* of my sparks* to bring me to see you. Why! I believe you think they are as plenty as herrings, when, alas! there is as great a scarcity of them as there is of justice, honesty, prudence, and many other virtues. . . . I should really rejoice to come and see you, but if I wait till I get a (what did you call 'em?) I fear you'll be blind with age.[6]

At about the same time she wrote to Isaac Jr. that knowledge was essential to happiness, and that youth was the best season in which to acquire it. "In youth the mind is like a tender twig which you may bend as you please," she explained, "but in age like a sturdy oak and hard to move."[7]

As she encouraged Isaac to continue to read and to learn, she was beginning to feel that women, too, had an important role to play in the "great theatre" of life. After all, she argued, they were the ones responsible for the care and early instruction of their children. Therefore it was essential that they be educated as well as their brothers. She pleaded to be allowed to study with the "great masters" who taught the male members of her family. That she could not would remain one of the crushing disappointments of her life.

---

* Eighteenth-century term for suitor, or boyfriend.

~ CHAPTER II ~
"Ballast is what I want"

One of the visitors to the parsonage at about the time Abby was eleven was a tall, thin, gentle man with an infectious wit, who loved to talk. His name was Richard Cranch. Now thirty years old, Cranch had come from England ten years before. He was a self-taught theologian, one who studies religion, and a student of literature. He was also a watch repairman. Most important, he loved to teach, and he infected the three sisters with his zest for life and for literature. He put the right books into their hands and taught them to love the poets as he did. He was probably the first man (other than Parson Smith and young Isaac) to take Abigail's passion for learning seriously. Abby adored him.

Each time he arrived at the parsonage she would insist that he listen to some new lines of poetry that she had memorized from Shakespeare, Milton, Pope, or Thomson. Pope, she told him, was a joy, but James Thomson was her favorite. Thomson described the world she knew and made her see it in a fresh new way. His descriptions of the first spring showers, of summer thunderstorms, and of the terrors of a wintry night showed an honest understanding and love of the details of nature. From him she learned that each season brought moments of beauty and pleasure, but also times of destruction and sadness. Years later Abigail would often quote a line of poetry to help her express a deeply felt sentiment.

Another frequent visitor to the parsonage was Abigail's cousin Cotton Tufts, a tall, lanky, rather homely looking man twelve years older than she. In 1752, at the age of twenty, he had begun to practice medicine in Weymouth. Like Richard Cranch, he was compassionate, witty, devout, and hungry for knowledge, and he became an excellent physician by the

Cotton Tufts, Abigail's uncle, was her dear friend and performed many services for her throughout his long life.

~

standards of the day. He often came to borrow books from the Smith's library, then stayed to talk. There, he met Lucy Quincy, Mrs. Smith's sister, and married her on December 2, 1755. Thus, he became both cousin and uncle to the Smith children. Abigail called him Uncle Tufts. He became particularly devoted to her, and they remained close friends for the rest of his life.

By 1761 another young man began to appear regularly at the parsonage. Richard Cranch was now openly "courting" Mary, and he came frequently, sometimes bringing with him his friend, a short, brash, arrogant, somewhat overweight young lawyer with clear blue eyes named John Adams. John, at twenty-six, nine years younger than Richard, first came simply to combine legal business with the pleasure of the half-hour ride from Braintree. But he soon felt at home in the family, enjoyed the stimulating conversation at Parson Smith's fireside, and particularly loved the opportunity granted him to borrow books.

On his first visit to the parsonage two years before, John had not been at all impressed by the Smith girls. He had just broken off a romance with the beautiful, flirtatious Hannah Quincy, a distant cousin of theirs. By comparison, Mary and Abby were "wits," he admitted, but "quite lacking in tenderness."[1] They, in turn, thought he talked too much. He was certainly not the sort of man to set a girl's heart pounding.

By now, Abigail, at seventeen, had grown into a pretty, delicate-looking teenager with a slender figure and clear, pale skin. But she had lost none of her childhood stubbornness or curiosity. She was quick-witted and direct, and often spoke her mind. She and her sisters, even eleven-year-old Betsy, were good talkers *and* good listeners, and they delighted in stimulating conversation. Although nine years younger than John, Abigail showed no deference to the rather cocksure opinions of this enthusiastic young lawyer bursting with ideas and ready to talk about everything. Too often, she commented to Mary, he spoke first and thought later. But he was able to send them into gales of laughter with his easy mimicry of local characters.

John increasingly found "business" taking him the four miles to Weymouth. As his visits became more and more frequent, Abigail slowly began to find something strangely attractive

Richard Cranch, self-taught student of religion and literature, infected the three Smith sisters with his love of life and literature. He married Abigail's elder sister, Mary.

~

about him. She began to think that in some ways they were much alike. In fact, the three men, Richard Cranch, Cotton Tufts, and John Adams, and the three sisters were forming a bond that would last until death.

Often, when John arrived, he would find Abby, dressed primly in a brown or gray dress, with her head bent low in a book. He had been brought up to think that "the principal design of a young lady from her birth to her marriage was to procure and prepare herself for a worthy companion in life."[2] Not so Abigail. John had never met a woman like her. Although at times she seemed shy, she often stood up to him, not boldly, but with a gentle strength of will that was a match for his impetuous force. And he liked her vivaciousness and her lively mind. It made her even more attractive to him. Soon he confided to his diary that the Smiths' middle daughter was "a constant feast . . . prudent, modest, delicate, soft, sensible, obliging, active."[3]

And Abigail was beginning to discover the tenderness and enthusiasm that were hiding behind John's mask of arrogance.

John Adams and Abigail Smith were falling in love.

Their courtship unfolded slowly, for John had a career to make, and they would have to be patient. In the meantime Abby learned all she could about this young man. As John related stories of his childhood to her, she came to recognize his strong sense of competitiveness. As a young boy he had whittled boats to launch on the pond, he told her, then tried to sail them farther, fly his kites higher, and roll his hoops faster along the rutted roads than his friends. He played marbles and quoits, a game similar to ringtoss, and he loved to swim in the summer and go sledding and skating in winter. His favorite sport was hunting.

From the age of ten he had had a fondness for girls, and in his early teens he seemed to attract the opposite sex. He loved to "gallant the girls," he told her. But his parents had solemnly instructed him in the proper behavior that must guide his relations with the females of Braintree, and he had heeded their advice.

When he was young, he admitted, he was not interested in books. He much preferred to run barefoot around town with his noisy pack of friends, particularly his closest friend, John Hancock, a minister's son who was a year younger than he.

John went on to tell Abigail how he had begged his father to abandon his dream of sending his oldest son to Harvard. John's younger brothers, Peter Boylston and Elihu, were never offered the opportunity for an education.

When his father asked John, "What would you be, child?" John had responded instantly, "Be a farmer."

His father would show him what it meant to be a farmer. The next morning the two set out together to get thatch. They worked all day in the hot sun, up to their knees in mud, bending and cutting and tying the thick bundles of thatch. It was tiring work, but John stuck to it, trying to match his father's pace.

That night, after dinner, as John rested his aching muscles, his father challenged him: "Well, John, are you satisfied with being a farmer?"

"Yes, Sir, I like it very well."

"Aye, but I don't like it so well," his father replied, "so you shall go to school."[4]

By the age of sixteen, the young farm boy had discovered the joy of learning, and recognized his own extraordinary capacity for plain hard work. He was ready to apply for admission to Harvard College. But he disappointed his father by allowing his religious doubts to close off the ministry as a career. When he graduated from Harvard in 1755, he taught school for a while. Soon the law began to attract him. Whenever he could, he attended court sessions, listening with fascination to the lawyers' clever verbal debates. Finally, he decided to study law.

Once he had made the decision, he drove himself relentlessly, reading books on many subjects, as well as common law, canon law, and civil law. At this time there were no law schools. Young men interested in pursuing a career in this field "read" law, usually under the direction of an established attorney. When Jeremiah Gridley, the leading lawyer in Boston, learned that John had been reading Coke's *Institutes*, the great lawbook that records some five hundred years of English law, and the new publication of Blackstone's *Analysis of the Laws of England*, he was sufficiently impressed to agree to sponsor him as a lawyer. On November 6, 1758, John Adams was admitted to the bar.

But the dignified Mr. Gridley cautioned John to "pursue the study of law rather than the gain of it."[5] He also advised the young man not to marry early. The law must be his mistress and a demanding one, he warned him. John took his advice to heart. He accepted the interesting cases rather than the lucrative ones, and he plunged into the study of the great English casebooks and the treatises written in Latin that he had to labor over sentence by sentence.

But he was frequently melancholy, and often uncertain of what it was he really wanted to do with his life. He recognized that he was a bright, passionate man, but he had an unlimited need for approval and recognition. He called himself "puffy, vain, conceited." He was content with nothing less than perfection in himself. "Ballast is what I want. I totter with every breeze. My motions are unsteady," he had written in his diary soon after he was admitted to the bar.[6]

Now, with his father's recent death (on May 25, 1761), John inherited a small house and farm and became a "man of substance." At twenty-six, with a rapidly growing law practice, he was finally free to marry. And he had made up his mind that he would marry Abigail Smith. He sensed that she would be the ballast he needed.

~ CHAPTER III ~
"You may take me"

John's law practice made it necessary for him to be away from Braintree frequently. Young lawyers "rode the circuit," going to the larger cities such as Boston or Worcester to try their cases in the courts there.

When John and Abigail could not be together they wrote letters to each other, letters full of wit and devotion, to bridge the days until they could be together again.

To John, she was "Miss Adorable," or "Miss Jemima." To her he was first, most correctly, "Mr. John Adams," then, "My friend" and "Jonathon." Later they used classical names, as Abigail did with her friends. She had already taken the name Diana. She called John "Lysander," after the great Spartan admiral known for his courage and ability. Their letters were gay, uninhibited, and full of passion, with no hint of their Puritan descent or their Calvinist upbringing.

John told her he dreamed of her charms. He talked of the two or three million kisses he had given her, then ordered her to "give [him] as many kisses and as many hours of your company after nine o'clock as he shall please to demand and charge them to my account."[1]

Abigail struggled to maintain the coy restraint her role required. But she managed to tell him plainly that she cared for him "with the tenderest affection."

"At night," she said, "I no sooner close my Eyes than some invisible Being bears me to you."[2]

Sometimes she could tease him: Had John heard that two apparitions had been seen about the Smith house, one of which resembled him?

16

"How," she wondered, had it "ever entered into the head of an apparition to assume a form like yours?"

She went on to tell him that she would accompany him on a trip to the circuit court in Worcester the following week, "provided I shall not be any encumberance to you, for I have too much pride to be a clog to anybody."[3] She did go with him, staying with friends there. When they returned, Abigail joked that the rocky, bumpy roads between Boston and Worcester were good practice for the hazards of matrimony.

Their love was growing giddy and passionate. Increasingly their meetings started with conversation, but quickly turned to lovemaking that pushed hard against the bounds of prudence. Both had so much sexual yearning, called "excessive sensibility," that they actually became ill from anxiety and anticipation as the years of courtship continued.

When a snowstorm prevented John from visiting Weymouth, he wrote to Abby that it was a "cruel but perhaps blessed storm"—"cruel for detaining me from so much friendly and social company, and perhaps blessed to you, or me or both, for keeping me *at my distance.*" He ended the letter, "Yours (all the rest is inexpressible)."[4]

He was drawn to her, he said, like steel to a magnet.

But Abigail's mother was not pleased about this attraction. She had given her blessing to the marriage of her eldest daughter to Richard Cranch on November 25, 1762. But she looked on John Adams as a struggling country lawyer whose lack of grace and polish, rude outbursts, and moody silences were not a fit match for her fragile but gifted middle daughter. She had hoped that Abigail would marry into a more "noble" family.

John Adams, Mrs. Smith complained, was descended from a relatively insignificant background. His father was a farmer who also worked as a cordwainer, making custom leather shoes during the winter months to make ends meet.

But John Adams, Sr., or Deacon John, as he was affectionately known by his Braintree neighbors, was, in fact, a pillar of his rural community. He was deacon of the North Precinct Meetinghouse, a lieutenant in the Braintree militia, and the town constable whose forceful personality and tact enabled him to collect taxes from his neighbors.

"Almost all the Business of the Town [was] managed by him for twenty years together," John wrote of his father years later.[5] The young John

Adams attended many town meetings with his father, learning much about the process of democratic government along the way.

It was at these town meetings that the young boy had first come to know Abigail's grandfather, Colonel John Quincy. As John Adams was growing up, John Quincy was the great man of the town of Braintree, its leading citizen. The older man had a strong sense of public service and of concern for the commonwealth. He had been speaker of the Massachusetts Assembly for many years, was a colonel of the militia, a member of the Governor's Council, squire of the Braintree Parish, and a negotiator of Indian treaties. In fact, the Ponkapoag Indians often tramped the twelve miles from their reservation to his home to tell him their troubles and ask for advice. Despite his greatness, John Quincy was a simple man, stern but kindly, and, above all, independent. The young John Adams tried hard to emulate him.

John Adams's grandmother, Hannah Bass, was the granddaughter of Priscilla Mullins and John Alden, who had sailed to Plymouth on the *Mayflower* in 1620. It was this grandmother, according to her grandson, to whom he owed a debt for his education. This remarkable woman, who died in 1705 at the age of thirty-eight, had been an enthusiastic reader and far more learned than most men and women of her day. A document written by her, expressing a strong plea for learning, was the reason, John felt, his father had insisted that his eldest son attend Harvard.

John's mother, Susanna, was descended from the Boylstons of Brookline, one of the colony's most vigorous and successful families. Several of the Boylston men were known and respected for their contributions to medical science. Susanna's lively disposition and fine mind made her always an inspiring companion. It was she who taught John to prize reading, setting an example for him by reading every book and newspaper that came to hand. She and Abigail would become good friends.

But Elizabeth Smith was not impressed. She was painfully aware that eyebrows in Braintree and Weymouth were being raised because a young woman of Abigail's lineage had accepted a lawyer as a mate. In the province of Massachusetts Bay, as in all the American colonies, full-time lawyers were looked down upon. It was thought by many that legal services could be provided as a sideline by farmers, ministers, and businessmen. Mrs. Smith hoped for more for her lovely daughter.

But the Reverend Smith saw in John Adams the same promise his daughter did. He was, for a time, her only support. Gradually, though, Mrs. Smith came to realize that while John's family was neither wealthy nor fashionable, they were good people and "solid." Finally, she gave in graciously to Abigail's quiet, unshakable determination. Now the young couple began to talk of wedding plans.

Soon a new stumbling block appeared. In the fall of 1763 a smallpox epidemic broke out in Boston. John and Abigail realized that anyone who traveled as much as John did was likely to contract the disease, so they made the difficult decision for him to be inoculated. They abandoned their hopes for a spring wedding.

This was not an easy decision to make. At that time inoculation was a simple yet dangerous procedure. A physician made a small slit in the arm, inserted a drop of pus taken from an infected person, and closed the incision with a bandage. This was intended to build up resistance to the disease in the blood. But the patient was being infected with the great killer disease of the age. Results, they knew, could range from the complete absence of any signs of smallpox to serious disfigurement or even death. The risk was great.

One of John's brothers went with him to Boston. John would be away from Abigail for at least five weeks. He left her in "tears and anxiety." She wrote to him every day.

In the letters they exchanged during this period they expressed their deepest feelings for one another, sometimes under cover of light banter, but other times quite openly. Years later, Abigail would write, "My pen is always freer than my tongue. I have wrote many things to you that I suppose I never could have talk'd."[6] In the eighteenth century it was not considered appropriate for women to write for publication. Letter writing was the genre available to them. It was here that Abigail displayed her talent as a writer and her spirit as a person.

In his letters, John often played the role of reformer, suggesting to Abigail ways in which she might improve. But the sharp sting of his criticism prompted her to tell him that compliments were "a commodity . . . that you very seldom deal in." She hoped that when they were married his "benevolent mind will lead him to pardon what he cannot ammend." He was "too severe" in his judgments of people, she chided, and did not "make quite so many allowances as human nature requires."[7]

". . . as a critick I fear you more than any other person on Earth, and tis the only character, in which I ever did, or ever will fear you." Proud of herself for having said that, she went on: "What say you? Do you approve of that Speach? Dont you think me a Courageous Being? Courage is a laudable, a Glorious Virtue in your Sex, why not in mine?"[8]

But she would never ignore John's appreciation of "the kindness, the softness, the tenderness that constitute the characteristic excellence of your sex."[9] She had learned well the importance of grace and softness from Grandmother Quincy.

Two weeks later she told John again that he inhibited her: "I feel a greater restraint in your Company, than in that of allmost any other person on Earth." But she went on to say that "for Saucyness, no Mortal can match him, no, not even His Diana."[10]

At the same time, John, writing to her, ended one letter: "I am, . . . and forever after will be your admirer and friend, and lover, John Adams."[11] The very next day he told her: "Letter-writing is, to me, the most agreeable Amusement I can find, and writing to you the most entertaining and agreeable of all letter-writing."[12]

But John was fearful that germs from the smallpox that were in the air in the house might cling to his letters and infect Abigail. So he asked her to be sure they were fumigated before she read them. Tom, the Smiths' servant, would smoke them. John assured her that he faithfully smoked all his letters to her before sealing them, and "I write at a desk far removed from any sick room, and shall use all the care I can, but too much cannot be used."[13]

He was convinced there was real danger in writing.

Abigail responded, "Did you never rob a Birds nest? Do you remember how the poor Bird would fly round and round, fearful to come nigh, yet not know how to leave the place—just so they say I hover round Tom whilst he is smoking my letters."

She ended her letter, ". . . excuse this very bad writing, if you had mended my pen it would have been better, once more adieu. Gold and Silver have I none, but such as I have, give I unto thee."[14]

Criticism and self-criticism continued to be frequent themes in their correspondence. John's "Catalogue of your Faults" which he sent to her at the beginning of May, is perhaps the most delightful portrait of Abigail that exists. In this letter John cautioned Abigail not to be "vexed, or fretted, or thrown into a Passion," but to "resolve upon a Reformation—for this is my sincere Aim." Having said this, he proceeded to list her faults: "In the first Place . . . you have been extreamly negligent, in attending so little to Cards." He hoped she would make a "better Figure in this elegant and necessary Accomplishment."

Second was "a certain Modesty, sensibility, Bashfulness . . . that enkindles Blushes . . . at every Violation of Decency in Company."

In the third place, she had never learned to sing. And fourth, "you very often hang your Head like a Bulrush. You do not sit erect as you ought," so "you appear too short for a Beauty, and the Company loses the sweet smiles of that Countenance and the bright sparkles of those Eyes. This Fault is the Effect and Consequence of another, still more inexcusable in a Lady. I mean an Habit of Reading, Writing and Thinking."

Yet another fault was that of sitting with legs crossed. This, he felt, "ruins the figure," and "injures the Health." This was the result, also, he added, of thinking too much.

Her sixth imperfection was walking with the toes bending inward, commonly called parrot-toed.

He ended by telling her that for three weeks he had searched for more faults, "but more are not to be discovered. All the rest is bright and luminous."[15]

Abigail was not perturbed. She replied:

"I thank you for your Catalogue, but must confess I was so hardened as to read over most of my Faults with as much pleasure, as an other person would have read their perfections."

But, said she, she would persist in some of them, particularly avoiding "that Freedom of Behaviour which . . . consists in Violations of Decency. . . . And permit me to tell you Sir . . . that there is such a thing as Modesty without either Hypocricy or Formality."

A neglect of singing she did acknowledge as a fault, but attributed it to "a voice harsh as the screech of a peacock."

The fifth fault she would endeavor to correct since he desired it. But, she told him playfully, "a gentleman has no business to concern himself about the Leggs of a Lady."[16]

As they probed into each other's personal qualities, they tempered their criticisms by their sense of humor. While they shared an intense need for self-examination, their dialogue seems to have strengthened rather than threatened their relationship. Their courtship had all the ideal qualities of deepening affection, ardent yearning, and increasing compatibility. And over all was their deep love for one another.

Finally, their long separation came to an end. John returned home to a joyous reunion late in May. Immediately, they set a wedding date for the coming fall. They would live in the simple saltbox house John had inherited, just a few steps away from the cottage on the Coast Road where his mother lived, and where he had been born.

A long lovers' summer stretched before them. John, always a farmer at heart, set about improving his land. He had the swamp drained and a stone fence built. He spent much time plowing the orchard, pruning the apple trees, mending fences, carting manure, and digging and planting corn, potatoes, onions, and cabbages. Clients who came to see him were apt to find him in the fields. Early in the fall he left, with "a disordered stomach, a pale face, an aching head and an anxious heart," to attend a session of the Inferior Court at Plymouth. From there he wrote to Abigail on September 30:

> Oh my dear Girl, I thank Heaven that another Fortnight will restore you to me—after so long a separation. My soul and Body have both been thrown into Disorder, by your Absence. . . .
>
> But you who have always softened and warmed my Heart, shall restore my Benevolence as well as my Health and Tranquility of mind. . . . Believe me, now & ever yr. faithful Lysander[17]

But Abigail was suffering also. By this time both were beginning to feel the strain of waiting. Both were experiencing nervous exhaustion. John, still unable to find a suitable girl to help Abigail with her household chores, was restless and filled with many anxieties.

Abigail, in the meantime, had been occupying herself by sewing linens for her trousseau and attending a round of prenuptial activities from which John was excluded. Early October found her at her uncle Isaac's house in Boston, shopping for furniture for their home. She, too, was now "extremely weak and . . . low spirited . . . hardly myself."[18] Her doctor ordered her to bed.

On October 3 a cart arrived, sent by John to carry her purchases to Braintree. Abigail wrote to him the next day: "The cart you mentioned came yesterday, by which I sent as many things as the horse would draw the rest of my things will be ready the Monday after you return from Taunton. And—then Sir if you please you may take me."[19]

October 25, 1764, dawned clear and cold. A sparkling Abigail Smith, just shy of her twentieth birthday, and a beaming John Adams, twenty-nine, exchanged their marriage vows in the Weymouth Parsonage. Parson Smith officiated. When the ceremony was over, and the last of the punch had been drained, Abigail, young and lovely in a long scarlet cloak and hood, ran down the stairs from the room she had shared with her sisters and out the door to where her new husband was waiting for her. Together, Mr. and Mrs. John Adams waved to the guests gathered in the doorway to see them off, then rode down the familiar winding road toward Braintree and their new home.

~ CHAPTER IV ~
"the weaker sex"

A bigail loved the weathered gray clapboard house, simple and unadorned, at the foot of Penn's Hill. While it appeared from the outside to be much smaller than her home in Weymouth (it looked much like a doll's house to her), it was, in fact, quite roomy inside. There were four rooms downstairs: a parlor, a large kitchen with an enormous fireplace, a little room off the kitchen for the young servant girl lent to them by John's mother, and a large front room that John remodeled into a law office by replacing a window with a door. When Abigail climbed the narrow, steep stairway that curved around the main chimney to the second floor she found two front bedrooms as well as two tiny rooms nestled under the eaves.

Abigail happily saw to the arrangement of her new furniture in the house. She proudly had the English grandfather clock that was a wedding gift from her family placed in the parlor. She set the bed warmer that her friends had given her near the fireplace in the bedroom. She rapidly made the transition from lover and bride to housewife and expectant mother, for almost immediately after the wedding Abigail became pregnant.

She cherished the first quiet months of life with her new husband. Days were spent attending to household chores, cooking, planting her garden, and sewing linens and tiny clothes for the baby.

John's legal practice was growing rapidly, but he still found time to work on his farm. Often Abigail watched as John directed his hired farmhands or worked the land himself. Always an enthusiastic farmer, John communicated his love of the land to his new wife, all the while urging her to be careful how she spent their money.

John Adams's birthplace, right, at the foot of Penn's Hill in Braintree, Massachusetts, later called Quincy. After their marriage, John and Abigail lived in the house above. Oil painting by Frankenstein, 1849.

~

The Braintree house today

~

The farm produced most of the young couple's daily needs—fresh vegetables and fruit in season, poultry, and milk. Since there were no stores in Braintree, Abigail went into Boston to purchase fish, meat, and staples such as flour, sugar, tea, and spices.

Abigail was delighted with her new life. She was happy, also, to be out from under the watchful eye of her mother. But she missed the daily companionship of her sisters. She visited her parents and her grandparents almost every week, and saw her sister Mary as often as possible. It was Mary, married to Richard Cranch for two years now, to whom she frequently turned for advice.

Sometimes Abigail and John went for long walks together, returning to climb Penn's Hill to admire its commanding view of the sea and the surrounding towns.

Evenings were spent quietly reading, Abigail systematically devouring one after another of the books in John's library, while John studied his law-books. When the weekly newspapers arrived they read them together and discussed the events that were taking place in the colonies. Rumblings of unrest were growing more frequent, and John voiced his concern to his wife.

In 1760, upon the death of King George II, the twenty-two-year-old Prince of Wales had become George III, king of England. A shift in relations between England and the colonies had become evident almost immediately.

The new king's first minister, William Pitt, expected financial assistance from America. He tightened up customs duties and reintroduced the Writs of Assistance. These writs allowed customs officers to break into ships, shops, homes, or warehouses suspected of containing smuggled goods without a specific warrant. The colonists were angry. This was a breach of the constitutional liberties of all Englishmen. Arbitrary search was the weapon of tyrants, they said. It must be resisted at its very beginning.

John had listened to James Otis, a brilliant young lawyer, argue against the writs in February of 1761 in the Boston Town House. He had been among those who pressed for places in the old Council Chamber that day. Sensing that this would be a historic case, he had come prepared to take notes with paper, pen, and a pot of ink.

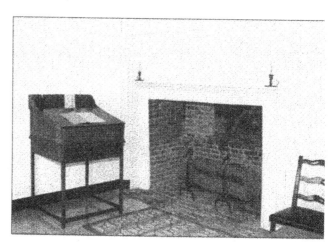

John Adams's desk

~

26

John had been stirred when James Otis stood and passionately declared: "This writ is against the fundamental principles of English law. . . . An act against the Constitution is void." The right of property to an Englishman, native or colonial, was the primary right on which all others rested. Calling the writs nothing more than disguised search warrants, Otis had become the first to raise the issue of the colonists' ability to question Crown policy.[1]

Two years later (in 1763), England's Seven Years' War with France, known in this country as the French and Indian War, came to an end. But England's war debt was huge, and the English treasury had been badly drained. So the authorities in England decided to replenish it by taxing the colonists in America. The colonists, and particularly those in Massachusetts, objected. They began to rebel by disobeying the laws. They refused to pay the taxes.

King George III of England, by Allan Ramsey, 1760–1770. A formal state portrait of the young king, who had just turned twenty-two when he ascended the throne in 1760.

~

Abigail was delighted with these opportunities to hear John's opinions, and to voice her own. She understood that her husband considered her an intellectual equal, and she soon became a sounding board for his ideas.

As they continued to read the newspapers and discuss the growing unrest, John and Abigail were learning more and more about each other each day. But the coming of winter, with snow that blocked the roads, cut Abigail off from visits to her family, and she became very lonely. Then, just three months after their wedding, John left his pregnant wife at home in Braintree and went off to attend the January session of the Superior Court in Boston. It was the first of the many separations that would shadow and shape their marriage.

W hile John was attending this court session, his old mentor, Jeremiah Gridley, invited him to join a newly formed private club of some of the most learned and distinguished lawyers in Boston, called the Solidality. John told Abigail how flattered he was to be considered their equal. At their meetings, he told her, they would study and discuss legal history and theory. These discussions would become for John the whetstone on which he would sharpen and define his thinking on the relationship between the colonies and the mother country.

John continued to attend court sessions throughout the remainder of Abigail's pregnancy. While she was not completely alone—she had a servant girl, and her mother-in-law, whom she liked, lived just a few steps away—still she missed John terribly.

Then, on the hot Sunday morning of July 14, 1765, Abigail gave birth to a little girl. On the same day Parson Smith rode over from Weymouth and christened the baby Abigail. The family would always call her Nabby. John was not at home for the birth, as he attended court sessions for most of July, and the baby arrived a few weeks prematurely. But Abigail's mother and sisters were with her, as women of the family and friends always gathered at a birth to offer encouragement. Sympathetic support of other women was the chief solace to the mother in delivery. While a few colonial physicians had received obstetrical training in Europe and might be called upon to assist in life-threatening emergencies, for the most part female midwives supervised deliveries.

Abigail had been taught that childbearing was considered the main preoccupation of women from marriage to menopause, and she understood full well the very real possibility of death in childbirth. But most men took childbirth for granted. Even Dr. Cotton Tufts, Abigail's physician uncle, noted the birth of her baby in his diary as casually as he noted the weather for the day.

Abigail remained in bed for about three weeks, as was the custom. While she regained her strength her mother, mother-in-law, and sisters took over her household tasks and looked after little Nabby.

28

Safely through her "ordeal," Abigail wrote happily to her friend Hannah in Boston, "Your Diana become a Mamma—can you credit it?" The baby's "pretty Smiles already delight my Heart, who is the Dear image of her still Dearer Pappa."[2]

The year 1765 was also the year of the Stamp Act. On March 22 Parliament had announced that revenue stamps costing between a halfpenny and twenty shillings must be affixed to all legal documents, including such things as leases, diplomas, and marriage licenses, as well as to newspapers, broadsides, pamphlets, even playing cards. The Stamp Act, scheduled to take effect the following November, would be the first *direct* tax England had imposed on Americans.

By the time Nabby was born, word of the tax had crossed the ocean and reached the colonies. There were violent protests throughout the thirteen colonies, with Boston leading the way.

"There is no room for delay," John's cousin Samuel Adams warned fellow colonists in an impassioned speech. "Those unexpected proceedings may be preparatory to more extensive taxation; for if our trade may be taxed, why not our lands and everything we possess?"[3]

Sam told John and Abigail that taxes in any form, without legal representation, change the people from free subjects to slaves, and destroy the right of the colonists to govern and tax themselves.

John Adams, the young lawyer who still pursued the study of law rather than the gain of it, concluded immediately that the Stamp Act was illegal and unconstitutional. It attempted to impose on Americans the tyrannical system from which their forefathers had fled.

But John's discontent was not simply the product of his study of the law. Parliament's attempt to tax the colonists—to take away their property without their consent—struck at one of his deepest feelings, a feeling he shared with many other Americans. For a threat to property was a threat to his beloved farm. He knew what it meant to turn wilderness into pasture and plowland. His love for his land at Braintree gave him something in common with all the men in America who farmed their own land.

Soon the Massachusetts courts were closed because many judges would not use the required stamps on their court documents. Trade across the Atlantic came to a standstill, since no ship could leave an American port for England without properly stamped papers.

Now John Adams was one of those (together with James Otis and Jeremiah Gridley) who called upon the governor to open the courts and ignore the Stamp Act. It was their duty, John told Abigail heatedly, to pronounce such an unconstitutional act null and void.

The closing of the courts, and the forced idleness that resulted from it, gave John the time for even more studying, and he composed a series of newspaper articles for the *Boston Gazette*. Writing with "a heart that burns for its country's welfare," he traced the rise of human freedom in the face of political and religious tyranny, and he demonstrated the injustice and unconstitutionality of the Stamp Act. While acknowledging his loyalty to the king, he reaffirmed his belief that "we never can be slaves."[4]

As one of the colony's up-and-coming young lawyers, and as an eloquent public speaker, John quickly became one of the principal spokesmen for the American point of view. But with the courts shut and business at a standstill, his law practice halted. As he and Abigail sat quietly together, reflecting on the situation, they recognized that they would have to cut down on expenses. Their future looked bleak, he told his young wife, just when he was finally beginning to gain a "small degree of Reputation."[5]

On Christmas Day John and Abigail and five-month-old Nabby went to tea with Grandmother and Grandfather Quincy at Mount Wollaston, then returned home to dine by themselves. Later, sitting by the fire, watching with pleasure a lightly falling snow, they talked at length about this "hideous" taxation without consent. "A person ought to be very cautious what kinds of fuel he throws into a fire," John mused to Abigail.[6]

On March 28, 1766, the Stamp Act was finally repealed, and life for the Adamses began to assume a degree of normalcy. But in May, when all of Boston was celebrating its repeal, they were unable to join in the festivities. Abigail had "hooping cough," caught from her ten-month-old daughter. Remaining at home in Braintree, they could only listen to tales of the clanging bells, booming cannons, beating drums, and of the Boston houses illuminated by candles in every window.

By now John had become a well-known political figure. His law practice continued to grow, but he was away from Abigail and Nabby for a week or two every month "riding the circuit" to attend court sessions in other districts of the colony. His financial situation improved, and he was pleased that he could now buy more land. But as his practice and his farm expanded, so did his wife's responsibilities. Not only did Abigail have more animals to feed, but she was also entertaining many of the influential colonists who came to call.

Early in the summer John agreed to take Abigail on a much longed for visit to her sister Mary, who had recently moved to Salem, twenty-five miles north of Braintree. Abigail and Mary had never been separated before, and they yearned for each other. "When ever I receive a Letter from you it seems to give new Springs to my nerves, and a brisker circulation to my Blood," Abigail wrote to Mary in July. Telling her that they would come in August, Abigail assured her sister happily that no longer would "mountains arise to hinder me. Mole hills I always expect to find, but them I can easily surmount."[7] They would leave Nabby at home, to be cared for by relatives. It was too hot for the baby to travel, she explained. Besides, Nabby was cutting teeth and still had a bad cough.

The twenty-five-mile trip to Salem, which they made in an open chaise, took two days. On the way they had dinner with friends in Boston, then went on to spend the night in nearby Medford. They reached Salem by noon the next day.

Separation from Mary became even more difficult for Abigail after the visit. She would have liked Mary's little daughter Betsy and Nabby to grow up together. What she would give to "see them put their little arms around one an others necks, and hug each other."[8]

In November they were able to make another visit to the Cranches. On this trip John and Abigail had their portraits painted in pastels by a local artist named Benjamin Blyth. These paintings, the earliest done of the couple, tell us much about them. John's plump, round face and pink cheeks give him an air of youthful innocence. His is a likable but unimpressive face, somewhat bland and withdrawn, with no distinguishing feature.

By contrast, twenty-two-year-old Abigail, with her dark hair swept neatly back from her pale face, and just the hint of a smile on her lips, appears reserved and thoughtful, a poised and confident young woman. Her brilliant, penetrating, wide-spaced eyes betray none of her childhood mischievousness. Her low-necked, lace-trimmed dress, set off by three strands of pearls, and the bow in her hair, tell us, too, that she was no stranger to feminine fashion.

Abigail and John Adams in 1766, two years after their marriage. Abigail wrote, "My Good Man is so very fat . . . and I am lean as a rale." Pastels by Benjamin Blyth.

B y January of 1767 the roads were once again blocked by snow, and Abigail was unable to visit her family in Weymouth, or the Cranches in Salem. In fact, she didn't see Mary again until the following May. She was already experiencing the loneliness that would become a way of life for her.

To ease that loneliness Abigail began to read *Sermons to Young Women,* two volumes recently published by James Fordyce, a minister in London. Stressing the importance of feminine softness and modesty, Fordyce declared that God had created woman to be a helpmate to the husband on whom she depended for protection and support. As the "weaker sex" she must recognize that "war, commerce, politics, exercises of strength and dexterity" are the province of men.[9]

At the same time Fordyce urged young women to use their intelligence. They must become economists of their households, even while perfecting their artistic talents in needlework, drawing, and music. And they must read extensively in order to achieve their full potential.

As Abigail read and reread his books, she came to a clearer understanding of who she was, and her belief in the importance of an enlightened woman intensified. She accepted the role assigned to her. But she accepted it as a challenge to excel in that role.

～ CHAPTER V ～
"I should . . . have been a rover"

J ust three days before Nabby's second birthday, on July 11, 1767, Abigail bore a son. She named him John Quincy, after her beloved grandfather, who died two days later. Now, with two children to care for, and John often away at court, Abigail felt the responsibilities of motherhood more keenly. She had no difficulty in caring for her children physically. She had learned that well from her mother. The details of feeding, clothing, and caring for an infant were passed down from mother to daughter like recipes for making a pudding or preserving fruit.

Their health was a serious worry. Many children died in the first year or two of life. But even more of a worry to Abigail were her children's education and moral development. She believed that mothers were primarily responsible for training their children to become moral, God-fearing, useful adults. She was conscious of the new ideas that emphasized the importance of a mother's early care in her children's development. In his *Sermons*, James Fordyce had written that children were like plants that had to be raised and cultivated. These "plants" would grow according to the care they received. Fordyce reinforced her belief that women had a unique opportunity to influence the world by raising good citizens.

Her concern for her children, and her care of them, seemed to intensify her loneliness when John was gone. Returning home from a two-day visit to her parents with the children while John was away, she wrote to tell him how Nabby had rocked her two-month-old baby brother in his cradle, all the while singing, "Come pappa come home to Brother Johnny."

She went on to tell him how Sunday seemed to her a more "Lonesome Day" than any other on which he was absent. "For tho I may be compared to those climates which are deprived of the Sun half the Year, yet upon a Sunday you commonly afforded us your benign influence." To her sister Mary she described how her servants' eyes had sparkled with joy when she entered the house. She was grateful to be received at home "even by one's Servants," in the absence of her "Dearest of Friends, and the tenderest of Husbands."[1]

By this time Abigail was beginning to realize that her husband would never be happy simply as a successful lawyer. John had already confided to her that he craved a lifework that would be like the ripples spreading out in concentric circles from a small stone dropped in a lake. "Friend, Parent, Neighbor, first does it embrace, our Country next and next all human Race," he had written in his Diary. How could he pursue his studies and at the same time carry forward a career and a revolution, he agonized.[2]

Abigail appreciated his restless intellect, his quick perceptions, his warm and faithful heart. And she recognized his driving ambition. She knew he was torn between his need to earn money to support his family and his desire to play a role in the political scene. She tried to make him aware of her total confidence in him, regardless of the path he chose.

Early in 1768, when John suggested moving the family into Boston in order to be closer to his important clients and to the center of political activity, Abigail agreed immediately. She loved Boston, she had friends and relatives there, and Mary had recently moved there with her family.

John made arrangements to have his farm looked after, then rented a large house in Brattle Square, in the center of the city. He moved his family there in April. The house was just across the way from the Brattle Street Church.

Boston at that time was a lively, crowded city of about sixteen thousand people. At first Abigail had difficulty adjusting to its noise and dirt. The clatter of horses' hooves and heavy carts and wagons rumbling past the house on the cobblestones day and night were the worst offenders. At night, a watchman called out the time every hour, for not every house had a clock. Sometimes Abigail couldn't sleep at night. Then British troops, recently arrived in the city, chose Brattle Square for their daily drills.

The soldiers, conspicuous in the red uniforms that gave them the name "redcoats," were yet another reminder of British oppression.

Abigail missed the quiet and the clean, fresh air of Braintree. Its bare pastures, wide meadows, and homely countryside had woven themselves into the fabric of her life. But she was just a short walk from friends and family, and from the market where she shopped for food. From her house she could see the waterfront that she had enjoyed as a young girl. She could attend the Brattle Street Church, surrounded by many of Boston's wealthiest families, including John's old friend John Hancock. And she could read the four weekly newspapers as they came off the presses on Monday or Thursday, instead of waiting for someone to deliver them to Braintree days—or even weeks—late. It wasn't long before she found it stimulating to live in this "Noisy Buisy Town."

Shortly after they moved into Boston, Abigail became pregnant again. On December 28, 1768, she gave birth to a daughter, whom they named Susanna, after John's mother. They called her Suky. Abigail worried that Suky didn't seem as robust as Nabby and Johnny had when they were infants.

Occasionally Abigail attended court sessions to hear John argue a political case. Lawyer Adams was now in the thick of the resistance to England that was building steadily. The colonists had begun their exciting march toward independence, and John was a leading spokesman for colonial rights. He wrote newspaper articles and engaged in coffeehouse political debates. But it was as an able and hardworking attorney who took on significant, politically charged cases that he was establishing his reputation. He had recently been successful in defending both John Hancock and James Otis in cases arising from confrontations with the mother country. Abigail was proud of him.

Their home was always open to friends who wanted to discuss political ideas. James Otis, John Hancock, and Samuel Adams, John's distant, older cousin, came often. Sam was already advocating serious resistance to Britain. He had formed a secret organization of rebels called Sons of Liberty. In fact, there are some people who say that Sam Adams was the first man in America who believed that the thirteen weak little colonies could exist independent of the British Empire. John was more cautious. But he and Sam were good friends. John thought Sam was a genius at politics. Abigail liked Sam's wife, Betsey, and they, too, became good friends.

Tall, blond, handsome Dr. Joseph Warren came, too. He was a young physician who was rapidly achieving a fine reputation. He came to the house on Brattle Street not only to nurse the children through their inevitable colds and fevers, but to talk politics as well. Joseph Warren had recently come to be recognized as a political leader, along with Sam Adams and John Hancock. The whole family was drawn to him.

Once again Abigail found herself an eager gatherer of the news in her own parlor as she listened to the men's often heated political discussions. John called their fireside a "theatre of politics." Abigail rarely joined in the conversation while the men were present. It was only later, in the privacy of their bedroom, that she and John shared ideas. Abigail was secure in the knowledge that her husband respected her opinions and admired her ability to present her own views. She recognized the possibilities as well as the limits of her place as a woman in a man's world.

Samuel Adams. Shown here pointing to the Massachusetts Charter, "Radical Sam" could rally mobs or debate learnedly. He was one of the organizers of the Sons of Liberty and the Boston Tea Party. Oil by John Singleton Copley, 1770–1772.

~

Now she heard the men express their outrage at the newly imposed Townsend Acts, which placed a tax on shipments of goods coming into America from England without the consent of the colonial legislatures. The list included lead, glass, paper, paint, and tea, all important items for the colonists. When the men decided to retaliate by boycotting *all* products manufactured in England, Abigail began, as did many colonial women then, to weave her own coarse but serviceable cloth at home instead of buying the fine English fabrics she was used to. She used crude homemade pins in place of English pins. Most important, she began to serve coffee instead of tea, and experimented with brews of local leaves including sassafras, sage, strawberry, raspberry, and currant. These were called "liberty teas." Abigail thought she was being very "Heroick."

Massachusetts women did not vote or hold office or even attend town meetings. Their lives were centered in the private world of family. They were dependent on fathers and husbands to represent them in the public sphere. But now a subtle change was beginning to take place in Colonial America. Men were gradually coming to realize that women were a necessary link in the strategy of rebellion. Since wives were the ones who managed the household, without their support boycotts could not succeed. Women were becoming politically important.

The winter of 1769–1770 was a difficult one for Abigail. She was deeply distressed as she watched tiny Susanna growing steadily weaker. In spite of Dr. Warren's efforts, the baby seemed unable to gain weight. Abigail felt helpless. And she was pregnant once again.

She also fully shared her husband's serious involvement in the crisis that surrounded them. England had become for her the "cruel" mother country. Added to that, her dear cousin Isaac was leaving for England. Abigail was happy for Isaac that he was going, but she would miss him. She asked him to send her reports of the "curious or remarkable" that he saw in his travels. Wistfully revealing her own desire to travel, she told him that this was the best season of life for him to travel, "Ere you have formed connection which would bind you to your own little Spot."

In another letter, written after he had arrived in England, she told him, "From my Infancy I have always felt a great inclination to visit the Mother Country as tis call'd and had nature formed me of the other Sex, I should certainly have been a rover."

She continued:

Women you know Sir, are considered as Domestic Beings, and altho they inherit an Eaquel Share of curiosity with the other Sex, yet but few are hardy eno' to venture abroad, and explore the amaizing variety of distant Lands. The Natural tenderness and Delicacy of our Constitutions, added to the many Dangers we are subject to from your Sex, renders it almost impossible for a Single Lady to travel without injury to her character. And those who have a protector in an Husband, have generally speaking obstacles sufficient to prevent their Roving.[4]

When she learned that Isaac had met the brilliant English historian Catharine Macaulay, she asked him to learn all he could about her and to send her the history Macaulay had written. Catharine Macaulay, even as a woman, had achieved recognition as an advocate of the American cause. Despite the fact that Abigail was very much a "domestic being" at this point in her life, this unschooled daughter of a country minister was reaching beyond the nursery and the kitchen to explore the outside world.

Susanna continued to grow weaker. Abigail, despairing, tried all the herbal remedies she knew. She spent anxious nights holding her baby in her arms, watching for the slightest improvement. But to no avail. Her love didn't save her from loss. Susanna died on February 4, 1770, just thirteen months old.

Abigail was distraught. She found it impossible to talk or write about it. She kept her grief beneath the surface. Not until forty-three years later, in an attempt to comfort her daughter-in-law on the loss of *her* thirteen-month-old daughter, and help her to recognize that one could survive such a tragedy, did she share her heartache over the loss of this child.

As Abigail and John attempted to deal with their personal grief, tension was building in Boston. The city was like a powder keg ready to explode. The explosion came on the cold, clear Monday night of March 5, 1770.

When John left the house that morning to walk the short distance to his office near the Old State House, Abigail had cautioned him to be careful how he walked. There was a thin layer of ice on the ground. A few inches of snow fell during the day. By evening, when John left home again to attend a meeting of a political club he had recently joined, the snow had stopped and a bright new moon was shining. As he walked to the South End of Boston, he noted that the town was filled with people, mostly boys and young men milling about. Rowdy soldiers were parading the streets, their bayonets glittering in the moonlight.

Shortly after nine o'clock, Abigail, at home alone with the children, suddenly heard gunfire and the clanging of bells. Rushing to an upstairs window, she saw soldiers racing down the street. The children, awakened by the commotion, reacted differently. Nabby, at four, was terrified of the fire bells, and Abigail tried to comfort her. Little Johnny, on the other hand, cried to be allowed to go outside to see the guns being fired.

John, at his meeting on the opposite side of town, heard the same insistent clamor of bells. Fearing that they signaled a fire, he and his friends broke up their meeting, snatched their hats and cloaks, and dashed out to assist in extinguishing the blaze. In this city of wooden houses the danger of spreading fire was great. Out in the street they heard reports that British soldiers had fired on some Bostonians near the Town House, killing some and wounding others. But by now the conflict was over, and all was quiet.

John's immediate concern was to get to Abigail. She must not lift the children in her condition, or run out on the icy streets, he thought. And she would be frightened. He made his way across Brattle Square past soldiers with muskets shouldered and bayonets fixed, trying not to notice them and hoping they would ignore him.

By the time John arrived home, Abigail had both the children back in bed, and she was anxiously watching at the window for him to come home safely, and to allay her fears.

Word of the "Boston Massacre" would soon be spread to every colony by Sam Adams and Joseph Warren.

Earlier in the evening a group of teenage boys, most of them apprentices, had gathered in Kings Street, near the customhouse. They began to taunt the lone sentry on duty there. The sentry called for help. Immediately, Captain Preston, the commander of the regiment, and six soldiers marched down from the guardhouse. As more young men joined the group of citizens, many armed with sticks and clubs, they rapidly turned into an angry, jeering mob. Shouting "Lobsters!" and "Bloody backs!" at the soldiers, they pelted them with icy snowballs, oyster shells, and sticks. Suddenly, bells all over the city began to peal, sounding the alarm. Someone yelled, "Fire!" No one knew who it was. The soldiers, thinking they had heard a command from their captain, fired their muskets into the crowd. When the smoke cleared, three Americans were dead, two more fatally wounded, and several others injured. Three of the dead were just seventeen years old.

The shooting of Boston citizens by British soldiers on King Street on March 5, 1770, became known as the Boston Massacre. Engraving by J. H. Bufford.

The next morning John was visited in his law office by a customhouse agent who came on behalf of Captain Preston. Would Mr. Adams defend the captain and the other British soldiers? No other lawyer would take their case.

John knew full well the risk involved if he agreed. His reputation as a leading patriot would be tarnished, and he himself might become the target of an angry mob. But John was a strange revolutionary. He believed strongly in rule by law. He agreed to defend them. He and Abigail sat up late into that night discussing what he had done. The accused have a right to legal counsel, he told her. If the soldiers killed in self-defense, they deserve to be acquitted. A fair trial will be proof to the British that the colonists believe in the preservation of constitutional rights.

John Adams won his case. Years later he would call it "one of the best pieces of service I ever rendered my country."[5]

In June the Boston Town Meeting elected John a representative to the Massachusetts legislature. He was being asked now to play a more active role in politics. He was aware of the importance of the trust being placed in him, but concerned about his ability to fulfill that trust.

He poured out all his apprehensions to Abigail. It would mean time away from his law practice, which would reduce his income just when his family's needs were growing, he told her. Their second son, Charles, had been born just a week before, on May 29. And he was throwing away as bright a prospect for wealth as any man ever had. This could signify his financial ruin—as well as the loss of his life. He could be tried by the British for treason. But his Puritan sense of duty compelled him to accept.

In a flood of tears, Abigail assured him that she understood the danger to him, to her, and to their children, but he must not decline the election. She was "very willing to share in all that was to come, and place her trust in Providence."[6]

~ CHAPTER VI ~
"The flame is kindled"

During the summer of 1770, while John spent almost all of his time attending sessions of the legislature, handling his law practice, and participating in political debates in the evenings, Abigail was home alone tending to her domestic duties and to the children. But she managed to find time to follow political events closely.

Before the end of the year John confided to her that he was experiencing chest pains. A racking cough was depleting his energy. Overwork and anxiety about politics were taking their toll. He was worried about his health. He needed his farm and the fresh country air to recuperate, he told her. They made the decision to move back to Braintree in the spring. John would keep his law office in Boston and commute there on horseback. And he would abandon politics. "Farewell politics!" he wrote in his diary.[1] He would keep his promise for a year and a half, while the city of Boston remained relatively calm.

Even without the demands of politics, John frequently left Abigail alone while he rode the circuit, trying to earn a living for his growing family. On one occasion, though, it was Abigail who was away from John and the children. Her loneliness for him then was no less acute. When a snowstorm prevented her from returning home from a visit to her parents, she wrote to John:

Alass! How many snow banks divide thee and me and my warmest wishes to see thee will not melt one of them. I never left so large a flock of little ones before. You must write me how they all do. . . . I feel gratified with the immagination at the close of the Day in seeing the little flock round you inquiring when Mamma will come home—as they often do for thee in thy absence.

And she was always hungry for political news: "If you have any news in Town which the papers do not communicate, pray be so good as to Write it." She ended by asking him to tell the children that Grandmama was sending "mittins" for them, and begged John not to disappoint her by not writing "a few lines to comfort the heart of Your affectionate Abigail Adams."[2]

By the summer of 1772 the commute to Boston to maintain his law practice became too exhausting for John. Once again, he and Abigail decided to move back to the city. At the end of August John purchased a large brick house on South Queen Street, opposite the courthouse and near his office. On Tuesday, November 24, his wife arrived with their four children. Nabby was seven, John Quincy five, and Charles two-and-a-half. Two-month-old Thomas Boylston, born in Braintree on September 15, was cradled in his mother's arms. Abigail was twenty-eight.

The Old State Meeting House in Boston, where the first stirrings of resistance to Great Britain took place. Oil by James B. Marston, 1801.

~

Within the year the uneasy calm that had pervaded Boston for close to two years disintegrated. Most of the taxes imposed by the British had been repealed, except the hated tax on tea. England had granted the powerful East India Company a monopoly on all tea exported to the colonies. The colonists were outraged. In October of 1773, when they learned that ships carrying the tea were sailing toward New England, they knew something had to be done. Sam Adams, with his genius for agitation, alerted the Sons of Liberty. Meetings were held and fiery speeches made denouncing the tax on tea as "British tyranny."

Early in December, when the ships finally arrived in Boston Harbor, the patriots would not allow the cargo to be unloaded. To accept these shipments would be to admit the right of Parliament to tax the colonists. The governor ordered that the tea be landed and the duty paid. Appeals to him to lift the tax were made and refused. The colonists then demanded that the ships return to England with their cargoes of tea.

A frightened and trembling Abigail, her heart beating at the sound of every whistle or bell, described the situation to her new friend, Mercy Otis Warren:

The Tea that bainful weed is arrived. Great and I hope Effectual opposition has been made to the landing of it. The flame is kindled and like Lightning it catches from Soul to Soul. Great will be the devastation if not timely quenched or allayed by some more lenient Measures.[3]

Her mind, she told Mercy, was shocked at the thought of shedding human blood, "and a civil War is of all Wars, the most dreadful." Still she knew that many would willingly give their lives for the cause.

On Thursday, December 16, Abigail was home alone while her husband was away at court. By nightfall several thousand angry Bostonians were crowding in and around the Old South Church in the cold winter darkness, awaiting the governor's reply to their final appeal to do away with the tax.

When it became clear that the duty must be paid, pandemonium broke loose. Sam Adams arose to speak: "This meeting can do nothing more to save the country."[4] As if his words were a signal, a war whoop sounded and the shout went up: "Boston harbor a teapot tonight!" Sons of Liberty, disguised as Mohawk Indians, took the action that would change the course of history. They rowed out into the harbor and quietly boarded

John Adams considered the Boston Tea Party an "Epocha in History." It was, he insisted, "absolutely necessary."

the ships. Then they proceeded to dump 342 chests of tea into the water. The silent crowd watched approvingly as salty tea was brewed for the fish.

Parliament retaliated with measures that would brew a revolution. The most drastic of these, the Boston Port Act, closed the tea-stained harbor to all trade, effectively cutting off the town's lifeline to its neighbors and to the world. To exclude Boston from the sea, the very element that made her great, was a devastating punishment. Then on May 13, 1774, General Thomas Gage sailed into Boston Harbor to take over as military governor and commander in chief of British forces in America. Three regiments of British troops followed.

Abigail's husband pronounced the "Boston Tea Party" a bold and daring act. He considered it "an Epocha in History."[5] In spite of the British retaliation, it was, he insisted, absolutely necessary.

Earlier that year, John had purchased his father's homestead from his brother Peter, who had inherited it. Now he moved his family back to Braintree. He would prepare them as best he could for the "Age of Tryal" that was upon them. It would mark the beginning of a new era for John and Abigail Adams.

In a sense it marked, as well, the beginning of a long and fulfilling friendship between Abigail Adams and Mercy Otis Warren. Abigail had met Mercy during the spring of 1773, when she accompanied John on one of his trips to Plymouth to attend a court session there. An elegant lady and the mother of five sons, Mercy was the sister of James Otis, one of John's heroes, and the wife of James Warren, a leading Massachusetts radical and brother

Mercy Otis Warren was an elegant lady with one of the sharpest minds in America. She wrote plays and history. Mercy corresponded with both Abigail and John, and became Abigail's good friend and confidante. Portrait by John Singleton Copley, about 1763.

of their good friend Dr. Joseph Warren. John often visited the Warrens when he was in Plymouth. Their home was the scene of frequent political meetings.

Mercy herself had become an active propagandist for the patriot cause in 1772, when she published a play entitled *The Adulateur.* She would later become a well-known literary and political figure, writing plays and history, all with clear political intent. Her plays were written to be read, not acted, for Mercy had never seen a stage production. Playacting was not permitted in Boston.

Soon after the visit Mercy initiated a correspondence with Abigail. Abigail, flattered that the older woman would write to her, replied: "Thus imbolden'd I venture to stretch my pinions."[6] Mercy was forty-five; Abigail was twenty-nine. But they shared fine minds and almost identical concerns about female circumstances. It was to Mercy that Abigail revealed her most feminine and feminist thoughts. In their letters they talked about writers, politics, and the roles thrust upon their husbands, as well as children and fashions. They frequently bartered yards of ribbons, laces, and fabrics. When Mercy injured a finger and couldn't use her hand, she told Abigail that she missed her needlework as much as her writing.

~ CHAPTER VII ~
"Partner in all the Joys and Sorrows"

The Boston Port Act had been intended to intimidate the colonists and isolate Massachusetts from the other colonies. In fact, it had the opposite effect. Committees of Correspondence had already been organized to spread ideas and information among the colonies in order to keep alive opposition to British policy. Now the colonies united in support of Massachusetts. They called for "a Meeting of Committees from the several Colonies . . . to consult upon the present State of the Colonies . . ." and to devise "a plan for a more lasting accommodation with Great Britain."[1] The meeting, to be held in Philadelphia in September 1774, would become known to history as the First Continental Congress. In June, John Adams was elected by the General Court to be one of five delegates from Massachusetts to attend.

After his election, and before the time when he would set out for Philadelphia six weeks later, John worked hard on his law cases "pursuing every shilling and copper" so he could leave Abigail with some little reserve of cash to tide her over in his absence. He worried constantly about the lack of money, and sent Abigail specific instructions on caring for the farm while he was away.

He decided to prepare himself as well as he could "for the storm that was coming on."[2] He expressed his feelings of inadequacy about his role in the Continental Congress to his friend James Warren: "I am at a loss, totally at a loss, what to do when we get there; but I hope to be there taught. It is to be a school of political prophets, I suppose, a nursery of American statesmen."

He went on to suggest to his friend that they recommend to their respective wives, "to teach our sons the divine science of the politics; and to be frank, I suspect they understand it better than we do."[3]

Depressed, full of fears for his country, and beset by a sense of his own inadequacy, he poured out his hopes and his fears in his letters.

To his wife he wrote:

I must intreat you, my dear Partner in all the Joys and Sorrows, Prosperity and Adversity of my Life, to take a Part with me in the Struggle. I pray God for your Health—intreat you to rouse your whole Attention to the Family, the stock, the Farm, the Dairy. Let every Article of Expence which can possibly be spared be retrench'd.[4]

John Adams had created a partnership with his wife.

On the next day, recognizing the potential importance of their letters, John asked Abigail "to put them up safe and preserve them. They may exhibit to our posterity a kind of picture of the manners, opinions, and principles of these times of perplexity, danger, and distress."[5]

On August 9, the day before John was to leave for Philadelphia with his fellow delegates, Abigail went into Boston with him. They stayed at her uncle Isaac's house.

Wednesday, August 10, was a hot, dry, dusty day. Early that morning Abigail and John said their private good-byes. Then Abigail joined the cheering crowds gathering in the streets to see the delegates off. Their trip would take nineteen days.

The delegates, impressive in their new clothes and freshly powdered wigs, rode through town in a coach-and-four. Two armed servants on horseback preceded them, and four in livery followed. Five regiments of British troops watched silently from their encampment on the common.

Later, as she turned back toward her uncle's house, Abigail, not yet thirty, and with four young children at home, tried hard not to think about what lay ahead. She was proud of her husband's election to Congress, and hopeful about colonial unity, but she was fearful of what she felt certain was coming. She dreaded war, but saw no alternative. She dreaded even more the loss of American freedom if her countrymen purchased peace "at the price of liberty."

Just a week after John left, Abigail wrote to him:

The great distance between us, makes the time appear very long to me. It seems already a month since you left me. The great anxiety I feel for my Country, for you and for our family renders the day tedious and the night unpleasant. . . . What course you can or will take is all wrapt in the Bosom of futurity. . . . Did ever any Kingdom or State regain their Liberty, when once it was invaded without Blood shed? I cannot think of it without horror.[6]

She couldn't know then that, except for brief intervals, ten years would elapse before they could live together again as man and wife.

Abigail didn't hear from John for five weeks. But she faithfully wrote letters of encouragement. "Your task is difficult and important," she told him. "Heaven direct and prosper you."[7]

For her part, Abigail saw that the children continued their studies, she somehow managed to hold together the threads of John's law practice, and she looked after the farm. As the threat of war became more serious, farming took on greater importance for all the colonists. With trade cut off and business in decline, families had to rely more heavily on their own production. Industry and frugality became the watchwords of the day. This was particularly true for the Adamses, for John could not provide financial support for his family while he served in Congress. There were many important decisions that Abigail had to make alone. And there was the ever-present menace of the British troops.

Abigail was lonely, but as much as she disliked their separation, she derived great satisfaction from her husband's role as a delegate: "I long impatiently to have you upon the Stage of action," she wrote to him. "I wish you every Publick as well, as private blessing, and that wisdom . . . to conduct you in this difficult day. The little flock remember Pappa; and kindly wish to see him. So does your most affectionate Abigail Adams."[8]

She wrote to John often. He wrote less frequently, and less emotionally. She could never count on getting an answer to a specific question. The postal service was poor—and expensive. It might take two weeks for a letter to travel the three hundred miles from Philadelphia to Braintree. When John, worried that his letters might be intercepted by the British, sent them by personal messenger, it took even longer.

Gradually Abigail gained confidence in herself and in her ability to make her own decisions about how to run the farm. But she depended on John's letters to keep up her spirits. They gave her comfort—and the news that she craved. They opened her eyes to new scenes, and soon she became a shrewd observer from afar.

John, in turn, depended on her letters for emotional support as well as up-to-date, detailed, and accurate information about events in New England. With her keen interest in political events, and her skill at observation, Abigail became his best informant. In fact, John once quoted from one of her letters in a speech before Congress. In Philadelphia John was surrounded by many men who advocated a cautious and conciliatory policy toward Great Britain. His wife reminded him that New England was ready to explode into war.

In order to better understand what was happening around her, Abigail began to fill her lonely days by reading about the struggles of the classical heroes against tyranny. She tried to make the ancient time come to life for her children by relating the stories she read to the present struggles. As Nabby sat with her and listened, Abigail encouraged John Quincy, now seven, to read aloud to her every day a page or two from Charles Rollins's *Ancient History*, "and hope he will from his desire to oblige me entertain a fondness for it," she wrote to her husband.[9] By this time Johnny had already learned from his mother how to read and write, and had begun the study of ancient languages.

A month later, when she still had not received any mail from John, she wrote:

> Dearest Friend
> Five weeks have past and not one line have I received. I had rather give a dollar for a letter by the post, tho the consequence should be that I Eat but one meal a day for these 3 weeks to come.

She went on to describe all the preparations for war that she was witnessing, such as mounting cannon on Beacon Hill, digging entrenchments and placing cannon on the Neck, and encamping a regiment there. "The people are much alarmed," she told him.[10]

She wrote also of a soldier seen lurking about the common who was thought to be a spy. Abigail thought he might be a deserter. And she wrote, too, of the soldiers marching past her window from the powder house who stopped to talk to her and asked if she would like some of the powder for protection. She declined. The powder was in good hands, she told the soldiers.

John had written on August 28, on his way to Philadelphia, but his letter was delayed in getting to her. In it he told her: "Tomorrow We reach the Theatre of Action. God Almighty grant us Wisdom and Virtue sufficient for the high Trust that is devolved upon Us."[11]

John fired off streams of instructions about the children's education. "For God's Sake make your Children, *hardy, active,* and *industrious,* for Strength, Activity and Industry will be their only Resource and Dependance," he said in another letter.[12] And they must be taught "not only to do virtuously but to excell."[13]

Abigail tried hard to comply with John's wishes. But they debated the best method of education for Johnny. Abigail wanted him trained at home by John Thaxter, who was her cousin and John's law clerk. She feared that sending Johnny to the town school would expose him to impure language and corrupt behavior. John disagreed. In her husband's absence she followed her own instincts, then diplomatically wrote to him: "When you return we can then consult what will be best."[14]

Abigail was mostly alone in Braintree after 1774, but she was thankful that Mary and Richard Cranch had settled there recently. Abigail and her sister enjoyed being neighbors and making trips together to visit their family at the parsonage where they had grown up. Years later, reminiscing about that time, John Quincy said his Smith grandparents had been a second father and mother to him, adding that he remembered his grandmother Elizabeth as the "guardian angel" of his childhood.

There were also visits to and from John's mother and his brothers. And John's two young law clerks, recent graduates of Harvard College, were living over John's office and taking their meals with Abigail. But nothing diminished the acute loneliness caused by the separation from:

My Much Loved Friend

I dare not express to you at 300 hundred miles distance how ardently I long for your return. . . . The whole collected stock of ten weeks absence knows not how to brook any longer restraint, but will break forth and flow thro my pen. . . . Many have been the anxious hours I have spent. . . .

Enumerating all her "fears and apprehensions," she went on to reflect that "whether the end will be tragical Heaven alone knows. You cannot be, I know, nor do I wish to see you an inactive Spectator, but if the Sword be drawn I bid adieu to all domestick felicity. . . ."

She ended her letter: "Your Mother sends her Love to you, and all your family too numerous to name desire to be remembered. You will receive Letters from two, who are as earnest to write to Pappa as if the welfare of a kingdom depended upon it."[15]

Johnny's letter followed immediately:

Sir:

I have been trying ever since you went away to learn to write you a Letter. I shall make poor work of it, but Sir Mamma says you will accept my endeavors, and that my Duty to you may be expressed in poor writing as well as good.

I hope I grow a better Boy and that you will have no occasion to be ashamed of me when you return. Mr. Thaxter says I learn my Books well—he is a very good Master. I read my Books to Mamma. We all long to see you; I am Sir your Dutiful Son, John Quincy Adams.[16]

As John's absence dragged on and few letters arrived from him, Abigail's loneliness intensified. Her imagination began to run wild. She feared the worst. Letters from Mercy Otis Warren reminding her that their husbands would be marked by the British as early victims, but cautioning her that they must never interfere with their husbands' patriotic duty, added to her fears. Mercy suggested, too, that they use Portia, patient and long-suffering wife of Brutus, a Roman political and military leader, as a classical example of courage. It wasn't long before Abigail, who had dropped the pen name "Diana" when she married, adopted "Portia" as her new name.

One evening in the middle of September, Abigail, her sister Betsy, not yet married and still living at home with her parents, and little Nabby returned from a daylong visit to Uncle Norton Quincy, living now at Mount Wollaston. She found Mr. Thaxter waiting at the door with a letter from John. "It really gave me such a flow of Spirits that I was not composed eno to sleep till one oclock," she wrote to her husband.

She went on to fill a long letter with descriptions of life at home. But fearing that it was carelessly written, she pleaded with him to "burn all these Letters least they should fall from your pocket and thus expose your most affectionate Friend."[17]

John replied: "The Conclusion of your Letter makes my Heart throb more than a cannonade would. You bid me burn your Letters. But I must forget you first."[18]

As politics took over the inner rhythm of John's life, Abigail entered into his world with so much sympathy and understanding that her moods began to swing with his. When he wrote, "There is in the Congress a Collection of the greatest Men upon this Continent, in Point of Abilities, Virtues and Fortunes,"[19] then she was happy that he was on the "Stage of action." But when he moved from exultation to despair, and told her, "I am wearied to Death with the Life I lead. The Business of Congress is tedious, beyond Expression,"[20] she suffered with him, and longed for his return.

October 25, 1774, was Abigail and John's tenth wedding anniversary. Abigail spent it home alone with the children in Braintree. Delegate Adams was too busy in Congress to note the occasion.

The next day Congress finished and John prepared to return home. He left "the happy, the peaceful, the elegant, the hospitable, and polite city of Philadelphia"[21] in the pouring rain on Friday, October 28. Sunday, October 30, was his thirty-ninth birthday.

On the evening of November 9, he arrived in Braintree to a joyous reunion with his family. As he lifted his excited, shouting children in his arms, and looked beyond them to his Abigail, a little plumper, perhaps, but delightfully so, and pink with pleasure at the sight of him, he was grateful to be home.

∼ CHAPTER VIII ∼

"I want some sentimental Effusions of the Heart"

T he First Continental Congress which had assembled in Carpenter's Hall in Philadelphia on September 5, 1774, had been summoned not for independence but for liberty as Americans understood that word. They were struggling to preserve the freedom the colonies already had. Independence was not a conscious goal. It was viewed as a last resort. Yet early in 1775, as her husband wrote a series of newspaper essays defending the rights of the colonies, Abigail wrote to Mercy, "We cannot be happy without being free, . . . we cannot be free without being secure in our property. . . . We know too well the blessings of freedom, to tamely resign it."

"Is it not better to die the last of British freemen than live the first of British Slaves?" she asked Mercy. When she read George III's speech at the opening of Parliament on November 20, published in the *Massachusetts Spy* on February 2, she continued her letter, "The die is cast. . . . Heaven only knows what is next to take place but it seems to me the Sword is now our only, yet dreadful alternative."[1]

Then, just two and a half months later, on the clear, cold morning of Wednesday, April 19, 1775, the first shots of the American Revolution were fired at Lexington and Concord. The war with England had begun. The dreaded message, carried frantically by word of mouth and galloping express, moved across the land in shock waves.

Abigail's worst fears had become a reality. Yet now she felt calmer than she had in months. The crisis she had been certain was unavoidable had finally occurred, and she refused to panic. John's presence at home helped.

But just one week later Delegate Adams was on his way to Philadelphia again to join the Second Continental Congress. When he left home he was sick to his stomach, feverish, and numb with horror and foreboding. The other delegates had left without him two days before. Now Abigail saw him off in a horse-drawn cart borrowed from her father, with a young man to look after him, a cake from her mother, and pleas to take his medicine. She tried to be "heroick," but confessed that her "heart felt like a heart of Led."[2]

Once again, Abigail and the children were alone, just half an hour's ride from the American lines encircling the British army in Boston. Boston had become, in effect, a British camp, closed off from the rest of New England. Many houses, including the Adamses' house on Queen Street, had been taken over by the British army. For the most part, the redcoats allowed no one to enter or leave the city. A short time later a few people were permitted to leave each day, but they could take with them very few of their possessions. These weary refugees from Boston, many with their little children in tow, needed a place to go. Abigail, as did many of her neighbors, housed as many people as she could—for "a day, a night, a week."

As Massachusetts was plunged into the fierce tumult of the American Revolution, every alarm sent minutemen marching past Abigail's front door, hungry, thirsty, looking for a place to rest. The indomitable Abigail tried to accommodate the soldiers also. One night she housed an entire company of militia on their way to join the encampments outside Boston. Some of the soldiers slept in the attic, some in the barn. A few spread blankets on the parlor floor. The next morning, as they drilled in the field behind the house, little Johnny proudly marched up and down with them.

"The house is a Scene of Confusion . . . you can hardly imagine how we live," Abigail wrote to John a month after he had left.[3] Three weeks later, when she still had not heard from John, she was unable to conceal her distress. She wrote to her absent husband:

I set down to write to you a monday, but really could not compose myself sufficiently: the anxiety I suffered from not hearing one syllable from you for more than five weeks; and the new distress ariseing from the arrival of recruits agitated me more than I have been. . . .

Perhaps, the very next Letter I write will inform you that I am driven away from our, yet quiet cottage. . . . Courage I know we have in abundance, conduct I hope we shall not want, but powder— where shall we get a sufficient supply?

. . . You tell me you know not when you shall see me. I never trust myself long with the terrors which sometimes intrude themselves upon me.

I hope we shall see each other again and rejoice together in happier Days. The little ones are well and send Duty to Pappa. Dont fail of letting me hear from you by every opportunity, every line is like a precious Relict of the Saints.

She continued with a practical request: would John purchase a "bundle of pins" for her? The "cry" for pins was "great."[4] "Pray, don't . . . forget my pins," she reminded him the following month.[5] "Not one pin to be had for love or money."[6]

"We live in Continual Expectation of Hostilities. Scarcely a day that does not produce some," she told her husband.[7] But she described herself as "very brave upon the whole," then went on to ask John how much Congress knew about the suffering of Boston: "Does every Member feel for us? Can they realize what we suffer? And can they believe with what patience and fortitude we endure the conflict?"[8]

Much to his wife's dismay, John occasionally showed her letters to fellow delegates in the hope that they would understand. He told a friend, "There is a Lady at the Foot of Pens Hill, who obliges me with clearer and fuller Intelligence, than I can get from a whole Committee of Gentlemen."[9]

Fearful that British redcoats might attack coastal towns like Braintree and Weymouth, John wrote to Abigail that if an attack actually came, she must "fly to the Woods with our Children. Give my tenderest love to them."[10]

In fact, the conflict did come to Braintree, causing many to flee when the British raided nearby Grape Island to take off hay for their horses. Both of John's brothers were members of the militia and shouldered muskets in this and other frequent conflicts. But Abigail was not one to panic. She knew that should she be in real danger, she could accept her brother-in-law Peter's offer of the safety of his home, further inland and away from the scene of the fighting. But for now, she would wait and see.

When the first major battle came, Abigail chose to remain, and even to be a witness. Before dawn on Saturday, June 17, she was awakened by the sound of far-off gunfire. All through the sweltering morning, as she went about her chores, the dull boom of cannon intruded on her consciousness.

Finally she took seven-year-old Johnny by the hand and together they walked to the top of Penn's Hill and climbed up on the rocks for a better view. In horror they stared across the blue bay and into the black, smoking mass that was all that was left of Charlestown. Her father's birthplace had been burned to the ground. John Quincy never forgot the scene.

Abigail and Johnny walked

Dr. Joseph Warren, the Adamses' good friend and family doctor. He fell "gloriously fighting for his country" during the Battle of Bunker Hill.
Oil by John Singleton Copley, 1774.

~

slowly back home, tears blurring their eyes. Soon riders on the Coast Road to Plymouth stopped at the farmhouse for a drink of water. They told of the great battle under way on Bunker Hill* in Charlestown. One brought word that the beloved Dr. Joseph Warren had been killed in the fighting.

Third only to Sam Adams and John Hancock as a political leader of the radical Whig party, Dr. Warren had gone into battle as a volunteer. He had insisted on fighting side by side with the soldiers, who were heartened by his courage. Hit on the right side of his head with a musket ball, he died instantly. Whispered accounts said he was beheaded. He had been a widower and the father of four young children.

* It was actually Breed's Hill.

It was Joseph Warren who, on April 18, had dispatched his good friend Paul Revere, a trusted express rider as well as Boston's most gifted silversmith, to warn Sam Adams and John Hancock that the British might make a sudden march to seize both them and the stores of powder in Concord.

Paul Revere, gifted silversmith and engraver, is perhaps best remembered as the trusted express rider who, on April 18, warned the colonists that the redcoats were coming. Oil by John Singleton Copley, about 1768–1770.

∼

Joseph Warren had been the Adamses' good friend and their family doctor in Boston. His skill in setting a "very bad fracture" had recently saved Johnny from the loss of a finger. Now he was dead at the age of thirty-four, his fine clothes soaked with blood. "Everybody remembered his fine, silk fringed waistcoat," a British officer later recalled.[11]

Nabby and Johnny were bewildered and sad. Abigail was distraught. She gave vent to her feelings in a letter to John the next day: "The Day; perhaps the decisive Day is come on which the fate of America depends. My bursting Heart must find vent at my pen." She went on to tell him of Dr. Warren's death: he "fell gloriously fighting for his Country. . . . Great is our Loss."

Quoting from the Bible, she continued: "The race is not to the swift, nor the battle to the strong, but the God of Israel is he that giveth strength and power unto his people. Trust in him at all times. . . . God is a refuge for us." At times of stress Abigail turned to her faith in God to sustain her.

She continued her letter: "Charlestown is laid in ashes. The Battle began upon our intrenchments upon Bunker Hill, a Saturday morning about 3 o'clock and has not ceased yet and tis now 3 o'clock Sabbath afternoon." She ended by telling her husband: "I cannot compose myself to write any further at present."

Two days later Abigail concluded her letter, alluding once again to the death of Dr. Warren: "The tears of multitudes pay tribute to his memory."[12]

John responded by telling his wife, "You are really brave, my dear, you are an Heroine."[13]

And she continued to be a heroine. One day Johnny came into the house to find his mother and his uncle Elihu, dressed in his minuteman uniform, a hunting shirt with a musket slung on his back. The two were in the kitchen, putting all his mother's treasured pewter spoons into a large kettle. As Johnny watched his mother calmly directing the activity in her quiet voice, he slowly began to understand that they were melting down her precious pewter to make bullets. As his eyes met hers across the room, he felt a surge of love and pride.

"Do you wonder," said John Quincy Adams sixty-eight years later, "that a boy of seven who witnessed this scene should be a patriot?"[14]

By July 1775 every bed in Braintree was filled by families forced to flee from occupied Boston. Abigail reorganized her household to accommodate an entire family in which there was an expectant mother.

"It would make your heart ake to see what difficulties and distresses the poor Boston people are driven to," she wrote to John.[15]

As she continued to help the displaced people, supervise the mowing of the hay, keep the caterpillars out of the fruit trees, worry that the drought they were experiencing that summer might damage the crops, and, of course, care for her "little brood," she still found time to write. But she playfully complained, "I have received a good deal of paper from you; I wish it had been more covered." She reproached John for his short letters, yet she acknowledged, "I must not grumble. I know your time is not yours, nor mine."[16]

As if to compensate, her letters to him grew longer, filled with details of the war in Massachusetts, and of their family and domestic concerns. She was pleased when John called her his "home-front reporter," telling her that her letters "contain more particulars than any Letters I had before received from any Body."[17]

More than ever now, letter writing became a way of life for her. "There are perticular times when I feel such an uneasiness, such a restlessness, as neither Company, Books, family Cares or any other thing will remove, my Pen is my only pleasure."[18] As she committed her thoughts to paper, she gained a clearer understanding of her own role as a wife and mother. Her letters became, in effect, a revealing source of self-analysis. They frequently varied in information and opinions, but never in their tenderness and thoughtfulness. She might be emotionally upset, but she was always conscious of her husband's enormous responsibility. And she was always intellectually keen, turning to examples from history to help her understand what was happening around her.

She seemed to feel that as a woman she could best show her patriotism by supporting her husband in his work for their country. She understood that John was genuinely torn between his public and private life, and that he suffered when he was forced to be away from his family for long periods of time. She didn't ask him to choose between them.

But there were times when she felt overwhelmed by all her responsibilities: "I want you for my protector," she pleaded.[19] A few days later she couldn't resist chiding him:

All the letters I receive from you seem to be wrote in so much haste, that they scarcely leave room for a social feeling. They let me know that you exist, but some of them contain scarcely six lines. I want some sentimental Effusions of the Heart. . . . I lay claim to a Larger Share than I have had.

She ended that letter:

Our little ones send Duty to Pappa. You would smile to see them all gather round mamma upon the reception of a letter to hear from pappa, and Charles with open mouth, What does par say—did not he write no more. And little Tom says I wish I could see par.[20]

She never lost her sense of humor. She told John that Charles, now five, asks, "Mar, who is for us and who against us?" John would laugh, she told him, to see the children run at the sight of his letters—"like chickens for a crumb, when the Hen clucks."[21]

~ CHAPTER IX ~
"Mrs. Delegate"

When the members of the Continental Congress reassembled after the Battle of Lexington, it was John Adams who led them patiently but relentlessly down the path to independence. Long before most of the other delegates were ready to think of independence, John had made up his mind. He had a clear picture from his wife of the devastating situation in Massachusetts. Her letters brought the reality of war home to him. He understood full well that Congress could no longer afford to offer an olive branch in one hand without pointing a musket with the other. When some members of Congress pressed for conciliation with Great Britain, Abigail's letters echoed in John's mind and he pressed for powder.

But no man in Congress had a clearer idea of what independence would entail: the risks, the obligations, the burdens that it would impose on Americans. To this end he persuaded Congress to enlist the Continental army under the command of George Washington. Strong leadership, he knew, would be critical to success in further battles. Washington was a Virginian, experienced in the military, financially able, and of impeccable character and firm, quiet judgment.

John recognized also that America's ability to protect her own commerce on the high seas would be vital to her survival as a nation, and he became a leader in establishing the American navy.

During this period John poured out his feelings to Abigail, expressing his hopes and frustrations. He was annoyed when other members of Congress were not as quick to see the facts as he saw them. It was all he could do to sit through their tedious debates, the "nibbling and quibbling," as he called it. "My Dear," he wrote to her,

It is now almost three Months since I left you, in every Part of which my Anxiety about you and the Children, as well as our Country, has been extreme.

The Business I have had upon my Mind has been as great and important as can be intrusted to Man. . . . When 50 or 60 Men have a Constitution to form for a great Empire, at the same Time that they have a Country of fifteen hundred Miles extent to fortify, Millions to arm and train, a Naval Power to begin, an extensive Commerce to regulate, numerous Tribes of Indians to negotiate with, a standing Army of Twenty seven Thousand Men to raise, pay, victual and officer, I really shall pity those 50 or 60 Men.[1]

Citing all his many duties and responsibilities as an apology for not writing longer and more frequent letters, John suggested to Abigail that she depend on Paul Revere for more detailed news of the activities of Congress.

On July 2, 1775, newly appointed General George Washington arrived in Cambridge, Massachusetts, to assume command of the Continental army. Two weeks later he paid a call on Mrs. Adams, carrying a letter to her from John. She had worried that Washington was an aristocratic Virginian and a slaveholder, but she knew John liked him, and when she met him she was quickly charmed. She "was struck with General Washington," she wrote to her husband. His appointment gave "universal satisfaction."[2] Like many other patriots, she instantly saw godlike qualities in him. She was delighted when the general invited her to visit the army camp at Cambridge, and to dine with him.

When Benjamin Franklin, recently returned from Europe, visited the Boston area, he was a guest at the home of Abigail's uncle Isaac. Abigail joined them for dinner. She was impressed by the philosopher and scientist, describing him as "grave, yet pleasant and affable." She pronounced him a "true patriot."[3]

Travelers and politicians up from Philadelphia also stopped at her house to visit. These meetings provided her with firsthand information about John and the activities of Congress. The men, in turn, were impressed by this woman of fiery political principles. In fact, while John and Abigail's political views were usually similar, she sometimes took an even more extreme position than he.

*George Washington,
in the uniform of a colonel
in the Virginia militia,
was nominated by
John Adams to be
commander in chief of the
Continental Army
at about the time this
portrait was painted.
Oil by Charles Wilson
Peale, 1772.*

~

As the wife of a revolutionary leader and member of Congress, Abigail became the center of attention in Braintree. As she began to meet more of the important political figures, she came to enjoy the increased respect being paid her by her neighbors, and her self-confidence grew. She sometimes liked to think of herself being called "Mrs. Delegate."

"Why should we not assume your titles when we give you up our names?" she asked her husband.[4]

When the Second Continental Congress recessed at the beginning of August 1775, instead of returning home John went directly to Watertown to attend the sessions of the General Court. He went home to Braintree on weekends only. Abigail spent the last three days of the session with him in Watertown. He returned to Philadelphia on September 12 for the reconvening of Congress, which was now enlarged by the presence of representatives from all thirteen colonies.

When John left for Philadelphia he left behind in Massachusetts a major epidemic of dysentery, an often fatal intestinal disease marked by fever, cramps, vomiting, and diarrhea. The epidemic was probably caused by the poor sanitation practices of the American soldiers.

While John was still in Watertown, Abigail had written "with a sad Heart" to tell him that his brother Elihu was dangerously ill with the disease. "Your mother is with him in great anguish." The next day she continued her letter to tell him that Elihu was gone.[5]

Now she was writing to John in Philadelphia: "Our House is an hospital in every part. . . . So sickly and so Mortal a time the oldest Man does not remember," she continued, asking John to send her an ounce of turkey rhubarb, some cinnamon, nutmegs, and cloves, and an ounce of Indian root so she could make some medicine.[6]

Abigail, little Tommy, and several of the servants were all desperately ill. Tommy, just three years old, wanted only his mother to care for him. Abigail, so weak herself that she could barely stand, dragged herself to his bed to give him what comfort she could. Through it all Elizabeth Smith came every day, going from one sickbed to the other, ministering to her daughter and her little grandson. Abigail had sent the other children out of the house in the hope that they wouldn't catch the disease.

Sickness and death were in almost every family. "The desolation of War is not so distressing as the Havock made by the pestilence. Some poor parents are mourning the loss of three, four, and five children, and some families are wholly stripped of every Member. . . . Sister Elihu Adams lost her youngest child last night with this disorder," a distressed Abigail wrote to her husband.[7] She ended every letter with a fervent prayer for his good health.

John was unaware of what was happening. It took more than a month for Abigail's letters to reach him. Absorbed in politics, he wrote no letter home for three weeks.

By the time Abigail had regained some of her strength and Tommy was safely recuperated, Elizabeth Smith had caught the disease. Now Abigail went to the Weymouth Parsonage every day to care for her. On the morning of October 1, Abigail brought her mother tea, raised her head so she might swallow a few drops, then heard her gasp and saw her look up at her with "a look that pierced my heart, and which I shall never forget; it was the eagerness of a last look." Abigail recognized "the last sad silence of a Friend."[8] Elizabeth Smith died at five o'clock that afternoon.

Abigail poured out her grief to John: "How can I tell you (o my bursting Heart) that my Dear Mother has Left me." Her father, she told him, set "the best of Examples of patience and submission. My Sisters send their love to you and are greatly afflicted. You often Express'd your anxiety for me when you left me before, surrounded with Terrors, but my Trouble then was as the small dust in the balance compaird to what I have since endured."[9]

Separated from him "who used to be a comforter towards me in affliction," she was overwhelmed by her sense of loss. "I know I wound your Heart. Ought I to give relief to my own by paining yours?" she worried. But her pen was always freer than her tongue, she apologized.[10]

Patty, Abigail's servant girl, died a week later. Patty had suffered terribly for five weeks, wasting away while Abigail stood by helplessly. Patty had wanted only Abigail to care for her. Abigail, still reeling from the blow of her mother's death, spent hours at her servant's sickbed.

For weeks after her mother's death, Abigail visted no one except her father and sisters. Running the farm took all her energy. Evenings, after she had read to the children and put them to bed, she sat alone by the fire, thinking about her mother and her absent husband. She was consumed by grief.

Like many teenagers, Abigail had been unable to understand her mother's worries about her as she was growing up. It wasn't until she had begun to raise children of her own that she fully understood her mother's concern. Now the memory of her impatience with her mother's overwatchfulness turned to remorse. She thought of Elizabeth Smith's boundless patience and tenderness, and of her wit and keen mind that marked Abigail as her mother's child. And she remembered her love.

As the epidemic continued to ravage the community, John remained unaware of what was happening. When he finally did learn of the devastating losses, his letters were filled with compassion and tenderness. "If I could write as well as you, my sorrows would be as eloquent as yours, but upon my Word, I cannot," he wrote his grieving wife.[11] He told her how painful it was to be too far away to "fly home" and share her burdens. He sent his love to her father and to Betsy, for he knew it must be harder even for Betsy since she was still at home with her father.[12]

"I feel—I tremble for You. Poor Tommy!" He hoped Tommy had by now "recovered his plump cheeks and his fine Bloom." And he rejoiced that Nabby and her brothers had escaped.[13]

Abigail was pleased when John wrote special notes of condolence on the loss of their grandmother to the children. He reminded Nabby, now ten years old, of all her grandmother's virtues, and hoped that as she grew older she would remember much of her advice and be careful to heed it. There was no substitute, he told her, for the experience, the wisdom, the love of a grandmother.

This Abigail knew full well. Thoughts of her own grandmother flooded her memory now. "The instructions of my own Grandmamma are as fresh upon my mind this day as any I ever received from my own parents and made as lasting and powerful impressions."[14]

~ Chapter x ~
"Remember the Ladies"

A s the Christmas season of 1775 approached, Abigail began to find her separation from John unbearable. She had been ill again, suffering from "Jaundice, Rhumatism and a most violent cold," she wrote to him. She was distressed, too, because a week of unusually cold weather and snow had ruined many hundreds of bushels of apples.

Although upset that John might not be home for Christmas, she could still write, "I hope the publick will reap what I sacrifice."

Her mind was filled with the great issues confronting the Congress: "If a form of Government is to be established here what one will be assumed?" she asked her husband. "Will it be left to our assemblies to chuse one? and will not many men have many minds? and shall we not run into Dissentions among ourselves?" she wondered. She feared that power was dangerous, and that even those most eager to protect the rights of the people might, when vested with power, abuse it. "The great fish swallow up the small," she warned.

"Ten thousand Difficulties" might arise in the formation of the government: "If we separate from Britain, what Code of Laws will be established. How shall we be governed so as to retain our Liberties? Can any government be free which is not administered by general stated Laws? Who shall frame these Laws? Who will give them force and energy?"

In the same letter Abigail told John that his dead brother's little daughter was living with her now. "I feel a tenderer affection for her as she has lost a kind parent," she wrote. As for their own children, they missed their father almost as acutely as their mother did. Little Tommy, she wrote, had gotten it into his head that his father was engaged in a battle and wouldn't come home until it was over.[1]

John, too, was distressed by the separation, and finally obtained leave to return home before Congress adjourned. He arrived in Braintree unexpectedly on December 21. But he remained for just one month.

During that time John and Abigail seriously discussed the possibility that John resign as a delegate. Ultimately, he left the decision up to his wife. She couldn't bring herself to ask him to stay.

"I found his honor and reputation much dearer to me, than my own present pleasure and happiness, and I could by no means consent to his resigning at present, as I was fully convinced he must suffer if he quitted," she wrote to Mercy Warren.[2]

They briefly discussed the possibility that Abigail accompany John back to Philadelphia, leaving the children in the care of relatives. Some of the delegates had their wives with them. But Abigail felt that it was difficult enough for the children to be without a father. She could not leave them without a mother, too. To move them all to Philadelphia was far too expensive.

For a short while after John left for Philadelphia everything was quiet in Massachusetts. In the Congress many of the delegates were still hoping for a reconciliation with Great Britain. They had not seen and felt the war firsthand as had Massachusetts.

Then on January 10, 1776, a pamphlet entitled *Common Sense* was published in Philadelphia. Written by Thomas Paine, an Englishman who had recently emigrated to America, it pleaded the case of the colonists in simple language. "The period of debate is closed," it said, putting before the people the common sense of independence.[3] The colonists were ready to hear what it said.

When Abigail received a copy from John, she wondered how any friends of the colonies could hesitate one moment at adopting its appealing sentiments. She would try to spread it around wherever she could, she told her husband, and hoped it could be "carried speedily into Execution."[4]

By the beginning of March the calm was over. On Saturday evening, March 2, as Abigail sat writing to John in the quiet of a sleeping household, she abruptly interjected: "But hark! the house this instant shakes with the roar of cannon. . . . I have been to the door and find 'tis a cannonade from our army. Orders I find are come for all the remaining militia to repair to the lines a Monday night by 12 o'clock. No sleep for me tonight."

"I went to bed after 12 but got no rest. The cannon continued firing and my heart beat pace with them all night," she continued.[5]

The next day, as minutemen ran past her door, she walked to the top of Penn's Hill, to the same spot where she had witnessed the Battle of Bunker Hill less than a year before. From there she could hear the roar of the cannon and see every shell being thrown.

This bombardment of shells into Boston from the American lines was the cover under which General Washington's men were placing artillery on Dorchester Heights, which overlooked Boston. Soon the British general realized his impossible plight, and he gave the order to his troops to evacuate. George Washington had won his first victory: he had forced the British out of Boston. The city was liberated on March 17. British presence there had come to an end after 145 years.

The day before they left, Abigail had sensed that the British were about to evacuate Boston: "the plot thickens; and some very important Crisis seems near at hand," she wrote. She described to John "the largest Fleet ever seen in America. You may count upwards of 100 & 70 Sail. They look like a Forest." British troops, government officials, and loyalists were sailing out of Boston Harbor, never to return. When chairs, tables, lids of desks, and other pieces of furniture began to wash up on the shores of Weymouth and Braintree in the next few days, Abigail believed the rumors she had heard that the British troops had taken with them everything they could carry and destroyed the rest.

Abigail was elated at the nearly bloodless victory, but she had mixed feelings. Perhaps, she reflected, it was necessary that the "Seat of War" be moved from New England to the southern colonies "that each may have a proper sympathy for the other, and unite in a separation."[6] Southerners, she reasoned, could not possibly fully understand the need for independence unless they, too, experienced British troops drilling in their cities and the sound of cannon disturbing their sleep.

But she worried that Virginians might not be able to stand against "our common Enemy" as had New Englanders. Virginians were slave owners, and Abigail questioned their ability to fight for freedom while denying liberty to nearly half their population.[7]

As she artlessly mingled news of the war just outside her door with tales about domestic concerns, Abigail wrote to her husband, "As to all your own private affairs I generally avoid mentioning them to you; I take the

best care I am capable of them." She went on to ask him to send her a "Grammer" and Lord Chesterfield's Letters. She had heard them "very highly spoken of." She ended with a postscript: "Pray convey me a little paper. I have but enough for one Letter more."[8]

Two weeks later she gently chided her absent husband: "I wish you would write me a Letter half as long as I write you; and tell me if you may where your Fleet are gone? What sort of Defence Virginia can make against our common Enemy? . . ."

But her spirits were brighter:

> I feel very differently at the approach of spring to what I did a month ago. We knew not then whether we could plant or sow with safety, whether when we had toild we could reap the fruits of our own industery, whether we could rest in our own Cottages, or whether we should not be driven from the sea coasts to seek shelter in the wilderness, but now we feel as if we might sit under our own vine and eat the good of the land.[9]

When John's mother worried that as the British moved south her son would not be safe in Philadelphia, John replied irritably that he wished she would stop fussing about him and not be so fearful. It would be nice, he told Abigail, if his mother had some of his wife's strength and courage.

By now John's prolonged absence was beginning to produce subtle changes in their marriage. Abigail was busy not only with domestic chores such as making soap and homespun clothes, but had quietly taken over management of the farm. She had to make decisions concerning breeding livestock, and even had to act on an unexpected opportunity to purchase a choice parcel of land. But the land had to be purchased in John's name, since by law a woman could not own property.

In a letter "wholy Domestick" Abigail outlined for John the scarcity of labor and the high wages they commanded because of the war, and the bills she had collected and paid. She gave her husband a full account of the weather and the crops. She hoped, she told him, that "tho you may have matters of infinately more importance before you," her letter would "come as a relaxation to you." She ended by telling him that when she had asked the children what they wanted Pappa to send to them, each had answered, "A Book." But Tommy particularly wanted a picture book, and Charles a history of the king and queen. Their mother wasn't surprised, since a book "is the only present Pappa has been used to make to them."[10]

John, for his part, was proud of the management skills of his "Farmeress." In fact, he teased her, her wise and prudent management of their house and farm might cause their neighbors to think their affairs were better conducted in his absence.[11]

Abigail responded that she was grateful for John's praise and, therefore, spurred on to fulfill her duties as efficiently as possible in the absence of her "dearest friend."[12]

Warmed by his approval, she began now to refer to "*Our* own private affairs" or "*our* house at Boston." Until then it had always been *your* farm or *your* business. John continued to speak of "*my* affairs at home." But both sensed the large measure of dependence he had come to place on her, and the resulting equality in their marriage.

Gradually, subtly, since the beginning of John's involvement in the Revolution, with its emphasis on individual rights, Abigail's perception of herself and of the role of women had been changing. Left at home alone for months at a time, she had begun to reflect on the importance of her position as a woman and on her own growing independence. Absorbed in the details of the war and the direction in which Congress was moving, she focused now on concerns that had been troubling her for many months. She expressed these thoughts in a letter to John that has echoed down through the centuries, and marks, in a sense, the beginning of change in the status of women.

Abigail had already spoken out for separation from England: "They are unworthy to be our Breathren," she had written.[13] Now she wrote to her husband:

I long to hear that you have declared an independancy—and by the way in the new Code of Laws which I suppose it will be necessary for you to make I desire you would Remember the Ladies, and be more generous and favourable to them than your ancestors. Do not put such unlimited power into the hands of the Husbands. Remember all Men would be tyrants if they could.[14]

*Abigail believed strongly that women deserved to be treated as equals.
"Remember the Ladies," she urged her husband in her letter to him
when she knew he was writing a new code of laws.*

~

As a lawyer's wife, Abigail had come to the conclusion that, under British rule, the major problem facing women was their legal subordination to their husbands. She knew that English law stipulated that only those who were *not* dependent on others had rights. Since women were dependent on their fathers or their husbands, they had no rights themselves.

Now, as America prepared to declare her independence from England, Abigail hoped that a new code of laws would be written that provided for an improvement in this traditional arrangement. She recognized that under English law many wives stood in the same relationship to their husbands as the indentured servant to his master. Their husbands controlled their property, directed their labor, and provided their support. Abigail sought for American women a separate legal existence that would guarantee the wife a share in the fruits of their mutual labor, recognize her voice in the education of daughters, and grant her the right to institute a legal action against an abusive husband. When Abigail asked that husbands' "unlimited power" over their wives be curbed, she was revealing her worry that even the kindest and most generous of men could not be trusted with arbitrary power. She was well aware of how power had made a tyrant of King George III.

"If perticuliar care and attention is not paid to the Ladies we are determined to foment a Rebelion," she warned her husband, "and will not hold ourselves bound by any Laws in which we have no voice, or Representation."

She continued her letter:

"That your Sex are Naturally Tyrannical is a Truth so thoroughly established as to admit of no dispute, but such of you as wish to be happy willingly give up the harsh title of Master for the more tender and endearing one of Friend. Why then, not put it out of the power of the vicious and the Lawless to use us with cruelty and indignity with impunity. Men of Sense in all Ages abhor those customs which treat us only as the vassals of your Sex. Regard us then as Beings placed by providence under your protection and in immitation of the Supreem Being make use of that power only for our happiness."[15]

Women were nurturers and healers, assignments of the highest order in nature and society, she agreed. Their roles were different from their husbands'. But women deserved to be treated as equals. Abigail was in no way denying wifehood or motherhood as the primary role of women. Nor was she asserting women's rights as equal participants in politics or the economy. She was calling for a legal system under which women could find maximum fulfillment in their ascribed roles as wives and mothers.

John's casual, even lighthearted response—"As to your extraordinary code of laws, I cannot but laugh"—was not cause for laughter for his wife. "Your Letter was the first Intimation that . . . a . . . Tribe more numerous and powerfull than all the rest were grown discontented," he continued.[16]

Abigail understood that her husband believed that women's delicacy, domesticity, and concern for their children rendered them more valuable as a private influence on husbands and sons than they could possibly be in any public position. Behind nearly every great man of history, John argued, there had been a woman of unusual knowledge and ambition. But it was not enough for Abigail.

"Whilst you are proclaiming peace and good will to men, emancipating all nations, you insist upon retaining an absolute power over wives," she retorted.

She was disappointed in John's reply, but she missed him desperately:

How many are the solitary hours I spend, ruminating upon the past and anticipating the future, whilst you overwhelmd with the cares of State, have but few moments you can devote to any individual. All domestick pleasures and injoyments are absorbed in the great and important duty you owe your Country "for our Country is as it were a secondary God, and the First and greatest parent. It is to be preferred to Parents, Wives, Children, Friends and all things the Gods only excepted. . . ." Thus do I supress every wish, and silence every Murmer, acquiesceing in a painfull Separation from the companion of my youth, and the Friend of my Heart.[17]

～ CHAPTER XI ～
"I want a companion a Nights"

While Abigail was urging her husband to recognize the changing role of women in the new republic, John was engrossed in agitating for a resolution in Congress calling for a "compleat Separation" from England. "It is now universally acknowledged that we are, and must be, independent States," he said. It only remained to determine whether there should be "a declaration of it."[1] In a steady, point-by-point argument, John Adams proceeded to show why independence, which was almost a certainty, must be *declared.* Thomas Jefferson, describing John's impact on the Congress, said he spoke "with a power of thought and expression that moved us from our seats."[2] Two other delegates called Abigail's husband the "atlas of independence." In the end, no one could stand before the torrent of his insistent demonstrations. Thomas Jefferson, whose "masterly pen" was highly regarded in the Congress, was chosen to draft the declaration.

The resolution of independence was adopted on July 2, 1776. The next day a jubilant John wrote to his wife: "Yesterday the greatest Question was decided, which ever was debated in America, and a greater perhaps, never was or will be decided among Men. A Resolution was passed without one dissenting Colony 'that these united Colonies, are, and of right ought to be free and independent States.'"[3]

Abigail received the news in Boston, where she was staying at her uncle Isaac's house with her children and several other members of the family, including her sister Mary and Richard Cranch and their children, her sister

Betsy, Cotton Tufts, Jr., and John Thaxter. They had just been inoculated against smallpox. For the war had brought with it an even greater threat than the British army: the movement of soldiers and civilians had stirred up a widespread epidemic of smallpox.

Earlier in June, John, sensing that prolonged separation from his family would continue to be the pattern of his life, had purchased a blank folio volume in which he began the practice of making a meticulous copy of every letter he sent home. In one of the first letters he recorded, John told Abigail: "The Small Pox is ten times more terrible than Britons, Canadians and Indians together."[4]

Abigail knew he was right, and that she should have herself and the children inoculated against the disease. It was a decision she could not reach lightly, for she understood full well the gravity of the situation. She knew that waiting to take smallpox "in the natural way" was courting death. She had tried to calm her own fears by reminding herself that the chances of survival were ten times greater with inoculation than if one contracted the disease naturally. Yet, she had agonized, how could she

The red brick state house, which later came to be known as Independence Hall, in Philadelphia, where John Adams first met Thomas Jefferson. It was here that the delegates to the Second Continental Congress met to decide to fight for "independency."

~

A View of Boston Taken on the Road to Dorchester, 1776.
Abigail and her family traveled this road on their way from Braintree to
Boston to be inoculated against smallpox. In order that the children might
have milk, Abigail took along a cow. Drawn by William Pierrie.
Engraved by James Newton. Hand-colored aquatint.

knowingly place her children in mortal danger or risk their serious disfigurement through inoculation? She had not forgotten her concern for John when he had been inoculated twelve years before.

Like many other women whose husbands were serving their country, she had had to make the decision alone. While she yearned for John's guidance and the comfort of his presence, she knew she had postponed the decision as long as she could. Now the war was forcing her to face the issue.

Finally, she had determined that she and her family would all undergo inoculation together, and they had accepted her uncle Isaac and aunt Elizabeth's invitation to use their home. When they loaded the cart that would accompany them to Boston, they included bedsheets and quilts as well as hay and wood. And in order that the children, who ranged in age from three to eleven years old, might have milk to drink, Abigail arranged to take along a cow.

The process of inoculation had changed little since John's experience. Abigail's family isolated themselves at Isaac Smith's home for several weeks. There they endured exhausting preparations, including a carefully restricted diet and medicines, and were then subjected to a mild form of the disease. Nearly every house in Boston had become a "hospital," filled with people following this procedure.

On receiving John's news of the Declaration of Independence, Abigail was able to forget for a moment all her many worries about the health of her children and her own inflamed eyes, so sore that she had not been able to write to John for almost a month. And on July 18, while waiting for the symptoms of smallpox to develop, she was able to join the crowds thronging to Kings Street to hear the Declaration read aloud from the statehouse balcony. At the conclusion of the reading the crowd broke into cheers, bells rang, cannons were fired, "and every face appeard joyfull." Later Abigail watched as the king's arms and other symbols of royal authority were taken down and burned. "Thus ends royall Authority in this State, and all the people shall say Amen," she wrote to her husband.[5] As shouts of "God save our American states" rang out, a jubilant Abigail realized that Massachusetts was no longer a colony. It was now a state in the youngest nation on earth. Fifteen years had elapsed since the protests had begun with the Writs of Assistance.

But Abigail didn't have much time to dwell on the joyous news of independence. Soon, two of her children were desperately ill. Johnny and Abigail herself had come through the experience with relative ease. But Nabby, Charley, and Tommy had had to be inoculated a second time. This time Tommy had responded with a very mild reaction. Nabby, though, suffered the worst horror of smallpox for those who survived it. She was covered with six or seven hundred eruptions, and her complexion was permanently scarred.

Charles's inoculation never took. After the third unsuccessful attempt, he finally caught the disease from being exposed to the large household undergoing inoculation. The normally bright-eyed, happy little boy, with soft curly blond hair and long eyelashes, was delirious for two days with an "exceeding high fever and most plentiful Eruptions."[6] Abigail feared for his life.

John, receiving Abigail's letters, was afraid to open them, not knowing what sad tidings they might contain. They have "fixed an Arrow in my

A detail of John Trumbull's painting, Declaration of Independence, showing, from the left, John Adams, Roger Sherman, Robert Livingston, Thomas Jefferson, and Benjamin Franklin.

～

Heart," he told her.[7] When a letter finally arrived assuring him that Charles was recovering, and that, in fact, "All my treasure of children have passed thro one of the most terrible Diseases to which humane Nature is subject, and not one of us is wanting,"[8] John was overcome with relief.

"I did not know what fast Hold that little Prattler Charles had upon me before," he replied.[9]

As the children continued to recover, Abigail's mind reverted to her concerns for the new nation. She was troubled about the lack of education for women. She wrote to John about daughters "who everyday experience the want of it. With regard to the Education of my own children, I find myself soon out of my depth, and destitute and deficient in every part of Education."

She hoped that the new constitution would provide a liberal plan to encourage "Learning and Virtue" in all children. "If we mean to have Heroes, Statesmen and Philosophers, we should have learned women," she continued. "The world perhaps would laugh at me, and accuse me of vanity, But you I know have a mind too enlarged and liberal to disregard the Sentiment. If much depends as is allowed upon the early Education of youth and the first principals which are instilld take the deepest root, great benefit must arise from litirary accomplishments in women." Educated women would be better able to function in their domestic role.[10]

Abigail had time now, too, to wander in Boston and absorb the latest news arriving from Philadelphia. And she could enjoy the luxury of a little privacy. At her aunt's she had a pretty room with a window that looked out on a flower garden. Here, at her aunt's desk, she could "keep my papers unmollested by any one." Here, she could read, write letters, reread John's letters to her until she had all but memorized them, or simply daydream about her "absent Friend . . . anticipating a joyful and happy meeting. . . ."

"I do not covet my Neighbor's Goods," she wrote to John, "but I should like to be the owner of such conveniences. I always had a fancy for a closet [room] with a window which I could more peculiarly call my own."[11]

And she could concentrate on domestic concerns once again. She worried about John's favorite mare, lamed by an accident. "You can hardly tell . . . how much I lament her," she wrote to him. Then she went on in her businesslike way, "She was not with foal, as you imagined, but I hope she is now as care has been taken in that Respect."[12]

After more than two months in Boston, Abigail was finally able to take her children back to Braintree early in September. As they crossed the quarantine line on the outskirts of Boston, they were reminded once again of the seriousness of this "deadly plague" as all their belongings were carefully smoked.

Now, happily anticipating John's homecoming, Abigail made arrangements for a servant to ride a horse to Philadelphia to bring him home. When John had left for the First Continental Congress he had traveled in splendor, accompanied by the other members of the Massachusetts delegation. His second trip was made in his father-in-law's single horse chaise. Thereafter he traveled to Philadelphia on horseback. In Philadelphia he shifted from one boardinghouse to another for the cheapest rates. Abigail had reported to him that other lawyers were making fortunes in his absence, and he tried hard to economize.

John had planned to be home in September. But the war took a turn for the worse, and now he wrote to his wife that he couldn't see his way clear to return as soon as he had intended. September stretched into October, and he didn't arrive in Braintree until the beginning of November. He was hopeful that Congress would appoint a delegate to replace him, and that he could remain at home for good. This didn't happen. The Massachusetts legislature once more chose him as their delegate, and once again John and Abigail were faced with the dilemna of public duty versus private happiness. Public duty won.

John's sacrifice was to separate himself from his family and his farm. Abigail's was to let—even encourage—him to go. His rewards were fame and the excitement of knowing that he was creating history. Hers were simply pride in her own ability to support her husband's need to serve his country, and to keep the family and the farm running smoothly under difficult conditions. And this time John would be going farther away. Congress had decided to move south to Baltimore, since Philadelphia was thought to be a likely target of the British troops. His letters would take even longer to reach her.

On January 9, 1777, when John rode off, bound for Congress, they had had only nine weeks together, and their parting was even more difficult than in the past. Abigail was pregnant for the first time in six years. She and John had planned this child, and John had promised that he would be at home for its birth. Now they realized that she would probably bring the baby into the world alone. They particularly hoped for another daughter. They had three sons and one daughter, and Abigail had never gotten over the loss of Susanna.

With John away, Abigail tried to keep her family fed, clothed, and out of debt. She wove her own cloth and made all the family's clothes. She did this not only in an effort to keep expenses down, but also as a matter of patriotism. Abigail and her friends believed that women's efforts on the home front were essential to ensure the ultimate success of the American cause. So they joined forces. Mercy Warren spun wool while Abigail and other Braintree women wove it into cloth: "I . . . work willingly with my Hands, and tho my Household are not cloathed with fine linnen nor scarlet, they are cloathed with what is perhaps full as Honorary, the plain and decent manufactory of my own family."[13]

By early spring Abigail was growing increasingly more depressed.

Long separations, real fear now for John's safety (Congress had moved back to Philadelphia from Baltimore), extreme shortages of goods coupled with high inflation, and a seeming loss in New England of the revolutionary spirit that had prevailed while the military action had centered there, all served to lower her spirits. And her figure was growing clumsy. In the seventh month of her pregnancy now, she moved about the cramped quarters of their little farmhouse with difficulty. Ten-year-old John Quincy told her, "Mar, I never saw any body grow so fat as you do."[14]

When a neighbor died in childbirth, Abigail began to worry about her own approaching delivery. She felt John's absence acutely, and worried about what would happen to her children should she die.

"I have a good mind to hold You to your promise, since some perticuliar circumstances were really upon that condition," she wrote, but then continued, "I must summon all the Phylosophy I am mistress of since what cannot be help'd must be endured."[15]

"Posterity! You will never know, how much it cost the present Generation, to preserve your Freedom! I hope you will make a good Use of it," her husband replied.[16]

By May troops were passing her house day and night, and she believed more fighting might take place. She had heard of brutal treatment of people who had fallen into the hands of the enemy. Should the British come again, she told John, she didn't know what she would do. "I should not dare to tarry here in my present situation, nor yet know where to flee for safety."[17] Her courage was beginning to desert her.

"No separation was ever more painfull to me," Abigail told John early in June, then wondered if this were a sign of weakness. But she was happy "in a daughter who is both a companion and an assistant in my Family affairs and who I think has a prudence and steadiness beyond her years." She ended her letter: "Good Night tis so dark that I cannot see to add more than that I am with the utmost tenderness Yours ever Yours."[18]

With the children asleep and the house quiet, the night was the hardest part of the twenty-four hours for Abigail to endure. Often she would awake from sleep with the impression of John's solid, sturdy body beside her, then realize that she had been dreaming.

Two weeks later, as the time for the birth of her baby approached, Abigail again expressed her loneliness: "I want a companion a Nights, many of them are wakefull and Lonesome. . . . I wish the day passt, yet dread its arrival."[19]

And her mother was no longer there to offer some measure of comfort.

On July 9 she wrote again, telling John that she had been "unwell" the past week, "with some complaints that have been new to me, tho I hope not dangerous."

"I was last night taken with a shaking fit, and am very apprehensive that a life was lost," she continued. "I would not have you too much allarmd. I keep up some Spirits yet, tho I would have you prepaird for any Event that may happen."[20] Uncle Tufts tried to reassure her that nothing was wrong.

At the same time that Abigail was expressing her fears for the life of the child she was carrying, John was writing to her from Philadelphia: "My Mind is again Anxious, and my Heart in Pain for my dearest Friend." He had been away three times when he should have been home, he told her: when the family had dysentery and so many had died; when they had endured the long and painful ordeal of smallpox; and now when she needed him most. He continued his letter:

Oh that I could be near, to say a few kind Words, or shew a few Kind Looks, or do a few kind Actions. Oh that I could take from my dearest, a share of her Distress, or relieve her of the whole.

Before this shall reach you I hope you will be happy in the Embraces of a Daughter, as fair, and good, and wise, and virtuous as the Mother, or if it is a son I hope it will still resemble the Mother in Person, Mind and Heart.[21]

Even as her labor pains began in earnest, Abigail was still writing to John, reaching out to him for comfort and closeness: "Tis now 48 hours since I can say I really enjoyed any Ease. . . . I pray Heaven that it may be soon or it seems to me I shall be worn out. I must lay my pen down this moment, to bear what I cannot fly from—and now I have endured it I reassume my pen."

The late frost had damaged the fruit trees, the corn looked well, and the hay crop would be good but manure was needed for the field, she told her husband in the midst of her weariness and the pains of labor. "Almighty God carry me safely through," she cried out.

The next morning, feeling more ill than ever, she continued her letter, "This day ten years ago master John came into this world. May I have reason again to recollect it with peculiar gratitude. Adieu."[22]

But this was not to be. Two days later, on July 13, John Thaxter wrote to John Adams:

Sir

The day before Yesterday Mrs. Adams was delivered of a daughter; but it grieves me to add, Sir, that it was still born. It was an exceeding fine looking Child.

Mrs. Adams is as comfortable . . . as can be expected; and has desired me to write a few lines to acquaint you that she is in a good Way. . . .[23]

Abigail was numb. The boys were dazed and silent. Twelve-year-old Nabby, who had longed for a baby sister to mother and to love, wept inconsolably. But three days later Abigail was able to write to John: "Join with me, my dearest friend, in gratitude to Heaven that a life I know you value has been spared. . . . I have so much cause for thankfulness amidst my sorrow."[24]

Abigail had probably developed toxemia, a serious condition in which elevated blood pressure, fluid retention, and the leakage of protein from the kidneys into the urine sometimes occur in the second half of a pregnancy.*

In spite of her "confinement" Abigail had written to John by every post, and was surprised to learn that her letters had not yet reached him. Now, as she slowly regained her strength, she continued to write, expressing her sadness at not being able to present him with a new baby on his return home. She began, too, to worry more about the health of her husband, about the war, and about the high prices for goods: "What do you think will become of us?" she wrote to John. "If you will come home and turn Farmer, I will be dairy woman. . . . and we shall grow wealthy. Our Boys shall go into the Field and work with you, and my Girl shall stay in the House and assist me." She feared that unless John returned home, what

---

* Today the disorder is readily treatable, but at the time of Abigail's pregnancy it went undiagnosed.

little property they owned would soon be lost, and she and their children would be "in danger of wanting bread."[25]

It wasn't until July 28 that John finally received Abigail's letters of July 9, 10, 11, and 16. "Never in my whole life was my heart affected with such emotions," he wrote. "Devoutly do I return thanks to God, whose kind providence has preserved to me a life that is dearer to me than all other blessings in this world." He went on to tell her how much he was affected by the "loss of this sweet little girl" even though he would never see her.[26] The tragedy seemed to draw them closer to each other and to their children.

Sensing now more acutely the weight of the burdens that Abigail was bearing alone, John tried, in some small measure, to help in the education of their children. Johnny had already written to him asking for advice on "how to apportion my studies and my play. . . . My head is much too fickle, my thoughts are running after birds' eggs, play and trifles," he told his father. If he would send him instructions, Johnny would try to follow them. "I am, dear sir, with a present determination of growing better, yours," he ended his letter.[27]

John replied to his oldest son, outlining the reading he wanted him to do, particularly in history. He must read the writings of the historian Thucydides, both in the original Greek which, he told his son, was the most perfect of all human languages, and in "a learned and exact" English translation.[28] John Quincy had just turned ten!

∼ CHAPTER XII ∼

"to rob me of all my happiness"

A t the same time that John and Abigail were dealing with the loss of their little girl, the war was gaining momentum. As John worried about his wife, fearing that the British might attack Rhode Island or Boston, she, in turn, worried about him, convinced that the British were heading for Philadelphia. For a month no one could figure out what was going to happen. Near the end of September Congress fled to Yorktown, Pennsylvania.

As John sent to Abigail "a feast of letters," describing in detail the progress of the war, he reflected on the importance of great women behind great men. The British general Howe, he speculated, lacked that support: "A smart wife would have put Howe in possession of Philadelphia a long time ago," he wrote. He told her, also, that her letters made him "merry."[1]

When Abigail asked her husband for a map on which she could trace the military operations, John asked James Lovell, another distinguished Massachussets delegate to the Continental Congress with whom he and Abigail had been friendly in Boston, to secure a map of Howe's route for her. This Lovell did. But instead of giving the map to John to forward to his wife, Lovell sent it himself. Abigail, seeing Lovell's handwriting on the envelope, was seized with terror. Had he written to tell her that John was ill, or that he had been captured or even killed by the British? She couldn't bring herself to break the seal. Finally, she forced herself to open the envelope and read the letter from the bottom up. Lovell, she found, had used the map as an opportunity to write to Abigail himself, telling her subtly of his affection for her. Abigail was overcome with many emotions. She was flooded with relief that her husband was safe. She was flattered and delighted by Lovell's compliments. But she was shocked at his recklessness. "Your having given your heart to *such* a man [John Adams] is what, most of all, makes me yours," Lovell told her. But this, he added, was only *part* of "the foundation of my affectionate esteem for you."[2] In the eighteenth century this was simply not done. Lovell's letter violated the standards of formal conversation between a gentleman and a lady.

Abigail's strict New England upbringing as a minister's daughter had established patterns of virtuous behavior that she could not ignore. In her next letter to John, she included a brief note of thanks to James Lovell, telling her husband only of the "very polite Letter" she had received from their friend.[3]

At the end of September General Howe finally did occupy Philadelphia, with no resistance. Abigail was angry: "If men will not fight and defend their own particular spot, if they will not drive the enemy from their doors, they deserve the slavery and subjection which awaits them."[4] By now it was several weeks since she had heard from John, and she had no idea where he was.

Then came the American capture of the British army under General Burgoyne at Saratoga, and Abigail could rejoice. She and Nabby rode to Boston to join in a celebration, and in prayers of thanksgiving at the Brattle Street Church. Once again they stayed with Uncle Isaac. Isaac Smith remained a kind and caring protector of Abigail and her children all the while that John was away.

As she wrote to her husband from her uncle's home, Abigail reflected that this was the thirteenth anniversary of their wedding day. They had been separated for three of those years. She had endured it, she told John, knowing that he was serving his country. She would not regret it, she continued, if the present generation "behave worthy of the blessings you are laboring to secure them."[5]

On November 7, 1777, Congress voted "that Mr. Samuel Adams, and Mr. John Adams, have leave of absence to visit their families."[6] The two cousins set out together on the eleventh, arriving home to a joyous reunion on November 27.

When John returned home Abigail was certain that he meant to keep a promise he had recently made to her that the next time he came home it would be for a long time. "My Happiness is no where to be found, but there."[7] He would take up his law practice once again, and attempt to get his finances in better shape. When he left for New Hampshire in the middle of December to try a law case, she understood that this would be a brief but necessary separation, and he would soon be back home. So she was not prepared for the packet of letters that arrived from Congress while he was away. Thinking that the letters might contain important information to be forwarded to John, and curious herself to know their contents, she opened them and began to read. Her husband had been elected commissioner to France. He was to join Benjamin Franklin and Arthur Lee, already in Paris, to negotiate a French alliance with America.

Abigail was stunned. This was almost more than she could bear. She had waited so long for his return. How could she give him up now, so quickly, and with all it entailed? A separation of three hundred miles was about to be multiplied to three thousand.

The journey to Europe could take two to four months, and would be for an unlimited period of time, filled with risks and hazards. Her life would be one continuous scene of loneliness, anxiety, and apprehension. John could be gone for years! Abigail was desolate. She spent sleepless nights wrestling with the conflict raging within her. As she wandered through the cold, silent house while the children slept peacefully, the only sound the grandfather clock in the parlor chiming the hours, she tried to reconcile herself to accept what she sensed was inevitable.

She knew that if she asked John not to accept he would remain at home. But she saw, also, that this appointment was for the public good. Neither she nor John could turn their backs on public duty.

She had never put restraints on her husband. She had always left him free to act for himself. She could not embarrass him now by asking him to refuse this post. She couldn't nullify the years of suffering and sacrifice she had already endured. Besides, she reasoned, John had been on the committee to draw up a "Plan of Treaties," and he had written the original documents under which the first commissioners had been sent to Paris. This was a logical extension of his work.

Finally, in an attempt to calm herself, she wrote a letter to James Lovell, from whom the letter announcing John's appointment had come. Lovell had included, along with the official announcement, a personal letter urging John to accept. In it he had referred to the unique bond that he knew existed between John and Abigail. But at the same time he indicated that Congress expected John to accept because of the need of his country for his great talents.

As Abigail wrote to Lovell of this cruel "plot to rob me of all my happiness," her rage turned slowly to the area of public duty. In the end, she apologized to him for her letter, telling Lovell that it had been a relief "to drop some of my sorrows through my pen." She would leave her husband free to act as he thought best.[8]

Next, Abigail turned to her friend Mercy Warren for comfort. That woman wept with her over the prospect of John's leaving behind his beloved wife and his little "brood." But the country needed John's services, Mercy counseled. Then she went on to congratulate her friend for being so "nearly connected with a gentleman whose learning, patriotism and prudence qualify him to negotiate at foreign courts at this very critical period."[9]

John, in the meantime, had heard the news in Portsmouth. He hurried back to Braintree. He, too, agonized over the decision. He knew he would be separated from Abigail and his children for at least a year, if not longer. His clients would not wait for him a second time. He would have to be prepared to give up the law for good. His family would have to manage on the income from the farm and what might be left over from the small amount paid to the diplomatic representative of an impoverished country. And, his going would entail a dangerous winter crossing of the Atlantic Ocean. British ships would be on the lookout for him. No doubt they had already been advised by spies of his appointment. He could be captured and hanged. He would sacrifice his career, abandon his family, and risk his life. But he knew he had to go.

John Adams wrote his formal acceptance of the post of commissioner at the court of France on December 23, 1777. It was read in Congress on January 19, 1778.

For a brief period John considered taking the entire family to France. Abigail wanted desperately to go. She had always had a secret longing to travel abroad. But she finally accepted the fact that a wartime passage was too dangerous, and that in addition to the normal hazards of a winter crossing, particularly for a woman, there was the tremendous expense to consider.

In the end, it was ten-year-old John Quincy who begged to be allowed to accompany his father. He would have a chance to see some of the world, to learn French firsthand, and to help his father with clerical work as much as possible, he pleaded. For this New England farm boy who liked outdoor sports as much as study, and who resisted all efforts to dress him neatly, it was an unheard-of opportunity. For John Adams, it would be the first step in training his son to be a statesman.

Abigail was devastated. Johnny performed many services for her. He was her post rider, delivering letters to and from Boston, and he was a good companion for her and for the other children. His lively conversation helped her through many lonely days. How would she manage without him? Now she would have two to worry about.

Could Johnny withstand the temptations of Europe that might "stain his morals even at this early period of life," she agonized; then she reasoned that "to exclude him from temptation would be to exclude him from the World in which he is to live."[10] When her young son reminded her that the country would need trained diplomats, and that she had talked to him of the good education to be had in Europe, she knew he was right. She recognized the advantages of a stay in Europe under the watchful eye of his father. And she knew that her patient but demanding instruction had prepared him well. It was the most difficult decision she had ever had to make.

Once it was made, there were a thousand things to be done in the short time until they were to sail. Both John and John Quincy must have proper clothes, and they must bring along their own bedding, food, and supplies for the long voyage. Abigail, with the quietly efficient Nabby to help her, set to work immediately. Often she worked late into the night. Clothes were outrageously expensive, so Abigail was determined to make John's shirts. But even fabric and thread were hard to obtain at any price. Somehow Abigail managed to buy or barter for brown sugar, mustard, tea, and chocolate. In addition, six live chickens and "two fat sheep" were among the items sent on board, as well as fourteen dozen eggs, five bushels of corn, and a barrel of apples to help combat scurvy, a dreaded disease caused by a deficiency of vitamin C.

When all the clothes and food were attended to, Abigail spent carefully saved money to purchase three reams of paper and twenty-five quills for John's pen so he could keep account books and continue his diary. They made the ink at home from powder and water poured into a stout bottle.

Soon Abigail had finished all her tasks, and John was ready to depart ten days ahead of schedule. With the packing completed and the good-byes to family and friends all said, waiting became the most difficult task of all.

Finally, the *Boston*, the ship on which they were to sail to France, and which had been refitted with faster sails, dropped anchor just offshore, near Mount Wollaston, where Abigail's uncle Norton Quincy was now living. It was from there that they would depart.

On February 13, 1778, a cold, blustery winter day, John and John Quincy said their private good-byes to Abigail, Nabby, Charley, and Tommy, then rode off together for Uncle Quincy's. Abigail reminded her son "never to disgrace his mother, and to behave worthily of his father."[1]

John gave this locket to Abigail just before he sailed for Europe in 1778. It shows a lonely woman watching a ship sail off. It is inscribed: "I yield whatever is is right."

~

Just before he left, John gave his wife a tiny locket picturing a lonely woman watching a ship sail off. Abigail, holding tight to her children's hands, watched "with full heart and weeping eye" as her husband and son rode out of sight. She had decided that it would be too painful for her to watch them actually board the ship that would carry them so far away from her. To let her husband go was hard enough, but to see her precious son embarking on this dangerous voyage as well was almost more than she could bear. It took all her fortitude to keep from breaking down in front of the other children.

At Mount Wollaston father and son had lunch with Uncle Norton and the captain of the ship, and John wrote a hasty note to Abigail assuring her that Johnny was acting "like a man."[12] Then they walked to a secluded stretch of shoreline, where, wrapped in great watch coats to protect them against the rough sea and high winds that drove the spray like hail against their faces, they boarded the tiny barge that would take them out to the *Boston.*

Two days later, with her husband and son gone, and all the hectic preparations of the last month over, the cold, hard fact of their absence hit Abigail. Now she regretted that she had not insisted on going along.

She sat at her kitchen table and wrote to John Thaxter: "Cannot you imagine me seated by my fire side bereft of my better half, and added to that a limb lopt off to heighten the anguish." She had given up her own happiness, she told Thaxter, because she believed that her husband's ability and integrity might be more useful to his country in this area now than at any other time. She knew, she told him, that she had once more discharged her duty to the public.[13]

She began to brood more and more on her loneliness, and on her own sacrifices for her country. She had endured four years of almost constant separations, and it was becoming increasingly difficult for her to accept them in the name of patriotism. As always in times of stress, she poured out her feelings in letters to her sisters and to her friends. In this way she seemed to gain the emotional strength she needed.

To her friend Hannah Storer she wrote, "I asked not my Heart what it could, but what it ought to do." But, she told her, few people knew the "Struggle" it had cost her. She considered herself a widow.[14] Hannah replied by assuring her that she could never have given up her husband as Abigail had. Her patriotism was not that strong.

Six months later she told John Thaxter, "I wish a thousand times I had gone with him."[15]

For four and a half months after John and John Quincy left, Abigail heard nothing except rumors that their ship had been captured by the British and that Benjamin Franklin had been assassinated in France, a fate that might await the other commissioners. She worried constantly. She was beginning to lose hope that her husband and son were alive.

But even as she waited anxiously for some word of their safety, she continued to write letters. She was certain, she assured John, that "that

Detail from a painting by Francis Holman, of the frigate Boston,
the ship that carried John and John Quincy to France

Being who . . . cloathes the lilies of the Feild and hears the young
Ravens when they cry," would protect him. This confidence, she wrote, "is
my food by day and my Rest by Night."

She continued her letter: "Difficult as the Day is, cruel as this War has
been, seperated as I am on account of it from the dearest connextion in life,
I would not exchange my Country for the Wealth of the Indies, or be any
other than an American tho I might be Queen or Empress of any Nation
upon the Globe." She needed neither "pomp nor power," she told John,
but gloried in the "important trust" placed in him.[16] Eventually, though,
she became so disheartened that she stopped writing: "My Heart so much
misgave me that I knew not how to hold my pen."[17]

Finally, in mid-June Uncle Isaac informed her that a London newspaper
arriving on one of his ships reported that the *Boston* had reached France.
On June 30 Abigail received her first letter from John. As she ripped open
the seal and saw his familiar handwriting, she knew that her husband and
son were safe, and she wept with relief.

Their passage had not been an easy one, John wrote. They had experienced rough seas and stormy weather several times, and twice they had come perilously close to being captured by the British. It was six weeks before they had pulled into the harbor at Bordeaux, France, and felt land beneath their feet.

From Bordeaux they had set out for Paris, five hundred miles away. There they stayed for a while with Benjamin Franklin in his house in Passy, just outside the city of Paris. Four days after their arrival in Passy John finally wrote to tell his wife of their safe arrival. Earlier letters of his, she learned, had been destroyed in order to avoid their capture by the British.

John told her, also, that "the Delights of France are innumerable. The Politeness, the Elegance, the Softness, the Delicacy, is extreme. In short, stern and hauty Republican as I am, I cannot help loving these People." He went on to tell her that the richness, magnificence, and splendor of the buildings, gardens, art, architecture, and music of Paris were beyond description. But he would gladly trade it all for the company of his dearest friend.[18]

John, for his part, had found no letters from Abigail waiting for him. Despite the many letters she had written, none had arrived. Normally slow communications were made even worse by the dangers of enemy ships. Often months would go by when they had no word of each other.

CHAPTER XIII

"And shall I see his face again?"

I n one of his earliest letters to Abigail from France, John told her how much he admired French women: "They are handsome, and very well educated," he wrote. But, he counseled her, "Don't be jealous."[1] Abigail responded by repeating her plea for female education. She was happy to learn of the accomplishments of French ladies, she wrote, but regretted the narrow education of women in her own country. While she acknowledged how liberal John was on the subject, and knew that he understood how badly neglected female education was, she reminded him that it was still fashionable to ridicule female learning. In fact, women were advised to keep any learning they might have a secret. Even John, on learning that Abigail was teaching Nabby the basics of Latin grammar, wrote to his daughter that while it wouldn't harm her, she must not tell many people, for it wasn't proper for young ladies to understand Latin and Greek.

In colonial America many men felt that intelligence was incompatible with "softness and delicacy." But educated women, Abigail contended, were not a threat, "since where there is most Learning, Sence, and knowledge there is always observed to be the most modesty and Rectitude of manners."[2] While she accepted the principle of male domination in the family and in society, it did not follow that she accepted intellectual inferiority for women. She had little respect for women who did not attempt to improve their minds. Books and ideas, she believed, represented the highest human achievements. "What is life or its enjoyments without . . . mental exertions—a mere vapor indeed," she wrote to her niece.[3] By midsummer she had sent Nabby to school in Boston.

As her husband moved through the glittering world of the French court, Abigail was at home with only her two young sons and two servants. She wrote to John as often as there was a ship to carry her letters, but she was lonelier than ever. She recognized that she would soon have to part with Charley, too, for he was eight years old now, and ready to begin grammar school. There was still no adequate school in Braintree, nor was there a qualified tutor. Abigail would have to send Charley to live with her sister Elizabeth,* married now to a minister and schoolteacher named John Shaw and living in Haverhill. John Shaw would be a fine tutor for Charley. But she was not yet ready to let him go.

It was at this time that two-year-old Louisa, the daughter of Abigail's brother William, came to live with her. William had become the black sheep of the family. He had resisted his father's efforts to get him to attend Harvard, and had failed in an attempt to establish a business in Boston. Now he had a sickly wife, a brood of children, and very little money. Abigail hoped to relieve some of his burden by taking Louisa. She was delighted at the chance to have a little girl to look after and loved her dearly. Louisa thrived under her care.

Writing to her husband now, Abigail questioned the necessity for caution in their letters, telling John that if the letters were captured by the enemy and ridiculed, it would serve only as further proof of the "savage barbarity" of the English.

"My Heart overflows, and longs to give utterance to my pen," she wrote. And she had many "domestic" questions for him. She continued by telling him that she had devised a means of earning a little more money. If John would send to her some saleable articles that she would list for him, Dr. Tufts's son would sell them for her. "Debts are my abhorrence," she wrote. "I never will borrow if any other method can be devised."[4] She spent money only on food and clothing, repairs to the house and farm, the education of her children, and taxes, which had increased to pay for the war. She was trying to be "frugal."[5]

---

* Since their mother's death, Betsy had begun to use her given name, Elizabeth.

J ust a few days before John and John Quincy had set sail for France, that country had entered into an alliance with the United States. Now the French fleet arrived in Boston Harbor after a storm-tossed voyage across the ocean. They would remain for two months while their ships were being repaired. Soon Count d'Estaing, chief officer of the French fleet, came ashore at Mount Wollaston to invite the wife of Commissioner Adams to dine on board his ship with her family and friends.

On the appointed day the admiral sent his barge to take the party of thirteen to the ship, where "an entertainment fit for a princiss was prepared," with music and dancing for the young folks.[6] Abigail reciprocated by cooking dinner in her cottage for several groups of officers. She was impressed with their polished manners and the social graces of the French. And she particularly savored the political news they brought her. Now she lamented the fact that as a young girl she had learned only to read French but not to speak it. She was delighted to learn that John Quincy was learning to read and speak the language.

Johnny wrote regularly to his mother, sister, and brothers, to his cousins and his friends, and to his grandfather Smith and his grandmother Adams. Abigail particularly enjoyed the letter that arrived from him telling her that he had begun to keep a journal, and that his papa had given him a blank book in which to keep copies of all his letters. Johnny worried, though, that he would be embarrassed "a few years hence, to read a great deal of my Childish nonsense, yet I shall have the Pleasure, and advantage of Remarking the several steps, by which I shall have advanced, in taste, judgment, and knowledge."[7]

John had also given his son a present of a pencil and a pencil book that he could carry with him at all times in order to make notes "upon the spot" to be transferred later to his diary. "This will give me great Pleasure both because it will be a sure means of improvement to myself and enable me to be more entertaining to you," he told his mother.[8]

Now fourteen-year-old Nabby was beginning to feel the pain of separation from her father and brother, too. She begged to be allowed to join them in France. For a brief moment Abigail was tempted to give in to her pleas. A new ship, the *Alliance,* would sail soon from Boston Harbor with Mercy Warren's son on board as lieutenant of marines. But in the end Abigail couldn't bring herself to let her daughter go.

To ease her own loneliness, Abigail began writing to John Thaxter, who was now serving as a secretary to Congress. He responded by sending her news of the war, asking her opinion on political issues, and sending her books published in Philadelphia, much as John had done. "I love to know what is passing in the world," she told him, "tho excluded from it."[9]

She wrote to James Lovell, also, asking him as a trusted friend to send her news of happenings in Congress, as well as any information he had from Paris. Lovell, as secretary of the Committee of Foreign Affairs,* communicated with the diplomats abroad, and so had information unavailable to Abigail from other sources. Lovell was happy to oblige. But his long correspondence with the wife of Commissioner Adams went well beyond official business.

Abigail trusted James Lovell because she knew that he had genuine respect and admiration for her husband. He also had been imprisoned by the British as a spy, and had endured long separations from his family. So when she asked him to "communicate to me some share of that hidden strength . . . that I may endure this misfortune with becomeing fortitude,"[10] she was simply attempting to establish a bond between them. But Lovell interpreted her request as an invitation to a correspondence of greater intimacy.

If Abigail wanted pity for her misfortunes, Lovell wrote, she should not send them in "the most elegant Dresses of Sentiment and Language. . . . Call me not a Savage," he wrote, "when I inform you that your 'Alarms and Distress' have afforded me *Delight*!"[11]

Abigail found his letters flattering, but improper. He was openly flirting with her, just as he had done the year before when he had sent the map to her. For several months she didn't write to him. Finally, she told him she considered him "a very dangerous man."[12]

Lovell continued to flatter the "lovely Portia." Abigail continued to scold, then attempted to tease in return. Their flirtation by mail persisted.

Abigail Adams was young—she was just thirty-four—and attractive. But she was a wife of fourteen years who had children entering their teens. She had been deprived of her husband's company for the better part of four years, and she craved companionship, attention, and affection. John's letters now were brief and infrequent, and without the expressions of love that had kept her going throughout the months that he had been in Philadelphia.

"How lonely are my days? How solitary are my Nights? Secluded from all Society but my two Little Boys, and my domesticks, [Nabby had left the week before to visit Mercy Warren in Plymouth for a month] by the

* Comparable today to the position of secretary of state.

Mountains of snow which surround me. . . ," she wrote to her husband two days after Christmas. They had experienced four extremely cold days, followed by the severest snowstorm she remembered. The wind howled for twenty hours, the roads were impassable, and it was impossible to go outside.

She told John she had been moved by a Scottish song she had heard a few days before. Charles had learned it and, to please her, he sang it to her.

His very foot has Musick in't,
As he comes up the stairs.

"How oft has my Heart danced to the sound of that Musick?" she asked.

And shall I see his face again?
And shall I hear him speak?[13]

As the cold and snow increased her isolation, her normally cheerful disposition gave way to loneliness and depression. "I have scarcely ever taken my pen to write but the tears have flowed faster than the Ink," she wrote.[14] February marked a year that John and Johnny had been gone, and there was no indication that they might return.

John, absorbed with the problems confronting him in France, wrote infrequently. His own feelings of self-doubt were aggravating an already troublesome situation. He had come to realize that when Parisians spoke of "the famous Adams," they meant his cousin Sam, not him. John felt ignored and unappreciated.

Further, he had become critical of Benjamin Franklin. Several years before John had looked upon Dr. Franklin as "a great and good Man." But the Benjamin Franklin whom John Adams found in Paris was a very different man, no longer worthy, in John's mind, of the respect paid him there. The two men had very different approaches to the difficult diplomatic negotiations in which they were engaged, while the other commissioners in Paris were embroiled in serious personal and ideological quarrels.

Abigail knew nothing of this situation, nor of John's state of mind, and interpreted his silence as neglect. She had received only three very short, unemotional notes from him in nine months. Some of the letters that he did write had gone down at sea when the ships that were carrying them were taken by the British.

Finally, Abigail could stand it no longer. She lashed out at her husband:

Could you after a thousand fears and anxieties, long expectation and painful suspences be satisfied with my telling you that I was well, that I wished you were with me, that my daughter sent her duty, that I had ordered some articles for you &c. &c. . . . . By Heaven if you could you have changed Hearts with some frozen Laplander or made a voyage to a region that has chilld every Drop of your Blood."[15]

The following month she apologized for her outburst, explaining, "Were you not dearer to me than all this universe contains beside, I could not have suffered as I have done."[16]

Benjamin Franklin, elder statesman, whose interests far transcended politics. John Adams wrote of him, "On Dr. F. the Eyes of all Europe are fixed." Adams complained of Franklin's "Love of Ease, and Dissipation," which the French found attractive.

~

John never understood the extent of her depression. Nor could he comprehend her hunger for tenderness and reassurance. "If you write me in this style I shall leave of writing intirely, it kills me," he wrote to her. "Can Protestations of affection be necessary? Can tokens of remembrance be desir'd? The very Idea of this sickens me. . . . I beg you would never write to me in such a strain for it really makes me unhappy."[17] He went so far as to ask Johnny to copy the letter over for him, then induced him to write his own letter to Abigail:

My Pappa "cannot write but very little because he has so many other things to think of . . . and when you receive them you complain . . . and it really hurts him," the eleven-year-old told his mother.[18]

On February 13, 1779, the anniversary of the "melancholy Day" that John and Johnny had left, Abigail wrote to her husband that she had just received four letters from him all at once, tied together in a handkerchief of his. It felt to her "like the return of an absent Friend."[19]

100

That month Congress appointed Benjamin Franklin sole minister to negotiate with the French. John Adams and Arthur Lee were relieved of their duties. John received no instructions from Congress. Finally, he decided to go home. He wrote to Abigail that he had been "reduced to a private Citizen" and would soon "present before you your own good Man." He went on to tell her how happy he would be, then:

> I must not write a Word about Politicks, because you are a Woman.
> What an offence have I committed?—a Woman!
> I shall soon make it up. I think Women better than Men in General, and I know you can keep a Secret as well as any Man whatever. But the World dont know this. . . .
> I never had so much Trouble in my Life, as here, yet I grow fat.[20]

John and John Quincy left Paris in March, but it wasn't until June 18 that they were finally able to board the French frigate *Sensible* and set sail for home. The letters John wrote between February and June, including one proudly telling her how respected Johnny was for his intelligence, constant good humor, and rapid progress in French, never arrived in Braintree. Abigail had no letters dated later than February.

She had no idea what was happening, although rumors abounded, including one that John would soon be named to another European court. The Americans had kept the war going until 1778 with secret French aid, but now both Holland and Spain had also entered into the fray against Great Britain. France continued to provide money, equipment, soldiers, and naval power. The American War for Independence had erupted into a multipower world war.

Not one to wait quietly for information, Abigail wrote to James Lovell asking if he knew what Congress had planned for her husband. But Lovell had no specific answer for her.

On August 2 Abigail was still trying to discover John and Johnny's whereabouts, when the *Sensible* dropped anchor off Braintree. A crew member rowed father and son ashore and deposited them on the beach, near the point from which they had embarked on a cold February day a year and a half before. Their arrival took Abigail completely by surprise.

Several days later a letter arrived from James Lovell telling Abigail that John was on his way home from France.

∼ CHAPTER XIV ∼
"Who shall give me back Time?"

August and September of 1779 were happy months for Abigail and John. After a separation of eighteen months, their delight in each other knew no bounds. They took long walks together in the late summer sunshine, they rode to Weymouth and to Mount Wollaston to visit family. Abigail harvested the last of her vegetables, and John inspected his fields and his fences. The children, too, enjoyed being together once again. Abigail let herself hope that her husband was home for good.

As was the custom, John delivered a formal report to the president of Congress outlining his views on the status and policies of the European powers as they affected America.

In September he was elected to represent Braintree at the Massachusetts Constitutional Convention. At that time state governments were crucially important new sovereignties in the world. They posed the question of whether a republican form of government could succeed in the vast territories of states like Massachusetts.

Now John was chosen to write the first draft of the Massachusetts Constitution. As a delegate to the convention, John spent much of his time in Cambridge, but Abigail was content, knowing that he was coming home on weekends. Then he read aloud to her everything he had written, and shared with her the discussions taking place in Cambridge. Once again, she felt a part of important events.

Suddenly, in October, her world was shattered once more. Word came from Philadelphia that Congress had unanimously chosen John Adams sole minister plenipotentiary to France.

This time John didn't hesitate. It was an appointment he wanted badly. This commission was even more important than the last one, and it was his alone. John Adams, not Benjamin Franklin, would be responsible for negotiating peace with Great Britain.

Abigail was devastated. It was cruel, she thought, to snatch her husband away from her so quickly after the agony of their last separation. She had had him for such a short time.

But John could not refuse the challenge. According to his stern code, the highest duty required the greatest sacrifice. Abigail understood this. She knew that her husband was driven to serve his

John Adams writing the first draft of the Massachusetts Constitution in his law office in 1779, by Albert Herter, 1942. (John Adams, seated at the table; Samuel Adams, in riding boots; and James Bowdoin, standing to left.)

~

country—and even more strongly driven to achieve public recognition for his contribution. It was this pursuit of fame that spurred him to nobility and political greatness. It was this that made it possible for him to leave behind all he professed to love—his wife, his children, his family, his farm.

Abigail knew he would be miserable if he remained at home and, therefore, so would she. She had to let him go and cling to his hope for the future. It was the best hold she had on her marriage to a man who was more committed to public service than to family life.

John accepted the appointment immediately "with the warmest sentiments of gratitude to Congress." The *Sensible*, still lying in Boston Harbor, was made ready to convey the new minister to France in proper style.

The possibility of Abigail's accompanying him was not even discussed. John had experienced the dangers and unpleasantness of a winter crossing. He would not expose his wife and daughter to them. "A lady cannot help being an odious creature at sea," they agreed. Seasickness, crowded quarters, and poor food made it impossible for a woman to maintain any sense of "delicacy."[1]

Sons were a different matter. John decided that both Johnny and Charles must accompany him. But this time, twelve-year-old Johnny was not anxious to make another voyage across the Atlantic. It was Abigail, though, who encouraged him. Johnny now knew the French language and could benefit even more from European travel, she told him. And while Charley was only nine, even younger than Johnny had been when he made his first trip, Abigail felt that a mother's heart should not stand in the way. Most important, she felt that at this time in their lives both boys needed their father's advice and attention.

To Johnny, Abigail explained that she hoped he would not be sorry that he made this second trip. "These are times in which a Genious would wish to live," she told him. The character of a great hero is formed by facing and overcoming difficulties. Wisdom is the result of experience.

She pointed out to her eldest son that he was "favour'd with superiour advantages," that "Nothing is wanting with you, but attention, diligence and steady application." Therefore, it would be "expected" of him that he do well.[2]

She reminded her young sons that they should be proud of a father who had played such an important role in the founding of the nation, and who was now being honored with another high post. But, she assured them, if she thought that they were capable of judging what was best for them, she would not urge them to go. They heeded her advice.

John and his two sons boarded the *Sensible* in Boston Harbor on November 13 after an especially difficult parting in Braintree. Accompanying them were Francis Dana, a young Boston lawyer who would serve as secretary to the delegation, and John Thaxter, who would be John's private secretary and tutor to the boys.

Just before they sailed John sent Abigail a note of comfort: "We shall yet be happy, I hope and pray. . . . Yours, ever, ever yours."[3]

Abigail replied immediately: "My habitation, how disconsolate it looks! My table I set down to it but cannot swallow my food." She would have gone to Boston in the hope of seeing them again, she said, in spite of the "cruel torture" of another parting, but she was afraid they might have sailed by the time she arrived and her trip would have been in vain. "My dear sons I can not think of them without a tear, little do they know the feelings of a Mothers Heart!" she lamented.[4]

It was hard enough to part with her husband and her oldest son, but letting her lovable little Charley go made the pain of saying good-bye almost unbearable. His tears, she wrote a year later, "have melted my Heart a thousand times."[5]

Blond, almost white-haired, Charles was quick and bright, considered the most handsome of four attractive children. He was an endearing little boy who had a gaiety and exuberance that contrasted sharply with the reserve of his parents and his brothers and sister. He was almost as precocious as his older brother, but even more charming. Loved by all who knew him, he was the pet of the family.

John Thaxter's departure, too, was a loss for Abigail. From the time when he had lived in their home as John's law clerk and as tutor to Johnny, she had begun to look on him almost as a son. Then, when John was abroad, she had come to depend on him for news of Congress and the war. She would miss his many kindnesses to her.

John fully expected that it would take no more than six months to a year at most to conclude a peace treaty with England. Mercifully, Abigail didn't know that it would be almost five years before she would see him again.

The first few months after John's leaving were not as difficult for Abigail as the months following his first departure had been. While he was home they had discussed the angry letters and the pent-up emotions behind them that they had sent back and forth across the ocean. Now Abigail resigned herself to waiting patiently for mail to arrive. John, for his part, made more of an effort to reassure his wife of his love for her.

The end of 1779 and the beginning of 1780 were quiet months for Abigail. She had rented the farm to two young men who now had complete responsibility for farming the land and paying taxes on it. This freed her from a great burden, and brought in some income as well.

Her husband and sons, meanwhile, had a swift and relatively easy voyage. Johnny and Charles were tutored in Latin and French on board the ship. And much time was spent in reading and conversation.

But their voyage almost ended in disaster. The *Sensible* sprang a leak and she crept into port at the northwestern tip of Spain with seven feet of water in her hold. The Adams party was forced to make the remainder of the journey—more than one thousand miles—by a hazardous winter trek, alternately riding in carriages, mounting donkeys, or walking across northern Spain and over the Pyrenees Mountains. But John saw to it that his young sons wasted no time during their six-week journey. He bought a Spanish dictionary and a grammar book, and they were "learning the Spanish language as fast as possible." They finally arrived in Paris on February 9, 1780.

"What could We do, if You and all the family had been with me?" John wondered to Abigail.[6]

The boys were immediately enrolled in school. They spent weekends and holidays touring Paris with their father, who spoke to them in French and quizzed them on their Latin.

John Quincy, John told Abigail, was becoming "more solid and steady than ever." Charles, lively and adaptable, was as well loved in Paris as at home. "Wherever he goes, everybody loves him. . . . He learns very well," his father reported. "He is a delightful little fellow. I love him too much."[7]

Abigail knew that John was encouraging Johnny to pay special attention to the study of Greek. "The most perfect models of fine writing in history, oratory and poetry are to be found in the Greek language," he told his son.[8]

John told Abigail of a book he had seen that was very beautiful. It included engravings and stories of the "Gods and Heroes of Antiquity. . . . Such a book would be very usefull to the Children in studying the Classicks, but it is too dear—3 Guineas, unbound."[9]

Johnny's mother, too, was sending advice across the ocean, counseling her oldest son to curb his temper, avoid any vices, and always tell the truth.[10] Two months later she reminded him that he had survived the trip to France only through God's providence. Now he must discharge his obligation to his God, to society, "in particular to your country," to his parents and to himself. And he must come to know himself.[11]

To her younger son Abigail wrote letters reminding him to be "modest" and "obliging." "You was a favorite in the neighborhood at home, all of whom wonder how Mamma could part with you." He must try to become "useful to society and happy to yourself," she encouraged him.[12]

The winter of 1780 was bitter cold, with snow so deep that Abigail was unable to visit Mary or her father. Below-zero temperature had frozen Boston Harbor for the first time in her memory. Fourteen-year-old Nabby, tired of being cooped up in the house, on a lark, went with some friends across the ice from Braintree to Boston. Uncle Isaac Smith was astonished to see her at his front door on one of the coldest days of the year. Her mother, though, stayed close to her fireside, reading and writing letters to her husband and sons.

This period was also one of the darkest periods of the war. Inflation was high, taxes were continuing to rise (Abigail told John that while two cows would formerly have paid taxes on their farm, now it would take ten), there was despair and disunion among the states, and mutiny over back pay was spreading in the army. Through it all, Abigail struggled to make ends meet. She looked after John's accounts and continued to acquire land when it became available, sometimes consulting Richard Cranch or Cotton Tufts, but more often relying on her own judgment. She never commented on the fact that she was buying property that, as a woman, she could not own. Abigail simply negotiated in her husband's name.

Writing to John about the forthcoming election for governor of Massachusetts, the first to be held under the new constitution, she commented: "What a politician you have made me? If I cannot be a voter upon this occasion, I will be a writer of votes. I can do something in that way." She couldn't vote, but she could assist at the polls.[13]

Now Abigail began to concentrate in earnest on selling some of the European goods John was sending her. With the seas becoming somewhat safer, he was able now to send home small shipments of European articles: good cloth, gay ribbons, laces, handkerchiefs, and tea. People in and around Braintree were happy to buy them. John sent, as well, as a gift for his wife, delft china that he knew she dearly wanted.

Eventually Abigail's business in this merchandise expanded and she learned exactly which items would turn a fine profit for her. When John suggested that she order goods directly, she found herself corresponding with merchants in Holland, Spain, and France.

As she continued to concentrate on their financial situation, she began to realize that she was enjoying these business dealings, and that she was good at them. But when she once accepted paper money, which was fast becoming as useless as blank paper, John reproached her from Amsterdam: "How could you be so imprudent!"[14]

At the same time that Abigail was ordering articles to sell, she asked John for silk gloves, some pretty cloth, and a little lace for dresses for herself and Nabby, "as a little of what you call frippery is very necessary towards looking like the rest of the world." But, she continued, Nabby had asked her to include a note to Pappa assuring him that she "has no passion for dress further than what he would approve." She would simply like to look "like those of her own age."[15]

In the same letter Abigail told her husband of the failing health of both their parents, and warned him of the imminent death from consumption of his brother's wife. "Sister Adams" did succumb later that month, just three days after giving birth to a little girl. John's mother took over the care of the family of five children. By November the baby, too, had died.

Now Abigail suggested that John send some small present to his mother "from your own Hand. "I always make her a sharer with me in whatever I receive from you," she told him, but his mother would be grateful for his attention. "It is not the value but the notice which would be pleasing."[16]

John's letters to Abigail at this time described the beauty that was to be found everywhere in Paris. But he was having a difficult time there. He and the Comte de Vergennes, the French foreign minister, did not like or trust each other. When Vergennes wrote a letter to Benjamin Franklin complaining about John, Franklin sent the letter to Congress. This hostility made Paris unbearable for John, and in July 1780 he decided to leave.

For a long time John had felt that Holland was the one country in all Europe whose friendship would be most helpful to the United States. Holland, he believed, was similar in many ways to his own country. If he could prevail upon the Dutch government to offer material assistance to America, he would improve his country's bargaining position and make it apparent to Vergennes that France was not the only resource of the United

States. He set off for Amsterdam on July 27, 1780 with his two sons in tow.

He found the country beautiful: "Such immense fields and heavy crops of wheat I never saw anywhere," he wrote. The Dutch people, too, were most congenial. They were thrifty and industrious, moral and learned, all of which appealed to John Adams.[17]

In Holland he was able, as a private citizen, to impress influential Dutchmen, assuring them of America's ability and determination to persevere in its fight for independence. But he soon regretted that he had taken his sons along with him.

On their arrival in Amsterdam, John had placed the boys in a Latin school there. But their lack of knowledge of the Dutch language proved a problem for them. "The disobedience and impertinence of your older son, who does his best to corrupt his well-behaved brother . . . can no longer be tolerated," the headmaster wrote to the boys' saddened father. John immediately removed them from the school and sent them, accompanied by John Thaxter, to the celebrated University of Leyden. They were so proficient in Latin and Greek that they were accepted there even though Charles was underage.

To their mother, John explained that the air in Leyden was purer than in Amsterdam, and the schooling less costly. Furthermore, he told her, the masters in the Latin school were mean-spirited, frequently pinching, kicking, and boxing the children.[18]

Abigail, unaware of their difficulties, wrote to her eldest son reminding him that he was in a country known for its industry and frugality, one that had given birth to many great and learned men. "Youth is the proper season for observation and attention," she lectured him. But above all, he must remember that "an Honest Man is the Noblest work of God."[19] In a later letter she reminded Johnny that he must curb his impulsiveness, he must become "a useful member of society," and a guardian of his own country's laws and liberty.[20] Johnny, in the meantime, was learning new Greek verbs and ice-skating every day.

On September 17 word arrived in Amsterdam that Congress had appointed John Adams as official representative to Holland. He immediately set about drawing Holland into an alliance with the United States, and attempted to negotiate a loan. But by the end of the year 1780 his efforts were as yet unsuccessful, and he had grown despondent. He didn't write to Abigail for three months.

At the end of April 1781, when he did write, it was to tell her that he had rented a house in Amsterdam, and that Charles had been ill with tertian fever (a type of malaria), but was on the mend. Abigail, however, received no mail from John or her sons for almost a year. Her loneliness was overwhelming. Her only comfort was to read and reread past letters. She dreamed of her husband and sons at night, then woke to solitude.

"Should I name my dear Boys a tear will flow with the ink—not a line have I received from them for more than a Year," she wrote in August.[21]

Two months later she told her husband:

Three days only did it want of a year from the date of your last Letter, when I received by Capt. Newman in the Brig Gates your welcome favour of May 22.

By various ways I had collected some little intelligence of you, but for six months past my Heart had known but little ease—not a line had reached me from you, not a syllable from my children—and whether living or dead I could not hear. That you have written many times I doubted not, but such is the chance of War.[22]

Most of what Abigail had learned during the year had come from the news-papers and her correspondents in Congress. She didn't like what she heard. As a result of the efforts of Vergennes and Franklin, Congress had appoint-ed four additional ministers to negotiate peace. When Abigail heard of this "dark process," she was furious. The blow to John, she knew, would be devastating. "When he is wounded I bleed," she wrote to James Lovell.[23]

Lovell was continuing to render small services to Abigail. Occasionally

Plaque on a building in The Hague that reads: "John Adams, the first American Ambassador to the Netherlands, lived at this site in a house which was the first embassy owned by the United States of America."

～

the shipments of goods from John arrived in Philadelphia instead of Boston. Then James Lovell would take charge of them, airing them out and then sending them on to Abigail. He sent her the *Journals* of Congress regularly, kept her informed of the happenings there and abroad, and gave her financial advice when she requested it.

And he continued to flirt with her: "How do you do, Lovely Portia, these very cold Days? Mistake me not willfully; I said Days," he wrote from Philadelphia.[24]

Abigail was hard pressed to know how to respond. First she teased, then she called him "a wicked man."[25] Finally, she told him which terms he could and could not use: "amiable and agreeable are bearable," but "lovely" and "charming" were not acceptable.[26]

Acutely aware of the risk of sending such letters through the mail, she worried that her reputation might be threatened. She begged Lovell to destroy her letters to him, as, she told him, she had already destroyed his. But, in fact, she had not. She put them away carefully with her other letters, and continued to write to him, signing herself "Portia." His outrageous compliments made her blush, but she admitted to reading them with great pleasure.

James Lovell had always been kind to and considerate of Abigail. She needed his services, and she respected him. She recognized that beneath the camouflage of impudence and wit was a sensitive and generous man. They continued to write to each other, and their correspondence ultimately developed into a caring and understanding friendship.

Now Abigail learned that John Quincy had left Amsterdam for St. Petersburg, Russia. He would accompany Francis Dana, who had been appointed minister to the court of Catherine the Great. Johnny would serve as his secretary and translator, since he was by now fluent in French, the official language of the Russian court, and Mr. Dana spoke only English. Also, his handwriting had improved and he could be helpful in copying diplomatic correspondence.

Little was known about Russia in 1781, except that it was a dictator-ship, and would take months of traveling to reach. For a fourteen-year-old boy it was quite an adventure, a journey "almost to the world's end," Johnny portrayed it. But his father let him go, reasoning that it would be good experience for a future statesman.

111

John Quincy Adams in 1783, at age fifteen, after serving in St. Petersburg as secretary to Francis Dana, first U.S. minister to Russia. Engraving by Sidney L. Smith from The Studio, March 1887, after the pastel by Isaac Schmidt, 1783.

Johnny's younger brother was not happy about it. He was ill, he missed his mother, and he was homesick. With Johnny about to desert him, Charles begged to be allowed to go home. His father agreed, and arranged for passage in August. But what should have been a relatively calm and simple summer crossing for the eleven-year-old turned into a frightening journey of more than five months.

From September, when Abigail first heard that her young son was on his way home, until December, she had no word of his whereabouts. For three months she feared that he had gone down at sea.

Only when she learned, through her uncle Isaac, that Charles was safe, but detained in Bilboa, Spain, did she write to her husband: "Alass my dear I am much afflicted with a disorder call'd the *Heartach*, nor can any remedy be found in America, it must be collected from Holland, Petersburgh and Bilboa."

Abigail could bear the separation no longer. She ended her letter by pleading with her husband to come home: "I will purchase you a retreat in the woods of Virmont and retire with you from the vexations, toils and hazards of publick Life."[27] Abigail had long been dreaming of buying land in Vermont both as speculation and as a refuge. John's response to her was, "Don't meddle any more with Vermont."[28]

When Charles finally arrived home in late January of 1782, Abigail found him taller and more polished than the boy who had left her. Her young adventurer had regained his health and kept his charm. He seemed to be growing into a miniature John Adams. His mother was overjoyed to have him back.

But Charles brought with him the news that his father had been seriously ill. In August, just after his sons had left, John Adams had been seized by a long and severe "nervous Fever." He had been in a coma for five days, and John Thaxter, acting as nurse as well as secretary, had despaired of his life. It was October before he was well enough to work again.

On October 19, 1781, the war had shifted from the battlefields in America to the negotiating rooms of Paris. The British general Cornwallis surrendered eight thousand troops and marched out of Yorktown as their bands played an old English tune, "The World Turned Upside Down." The war had come to an end. But it would be two years before a final peace could be concluded.

John Adams, now fully recovered, became a principal figure at the negotiating table. He recognized full well, though, the daunting task he faced: "I beg you would not flatter yourself with hopes of Peace. There will be no such Thing for several years," he wrote to Abigail. But he missed her: "What a fine Affair it would be if We could flit across the Atlantic as they say the Angels do from Planet to Planet. I would dart to Pens hill and bring you over on my Wings. . . . I would give a Million sterling that you were here."[29]

Abigail, on her side of the ocean, worried about her husband's health. Suddenly realizing that he might die while in Europe and she might never see him again, she begged him to resign and return home.

Hope, she told her husband, was her best friend and kindest comforter. She could not reconcile herself to living any longer "in this cruel State of Seperation." Women, she told him, must surely feel more intensely than men. "I never wondered at the philosopher who thanked the Gods that he was created a Man rather than a Woman."[30]

Women's sacrifices, she felt, went unrecognized and unappreciated. So "I will take praise to myself," she boldly decided. "I feel that it is my due, for having sacrificed so large a portion of my peace and happiness to promote the welfare of my country."[31]

Her sons' education was another worry. Charles, she told John, was following his studies with attention, but his tutor was leaving, there was no "Grammer School" in town, and she didn't want to be forced to send her boys away to school. "I know not how to think of their leaving Home. I could not live in the House were it so deserted. If they are gone only for a day, it is as silent as a Tomb."[32]

"Who shall give me back Time?" she lamented as she wrote to him on their eighteenth wedding anniversary. "Is there a dearer name than *friend*?" she asked. "Think of it for me." As she remembered "the untitled Man to whom I gave my Heart," she wished fervently that they could go back to living as they had in the early days of their marriage. "Should I wish you less wise, that I might enjoy more happiness?" she agonized.[33]

At the same time John was writing from The Hague that he had sent his wife a "most excellent and beautiful Scarlet Cloth—it is very Saucy." He suggested Abigail use it for a "Ridinghood" for herself and her daughter. He also sent blue cloth for suits for their sons. His letter ended: "I never know how to close, because I can never express the Tenderness I feel."[34]

John and Abigail began considering seriously the possibility of Abigail's traveling to Europe to join him. She told her husband she would "come to you, with our daughter" if he truly wanted her, but "I cannot accept a half way invitation." She would conquer her fear of the hazardous journey across the ocean alone if she could be certain that she could "render your situation more agreeable."[35]

John wanted his wife with him, but the uncertainty of the situation in Europe made him hesitate to send for her. Despite the coup he had achieved in April 1782 when, two years after he had first arrived in the Netherlands, the Dutch had formally recognized American independence, John worried that he might still be recalled home. He differed so in opinion from Dr. Franklin and Vergennes that "I do not expect to hold any Place in Europe longer than next Spring," he wrote to Abigail. If she came to him, they would run the risk of a return trip "in a Month or Six Weeks." It was better, he decided, to wait.[36]

In November of 1782 Great Britain made a sudden turnabout and unconditionally acknowledged the United States as a sovereign state and an independent nation. Still John remained uncertain about whether or not Abigail should come.

Now he urged her to try to learn what Congress was planning and "write it to me for my Guidance."[37] But, he cautioned, she must write under cover to some other friend. And she must write by every ship to Spain, France, Holland, or England. "I always learn more of Politicks from your Letters, than any others."[38]

Abigail continued to beg her husband to return to her. Conceding that his needs and desires must take precedence over her own, she acknowledged her pride in him: "I feel a greater regard for those persons who love me for your sake than I should if they esteemed me on my own account." She would submit, reluctantly, to his ambitions. "For myself," she wrote, "I have little ambition or pride—for my *Husband* I freely own I have much." [39]

It wasn't until a year later that Great Britain formally recognized the independence of the United States by signing the Treaty of Paris on September 3, 1783. Now Abigail wrote to her husband, "If Congress should think proper to make you another appointment, I beg you not to accept it." John's health was still suffering, his children needed his care, his advice, his instruction, and she felt "unequal to the task of guiding them alone."[40]

Two months later, sitting at her little desk in the candlelit quiet of the solitary night, she wrote: "I know not whether I shall believe myself how well you love me, unless I can prevail upon you to return in the Spring."[41] Indeed, people in Braintree had begun to wonder aloud at how a man who professed to love his wife could remain away for so long.[42] "Come home," she pleaded, "take the farm into your own hands and improve it, let me turn dairy woman in getting our living this way."[43]

But John wasn't ready to come home. He was waiting—and hoping— for an appointment as the first American ambassador to the Court of St. James. With the war ended, John's bitterness toward England was gradually disappearing, and he felt a renewal of all his old ties of affection to her as the mother country. He was an American, but in his own way he was an Englishman as well. The power and majesty of British history were part of him. The English had their faults, he conceded, but they had the best constitution and the wisest and fairest laws of any nation in the world. For John Adams to be received at the British court by the British king would be the sweetest triumph he could imagine.

~ CHAPTER XV ~
"safely landed"

There was another reason that Abigail wished fervently that John were at home. She needed his advice about a young man who was courting her daughter. Nabby, she knew, would listen to her father. In the spring of 1782 Nabby, approaching seventeen, had met Royall Tyler, a handsome, well-read young lawyer from a well-to-do Boston family. Royall Tyler had recently opened a law office in Braintree and was boarding with Mary and Richard Cranch. Rumors abounded that he had wasted several years of his life and had squandered a fortune. Although he seemed determined now to apply himself to his profession, Abigail warned her daughter to stay away from him. Nabby, in turn, passed this advice on to her cousins, Betsy and Lucy Cranch. But when Royall visited the Adams house to borrow books from John's library, both mother and daughter were captivated by his charm. By the first chill of winter, his "company and conversation" frequently enlivened their fireside, and he seemed smitten with Nabby.[1]

Mother and daughter were a study in contrasts. Abigail, at thirty-seven, was vivacious and petite, although inclined a bit to plumpness, with expressive warm, dark eyes and a sharp mind. Nabby, on the other hand, was tall, blonde, and stately, demure and beautiful with her cool gray eyes. She listened quietly as her mother discussed literature, history, and philosophy with their visitor. Shy, quiet, and serious, Nabby was not as intellectual as her mother, nor was she as interested in politics. When she occasionally did join in their conversation, it was in her low, precise voice, and with a thoughtfulness and feminine grace that delighted Tyler. Nabby, though, was oblivious to her own charm. She characterized herself to her cousin Betsy Cranch as a "cold indifferent Girl" who longed to be in love.[2]

Abigail felt her daughter was too passive and unemotional. Remembering what it had felt like to be young and in love, she hoped Nabby would experience the same joy and excitement of an intense, romantic love that she had had. A "tender passion," she wrote to John, would make their daughter less reserved and more attractive.[3]

John countered by telling Abigail to stop criticizing Nabby for her quiet manners. They were her most attractive quality. If she spoke little in company, so much the better, "and I would have this observed as a Rule by the Mother as well as the Daughter," he admonished her.[4] John Adams wasn't always pleased when his wife expressed herself freely in mixed company.

But Nabby was more emotional than her mother realized. She missed her father desperately, but tried hard not to show it for fear of upsetting Abigail. Mother and daughter were particularly close to each other, and Nabby was anxious not to add to Abigail's unhappiness. Further, she was falling in love with Royall Tyler, but was struggling with her family's concerns about his appropriateness as a mate. Her father's letter to her only added to her confusion: "My Princess, take care how you dispose of your Heart.—I hoped to be at home and to have chosen a Partner for you. Or at least to have given you some good Advice before you should choose."[5]

A barrage of letters from John followed swiftly. "My child is too young for such thoughts," he cried to his wife. "I positively forbid any Connection between my Daughter and any Youth upon Earth, who does not totally eradicate every Taste for Gaiety and Expence."[6]

A week later he warned his daughter, "Regard the Honour and moral Character of the Man more than all other Circumstances."[7] Clearly, to John Adams, Royall Tyler did not meet the Adams standards.

In another letter to Abigail, John insisted that "Tyler has no Right to your Daughter, who deserves a Character without a Spot," then recommended that his wife seek "the advice of our Parents and Brothers and sisters and Uncles and Aunts etc. You must endeavor to know the Opinion of the Family." This Abigail had already done.

He ended with the plaintive hope that "I shall have my Daughter by her Hand before she gives it away."[8]

Nabby took her father's admonitions seriously, and began to break off her relationship with Tyler. At the beginning of the year she went to Boston to stay with her uncle Isaac and aunt Elizabeth for several months to try to forget him. There she met a young French officer who escorted her on a whirl of gay social events. But when the French fleet sailed for home at the end of April, the brief romance came to an end.

Tyler, in the meantime, had remained in Braintree, continuing to build his law practice. When Nabby returned home in the spring, he resumed his visits to the Adams cottage.

By now Abigail was satisfied that Royall had mended his ways, and considered him a fine young gentleman and an acceptable mate. But Nabby treated him as a good friend only, and Abigail assured John that their daughter would not renew a romantic involvement unless her father consented to the match.

John, for his part, continued to lecture his daughter. "It is by the female world," he told her, "that the greatest and best characters among men are formed. . . . when I hear of an extraordinary man . . . I naturally inquire who was his mother? There can be nothing in life more honourable for a woman, than to contribute by her virtue, her advice, her example . . . to the formation of an husband, a brother, or a son, to be useful to the world."[9]

Throughout this distressing period, Abigail had additional problems to worry her. It was at this time that fifteen-year-old John Quincy was traveling across Europe alone, making his way back to Holland from St. Petersburg. John Adams, "fatigued and lonelier than ever in this horrid Solitude,"[10] had sent for him. As Johnny journeyed through Sweden and Denmark during the coldest months of the year, there were periods of time when no letters got through to his father, who was frantic for news of him. Occasionally John Adams saw a newspaper clipping of his son's arrival in a particular city, but Johnny's mother had no news at all. By now it was almost two years since Abigail had had a letter from her son. He "has forgotten to use his pen," she complained.[11]

Johnny, though, as he waited for favorable traveling conditions in the major cities he visited, was spending his time profitably, talking with merchants interested in developing trade with America. He finally arrived at his father's house in The Hague on April 21, 1783. But John Adams was still in Paris, impatiently waiting for the signing of definitive peace treaties and new instructions. The best he could do was write to his son, admonishing him to improve his handwriting, to write down everything he saw or heard worth notice: "We think, and improve our Judgments, by committing our Thoughts to Paper." Johnny must study mathematics, which, John assured his son, he would find "as entertaining as an Arabean Tale." He must use his time wisely, and he must "never be too wise to ask a Question."[12] The two were finally reunited in July.

In November Abigail received two letters from "my wanderer," one detailing his return trip, the other filled with observations on Russia. Her joy knew no bounds. When a trunk filled with his books and papers arrived in Braintree a short time later, she was delighted to see evidence of his good study habits: the books he had chosen to read and the poems he had transcribed impressed her; and the many translations he had completed were proof of his efforts to continue his studies.

If Abigail was concerned that her daughter was too reserved, she worried that her eldest son was too emotional, too temperamental. As a child Johnny had been more unruly than the other children, so she was delighted to learn from her husband that "He is grown up a Man, and his Steadiness and Sobriety, with all his Spirits are much to his honour. . . . You will be as proud of him as I shall be of my Daughter, when I see her," he continued.[13]

In September 1783 Abigail's father had died, and once again, Abigail had grieved alone. Then, in December, while she was visiting her aunt and uncle, Elizabeth and Isaac Smith, in Boston, her uncle unexpectedly encountered Francis Dana, who had just disembarked from a ship from Russia and was on his way home to Cambridge. Isaac prevailed upon Dana to come home with him to see Abigail, who had no idea that Dana was returning home.

When Abigail saw him walk through the door, she burst into tears. "Tho God is my witness," she wrote to her husband, she did not envy Dana's family their happiness, "yet my Heart swelled with Grief, and the Idea that I, I only, was left alone, recall'd all the tender Scenes of seperation, and overcame all my fortitude. I retired and reasoned myself into composure sufficient to see him without a childish emotion."[14]

Dana stayed at the Smiths' for a short time only, just long enough to deliver to Abigail her husband's "pressing invitation" to come to him in Europe. Dana was anxious to get home to his own family, but he promised to visit Abigail in a few days "with his Lady," a promise she looked forward to with pleasure.

John Thaxter, too, had arrived home from Europe, bearing the same message from John. Abigail found him waiting for her when she returned to Braintree from Boston. He visited with her for half an hour, then hurried off to see his parents. Abigail felt the absence of her husband even more acutely.

Now Abigail learned that by a resolution of Congress on May 1, 1783, John had been appointed to a new joint commission to negotiate a treaty of commerce with Great Britain. Official word was delivered to him in Paris on September 7. He wrote to his wife immediately, extending a firm invitation to join him in Europe. But his letter didn't arrive in Braintree until the end of the year.

"Will you come to me this fall . . . with my dear Nabby?" he had written. He expected that his letter would reach her in October, and she could set out by November or December. "You may embark for London, Amsterdam or any Port in France. On your Arrival, you will finds Friends enough. The Moment I hear of it I will fly with Post Horses to receive you . . . and if the Balloon should be carried to such Perfection in the mean time as to give Mankind the safe navigation of the Air, I will fly in one of them at the Rate of thirty Knots an hour."[15]

By the time this invitation reached Abigail it was already winter. She would have to wait until spring to make the crossing. She had many misgivings. She agonized about the dangers of crossing the ocean without her husband to comfort her, about leaving her home and her country, her family, her friends. With her father gone, there was one less tie to bind her to Braintree. But could she bear the wrench of leaving her two young sons? She couldn't uproot the twelve-year-old Charles once again to take him back to Europe, nor could she disrupt his schooling. Taking ten-year-old Thomas would only serve to isolate Charles again.

And she worried about her role as the wife of a diplomat:

I think if you were abroad in a private Character . . . I should not hesitate so much at comeing to you. But a mere American as I am, unacquainted with the Etiquette of courts, taught to say the thing I mean, and to wear my Heart in my countenance, I am sure I should make an awkward figure, and then it would mortify my pride if I should be thought to disgrace you.

But "the desires and requests of my Friend are a Law to me. I will Sacrifice my present feelings and hope for a blessing in persuit of my duty." She resolved to go.[16]

In fact, she had already made all the necessary arrangements. Uncle Tufts would assume responsibility for the house and farm, and look after the family's financial affairs. A trusted servant would live in the house. Two other servants, a man and a woman, would accompany her to Europe.

Her sister Mary had agreed to take Abigail's place in caring for John's mother. Abigail had tried, she told her husband, to be as good, kind, and considerate a daughter to his mother as Parson Smith had assured her she had been to her own parents.

Charles and Thomas would live with her sister Elizabeth. Abigail knew that in Elizabeth's home her sons would have the love and watchfulness of parents. Warm, gentle Elizabeth would make her home a haven for the Adams boys. Her husband, John Shaw, would tutor them in preparation for their entrance to Harvard.

Her niece Louisa was another concern. Now seven, she had been living with Abigail for the past five years and remembered no other home. She was inconsolable. Louisa's only comfort was the promise that she would come back to live with them when they returned from Europe.

Nabby, Abigail decided, would accompany her to Europe. A separation from Royall would test the strength of their affection for each other. Nabby dutifully agreed.

Tyler, in the meantime, had written to John for permission to marry his daughter. John, never able to deny his daughter anything, had finally reconciled himself to the marriage. But his letter of consent, suggesting that Abigail allow the couple to marry and remain in Braintree, did not arrive until after Abigail and Nabby had sailed.

Their trip would be an adventure, Abigail decided. She hadn't forgotten her childhood dream to visit England, "that once great nation," she had written to John Quincy a few weeks before. The young Abigail who had long ago envied her cousin Isaac the opportunity to travel, and who had confided to him that had she been born a boy she would surely have been a rover, was still lurking inside her.

At the end of May Abigail booked passage on the *Active*, a vessel scheduled to set sail for England in late June. She had delayed her departure in the hope of having some further word from John, but no letters had arrived for the last six months, and her uncle Smith, on whose judgment she relied, advised her not to wait any longer.

Now Abigail learned that on May 7, 1784, Congress had finally officially appointed John Adams, Benjamin Franklin, and Thomas Jefferson to negotiate commercial treaties with a number of nations with which the United States still had no formal connection. Jefferson, on hearing that the wife and daughter of his good friend John Adams were planning to sail to Europe, "hastened" to Boston "in hopes of having the pleasure of attending Mrs. Adams to Paris and of lessening some of the difficulties to which she may be exposed." He arrived in Boston just one day before the *Active* was to depart.[17]

Jefferson had made arrangements to sail from New York on July 4 on a vessel bound directly for France. His twelve-year-old daughter Martha would accompany him. Now he urged Abigail to change her plans and go with him. Much as she recognized all the advantages to having a congenial male companion on the voyage, she couldn't bring herself to delay her trip. She had already suffered a painful leave-taking of friends and family, and could not subject herself to that again. Charles and Tommy had come for a last visit and difficult good-byes, and had returned to their Aunt Elizabeth's house on Monday.

On Friday, the eighteenth of June, as she and Nabby prepared to depart for Boston, Abigail described her house as a "house of mourning." All her friends and neighbors had come, dressed in their best clothes. They had lined up from the road to her front door and into her sunny parlor "like a funeral procession" to wish her well and pray for her speedy return. It was more than she could bear:

"Knowing I had to act my little part alone, I had posessed myself with calmness, but this was too much for me, so I shook them by the hand mingling my tears with theirs, and left them. I had after this to bid my neices adieu." And she must say good-bye to dear Uncle Tufts.

Parting with John's mother was the most painful. Abigail had kept the actual day of departure a secret from her, knowing the agony it would cause the elderly lady. Now, as she appeared at Susanna Boylston's door dressed in her travel clothes, her mother-in-law began to weep, and cried out: "O! why did you not tell me you was going so soon? Fatal day! I take my last leave; I shall never see you again. Carry my last blessing to my Son." Abigail left her in an agony of distress.

Nabby's parting from Royall Tyler was no less dramatic. As the family stood by and watched, the two said tearful good-byes, exchanged keepsakes, and pledged undying love to each other. Abigail was glad to escape to Boston with her sister Mary, who did her best "to amuse me and console me" on the way.

Saturday was spent writing some last letters to friends and in getting her baggage (including a cow from which they hoped to have milk, cream, and butter) on board. At noon on Sunday a carriage arrived at the Smith home to take mother and daughter to Rowe's Wharf, where "100 Gentlemen," dignitaries and townspeople, waited to pay their respects. "Mr. Smith handed me from the Carriage," and they were quickly ushered aboard the ship. The *Active* immediately set sail for England "with a fine wind." Abigail Adams was on her way.[18]

Considered a particularly safe vessel because of its copper bottom, the *Active* was relatively small. There was one large cabin where the eleven passengers took their meals and spent most of their time. Two smaller cabins, each about eight feet square, served as staterooms for the women. Abigail and her maid shared one. Nabby and the only other woman on board shared the second. The men slept in the main cabin. The women, though, had little privacy. They were obliged to keep the doors of their tiny quarters open in order to have any fresh air. They closed them only to dress and undress.

Two hours after he raised sail, the captain sent word to the passengers to prepare for seasickness, and almost immediately the little ship was rolling and tossing on the ocean. All the passengers reacted just as the captain had predicted. It wasn't until Tuesday that the sea calmed and their nausea and seasickness abated. As Abigail went up on deck for the first time, she reflected that John had been correct when he had said that there was nothing so disagreeable as a lady at sea. She was grateful that he was not there to see her in such a condition.

Several days later they encountered a northeaster off the coast of Newfoundland, and once again the ship was tossed mercilessly. Abigail compared the scene on board to a "great cradle rocking with amaizing force from side, to side . . . not a wink of Sleep to be had, bottles, mugs, plates, everything crashing to pieces." They could stay in bed only by holding on to the sides of their bunks with both hands, "every thing wet, dirty and cold, ourselves Sick." The sailors seemed to consider it nothing more than a breeze. If this were only a breeze, Abigail commented wryly, "good heaven defend me from a storm."[19]

By Friday they awoke to a calm sea, a fine wind, and a pleasant day. Now Abigail decided to focus on other things. Recognizing that the captain was an admirable seaman—throughout the storm he had not left the deck for food or sleep—but concerned with little else, she felt certain that she "might reign mistress on board without any offence." Horrified as she was by the dirtiness of the ship, which was made even worse by the "loathsome" smell from the fumes given off by the cargo of leaking fish oil and potash, she determined to remedy it.

She sent her own "Man Servant . . . with all the Boys I could muster, with Scrapers, mops, Brushes, infusions of vinegar &c. and in a few hours we found there was *Boards for a floor.*"[20]

Not satisfied with cleanliness alone, she now invaded the galley, where she taught the "laizy, dirty" cook how to "dress his victuals," and even made two puddings herself. She saw to it also that her cabin was cleaned every day, and that the milk pail, "which has been enough to poison anybody," was scrubbed.[21] But the poor cow they had brought along was so battered by the storm that they were obliged to put her out of her misery. She was "consigned to a watery grave."[22]

Abigail marked Sunday, the Fourth of July, as the "Anniversary of our Glorious Independence," and prayed that the new nation would become the guardian of "Religion and Liberty, of universal Benevolence and Phylanthropy." "We have a fine wind and a clear sky," she noted. "We go at 7 knots an hour."[23]

While her family at home, she was sure, was melting in the summer sun, on board the *Active* Abigail and Nabby were shivering under layer upon layer of clothes. The dampness and chill of the Atlantic had brought on a recurrence of Abigail's rheumatism. As the cold, wet days kept her confined to her cabin, where even her bed was damp, she began to think of the ship as a "partial prison." When they encountered a dead calm and the ship was motionless without a wind to fill its sails, she reflected that "a Calm is not desireable in any situation in life. . . . Every object is most Beautiful in motion, a ship under sail trees gently agitated with the wind & a fine woman danceing . . . man was made for action."

Despite her problems, Abigail managed to read, write, and reflect. She wrote even when she had to brace herself against the walls of her cabin. "If I did not write I should lose the Days of the Week," she entered in her journal on July 8. She commented on the beauty of the ocean in its various guises, and particularly of the night sky sparkling on the water. And she was moved to pray with the psalmist: "Great and Marvelous are thy Works, Lord God Almighty, in Wisdom hast thou made them all."

She found the gentlemen on board most attentive to her and Nabby, who, she proudly reported, "has behaved with a Dignity and Decorum worthy of her."[24]

As they neared the coast of England, with the sun shining and the seas gently rolling, Abigail thought of her imminent reunion with her husband and her eldest son, and her spirits soared. "And am I Gracious Heaven," she prayed, "there to meet, the dear long absent partner of my Heart? How many how various how complicated my Sensations! Be it unto me according to my wishes."[25]

Exactly four weeks after leaving Boston, they sighted land. "You will hardly wonder," she wrote to Mary, "at the joy we felt this day in seeing the cliffs of Dover."

But as they were about to disembark, the wind shifted and a sudden squall came up. A gale force wind blew fiercely, the surf ran six feet high, and the pilot boat that came to get them was no larger than the Charlestown ferry that made the run between Boston and Charlestown. Finally, after three sleepless nights of tossing on the *Active* and a "violent sick head ack," they decided to brave the storm. Mother and daughter were handed down into the pilot boat. There, each clinging tightly to one of the male passengers, they managed to keep from falling overboard until the waves crashing against their little boat tossed it broadside onto the beach. Like nymphs "just rising from the sea," they trudged through the wet sand to a nearby inn in the little town of Deal.[26]

Abigail Adams and her daughter had reached the "land of my fore-fathers." This was the land whose history and literature she had known and loved since childhood. Like her husband some nine months earlier, when he had first set foot on English soil, she felt that she had, in a sense, come home.

John Adams, painted by John Singleton Copley in London in the fall of 1783. Abigail saw this portrait of her husband before her actual reunion with him in 1784. Adams had just negotiated the treaty that concluded the war with England, and is shown pointing to a map of the new United States of America.

~

The next morning the little party set out for London at five o'clock. They traveled the seventy-two miles in four post chaises* through Canterbury, Rochester, Chatham, and Blackheath, where a highway robber had just been caught. Abigail was distressed that the "poor wretch," little more than a boy, must hang for his crime. But she was impressed by the "old Gothick Cathedrals" and she was enchanted with the English countryside, where the land was "cultivated like a garden down to the very edge of the road."[27]

They arrived in London at 8:00 P.M. on July 21. Within half an hour one of their traveling companions had managed to track down Abigail's cousins, William Smith and Charles Storer, and bring them back to Lows Hotel in Covent Garden, where she had taken temporary lodgings. They, in turn, soon had the women moved to another hotel overlooking the Thames River, where they were provided with a large "genteelly furnished" drawing room, a cook, a chambermaid, and a waiter.

* Horse and carriage.

"Heaven be praised I am with our daughter Safely landed upon the British Shore," Abigail wrote to her husband as soon as they were settled.[28]

John replied immediately from The Hague: "Your Letter of the 23d has made me the happiest Man upon Earth. I am twenty Years younger than I was yesterday." But it was "a cruel Mortification" that he could not meet her in London. In his place: "I send you a son who is the greatest Traveller of his age, and without Partiality, I think as promising and manly a youth as is in the World."[29]

In mid-May, still unaware of which ship his wife and daughter would sail on, John Adams had sent John Quincy to London to await them. Johnny remained there for over a month. Finally, despairing of their arrival, he returned to The Hague just days before they landed.

Now Abigail and Nabby resigned themselves to waiting for John and John Quincy. They found their welcome to London even more enthusiastic than they had anticipated. There were many Americans in London, most of whom called to pay their respects to the minister's wife and daughter. Abigail and Nabby received visitors from nine to three every day. Then, after dinner, mother and daughter went off to see the sights of London. Abigail soon pronounced herself in love with the city.

She and Nabby were surprised, though, at the informality of the dress among Londoners, who, they felt, lacked style and elegance. "A common straw hat, no cap, with only a ribbon upon the crown," was considered suitable for going calling. Feminine grace and softness are "wholly laid aside here," Abigail stated caustically.[30]

One of their first stops was at the studio of the young artist, John Singleton Copley. In October 1783, when John had been in London, he had commissioned Copley to paint his portrait in commemoration of the successful peace negotiations. His wife and daughter were anxious to see the painting.

"It is said to be an admirable likeness," Abigail remarked of the husband she had not seen for almost five years.[31]

On Friday, July 30, Abigail decided to remain at home to rest and write letters. That afternoon, as she sat at her desk, a servant rushed in and announced breathlessly, "Young Mr. Adams is come!" But Johnny had stopped at the house next door to have his hair "dressed."

A few minutes later a young man whom Abigail didn't recognize entered the room. Only his eyes seemed familiar. Abigail drew back until he cried out, "Oh my Mamma! and my Dear Sister!" Then, tears streaming down her face, Abigail rushed to embrace her son.

Abigail had sent a boy to Europe with his father. Now she was greeted by a tall, slim young man. At seventeen, his years of travel had given him a polish, but underneath was the same boyish good humor and bursting energy that his mother remembered.

"I think you do not approve the word feelings," Abigail wrote as she recounted the reunion to Mary, "but I know not what to Substitute in lieu, or even to discribe mine."

She went on to tell her sister how matronly she felt now, "with a grown up Son on one hand, and Daughter upon the other, and were I not their Mother, I would say a likelier pair you will seldom see in a Summers day."[32]

One week and one day later Nabby made an entry in her journal:

At 12, returned to our apartments; when I entered, I saw upon the table a hat with two books in it; every thing around appeared altered, without my knowing in what particular. I went into my own room, the things were moved; I looked around—"Has Mamma received letters, that have determined her departure?—When does she go?—Why are these things moved?" All in a breath to Esther.

"No ma'm, she has received no letter, but goes to-morrow morning."

"Why is all this appearance of strangeness?—Whose hat is that in the other room?—Whose trunk is this?—Whose sword and cane?—It is my father's," said I. "Where is he?"

"In the room above."

Up I flew, and to his chamber, where he was lying down, he raised himself upon my knocking softly at the door, and received me with all the tenderness of an affectionate parent after so long an absence. Sure I am, I never felt more agitation of spirits in my life; it will not do to describe.[33]

Abigail never described her own reunion with her husband. Five months later she wrote to Mary that "poets and painters wisely draw a veil over those Scenes which surpass the pen of the one and the pencil of the other; we were indeed a very very happy family once more met together after a Separation of four years."[34]

~ CHAPTER XVI ~
"one of the choice ones of the earth"

arly the next morning, the reunited family of four set out together for Paris. They crossed the English Channel at Dover, then traveled by coach the two hundred miles to Paris, where they arrived on August 13. Abigail pronounced the city "the very dirtiest place" she had ever seen. She smelled it even before it came into view.[1]

After several days of sight-seeing they rode out to Auteuil, four miles outside Paris on the road to Versailles. There John had rented—at a bargain price—an elegant house overlooking the River Seine and very near the Bois de Boulogne, a huge royal park where John loved to walk. The house, hidden away at the end of a chestnut-lined driveway, was enormous. It contained thirty bedrooms and several odd "apartments." Its rear windows and doors opened onto five acres of formal gardens.

While its size was overwhelming after the tiny saltbox cottage in Braintree, Abigail quickly grew to love it. Here she finally had the kind of private space she had long dreamed of. Her bedroom, with an adjoining "apartment" overlooking the garden, was the perfect place to read and write letters. She compared the luscious gardens to her little garden in Braintree as silks were to calico.

But it was a constant struggle to keep the house up to her high standards of cleanliness. She soon discovered that French servants were "Lazy Wretches" who considered themselves specialists: one would not touch what belonged to the business of the other. The chambermaid would not go near the kitchen, nor would the cook wash a dish. It required eight servants merely to get by, Abigail told Cotton Tufts. The red tile floors, which could not be scrubbed with water, provided some amusement. To clean them a servant with brushes strapped to his feet whirled around the room, "dancing here and there like a Merry Andrew."[2]

In spite of the drawbacks, Abigail loved being here. Just knowing that John was nearby made her heart leap. The family quickly fell into a pleasant routine. They enjoyed a hearty New England breakfast together each morning, after which John read or wrote, Abigail sewed, Nabby studied French, and John Quincy translated Tacitus and Horace. At noon John usually went for a walk through "his" woods—the paths of the Bois de Boulogne. Abigail could watch from her window until he disappeared from sight. While he was gone she and Nabby had their hair dressed and practiced their French on the young coiffeuse, nineteen-year-old Pauline. At two o'clock John returned and the family dined together, then John made the short ride to the neighboring town of Passy to meet with Benjamin Franklin and Thomas Jefferson.

He returned in time for tea, after which he and John Quincy studied math together. The table was covered with their mathematical instruments and their books, and "you hear nothing till nine o'clock but of theorems and problems, bisecting and dissecting tangents and segments," Abigail described it. Father and son made their way systematically through geometry (eight books of Euclid in Latin), trigonometry, algebra, decimals, fractions, arithmetical and geometrical proportions, and conic sections. After the lesson they all generally played a game of whist together "to relieve their brains" before they went to bed.[3]

The Adams family also did much sightseeing. At that time balloon ascents were the rage, and one afternoon they joined thousands of people at the Tuilleries to witness a launching. Perhaps, they speculated, man had indeed conquered the air.

Abigail was delighted with the theater. In New England there were no theaters: plays were read, not acted. In Paris Abigail could attend the theater as often as she liked.

Another great attraction of Paris was its ballet. But the first performance that Abigail attended shocked her Puritan sensibility. The grace and beauty of the dancers enchanted her, but her "delicacy [was] wounded" by their flimsy dress, she wrote to Mary. "With their feet flying and as perfectly shewing their Garters and draws as tho no peticoat had been worn,"

130

she was "ashamed to be seen to look at them." But her "disgust" quickly wore off, and she was able to enjoy the music and view the dancers with pleasure, although she never stopped worrying about the bad effects of stage life on a young girl's moral character.[4]

In November Abigail met Adrienne, the marquise de Lafayette, wife of the French hero of the American Revolution. She found her sweet and gracious, and was impressed by the fact that, unlike most French women, Adrienne dressed simply and neatly, and devoted herself to her children and her husband.

Abigail and Nabby had been upset by the "tyranny of fashion" since they had arrived in Paris. "To be out of fashion is more criminal than to be seen in a state of nature," she complained to Mary.[5]

In fact, Abigail found the manners of the French

Abigail loved the elegant house John had rented in the Paris suburb of Auteuil. She described it as "gay and really beautiful."

~

people not at all to her liking. The business of life in France, she wrote to her friend Mercy Otis Warren, was pleasure.[6]

She was particularly disturbed by the fact that the French did not observe the Sabbath. Sunday was for them a day of recreation, not worship. Nor did the French seem to take marriage seriously. To Abigail, marriage was sacred. She considered it the basis of a well-ordered society, along with religion, education, and hard work.

In spite of the joy of being with John, Abigail was beginning to feel lonely. Her servants had taken over all the domestic duties that she had always attended to herself in Braintree. Every detail of running the household—even shopping—was handled by the servants. The only task she insisted on performing herself was sewing. She trusted no one to do it as well as she.

Her social life outside her family was somewhat restricted also. While she could read French easily, she had never learned to speak it fluently. For someone who loved to talk as much as Abigail did, the language

131

barrier was truly frustrating. To "go into a foreign Country without being able to speak the language," she confided to Mary, made her feel totally isolated.[7] She advised Mary's daughter Lucy to perfect her French, telling her that she was reading a play a day, looking up words in a dictionary, and writing them down. She advised her niece to do the same.

She was often homesick and lonely in the big cold house. She missed her Braintree friends and family. Her new French friends would not make the trip out from Paris without a specific invitation. She told Lucy how she wished she could transport her to France in a balloon. She worried about the poor whom she had often helped at home, and wrote to Cotton Tufts to be sure to continue her contributions to them. "What a sad misfortune it is to have the Body in one place & the soul in another," she reflected.[8] For comfort she bought a tiny songbird, and soon grew very attached to it.

Even John informed her that he had no time to discuss domestic matters with her. He wanted everything to run smoothly, yet he was unwilling to share the responsibility. He had become "The Statesman." The only detail to which he paid attention was his son's education. He left Abigail to grapple with the problems facing an American minister living in a grand house that had no rugs for its cold floors, no linens, and no china, glassware, or silver for the table. To purchase all that was needed to entertain foreign dignitaries properly was enormously expensive, and Congress had made no allowance for it.

Cotton Tufts, who was managing their financial affairs at home, had been writing detailed letters to both of them. Now he began to write to John about politics and to Abigail about finances.

And Abigail missed her young sons. Charles and Tommy were making good progress in their studies, Elizabeth wrote to her. They were also taking singing and dancing lessons. Thomas was a very good child, and much loved. Charles, with his ear for music, was "grace in all his motions and attitudes." He had grown so tall that his mother would hardly recognize him. Soon he would enter Harvard as a freshman. But Abigail was not happy to learn that Charles was a favorite of all the girls.

The one person in France with whom Abigail loved to spend time was Thomas Jefferson. He and his twelve-year-old daughter, Martha, nicknamed Patsy, often came to dinner at Auteuil. Jefferson and John Adams, although they presented an odd picture, the one tall and angular, the other short, plump, and balding, were kindred spirits. Both had a passion for books and preferred quiet family life to the social whirl of French society. Most important, they had worked together in Congress on the committee for drafting the Declaration of Independence, and had formed a lasting bond.

A lonely widower just a year older than Abigail, Jefferson possessed a brilliant mind and wide-ranging interests. He and Abigail found much to talk about. Jefferson knew few if any women in Europe whose intelligence equaled hers, and the two took increasing pleasure in each other's company. Their association in France began an affectionate friendship. Jefferson and seventeen-year-old John Quincy also formed a strong and enduring attachment.

Early in May 1785 John Adams finally received the honor he had coveted for so long. News arrived that in February Congress had elected him the first American ambassador to the Court of St. James. Thomas Jefferson was named minister to France. Benjamin Franklin, now almost eighty, would return to Philadelphia. Colonel William Stephens Smith, formerly aide-de-camp to General George Washington and member of an influential New York family, was named secretary to John Adams in the legation and would accompany the Adams family to London.

Thomas Jefferson, whose passion for books and preference for quiet family life endeared him to Abigail. She called him "one of the choice ones of the earth." Marble bust by Jean-Antoine Houdon, 1789.

~

As was proper, Jefferson gave a dinner to celebrate their appointments. In addition to the Adamses, the guests included the marquis de Lafayette and his wife, Adrienne, several members of the French court, and Commodore John Paul Jones, the daring young naval hero of the American Revolution. It was Jones who, during a naval battle in which he commanded an American frigate against heavy odds, had replied to a British demand for surrender, "I have not yet begun to fight." Abigail expressed surprise that the famous sailor was not at all stout or warlike, as she had anticipated, but small and soft-spoken.

But she didn't like the etiquette of a French dinner party. The men, she complained, didn't sit down. They stood or walked from one part of the room to another with their swords on and their *chapeau de bras,* a very small silk hat, always under their arms. These they would lay aside when they dined. But when they were standing still they would shut out all the fire from the ladies, leaving them very cold.

Conversation at dinner didn't please her either. It was carried on only with the person sitting next to you. After dinner, the tête-à-tête of two and two in low voices made her think that everyone had private business to transact. She would have much preferred to engage in a lively exchange of ideas among men *and* women.

So her walk in the gardens at the Tuilleries with Mr. Jefferson after dinner was all the more enjoyable. As usual, there were four to five thousand people strolling there in the soft spring air. But she was captivated by her companion. This tall and engaging Virginian always had a funny story to tell or a witty observation to make. His fund of information on a multitude of topics was vast and stimulating, and he treated Abigail as an equal. He was naturally courteous, his instinctive southern gallantry always evident. It made their imminent parting even sadder. She would miss his company and his conversation.

"I shall really regret to leave Mr. Jefferson. He is one of the choice ones of the earth," she wrote to Mary when she told her of John's new role and their pending move to London.[9]

As they made their plans to move from France to England, Abigail and John decided that John Quincy must return home to finish his education. They felt it wise that he enter the junior class at Harvard so that he might graduate with classmates of his own age. It was a wrenching decision.

Johnny had been only ten when he first accompanied his father to Europe eight years before, and over the years the two had grown very close. Johnny had been his father's personal secretary. They had studied together, they had traveled together, and they had discussed politics and diplomacy for hours on end. John had watched with pride as his son grew from a boy to a man, and it was hard now to give him up. For Abigail, to lose Johnny again after such a short reunion filled her with sadness. But they knew that sending him home was in his best interest.

The most difficult parting for Johnny, though, was from Nabby. The two had known each other only as children. Now they had rediscovered each other and become very good friends. They had much in common: they walked together, went to the theater in Paris, went sight-seeing and shopping, and talked about the frustrations of their love lives. Nabby was in love with a young man three thousand miles away, and Johnny was infatuated with a young Frenchwoman but far too young to contemplate marriage. Brother and sister promised to write to each other often. And Johnny would carry letters with him for Royall Tyler. Nabby had not heard from Royall in several months, and she was concerned. She hoped, also, that her brother and her husband-to-be would become good friends.

Both Abigail and Nabby had been writing to Royall regularly. Abigail's first letter to him, written on board the *Active,* had advised him how he should conduct himself during the separation. A few months later she told him that she viewed him as the person in whose care and protection she would one day entrust her beloved only daughter.

Now she and Nabby were puzzled. Why had Royall suddenly stopped writing? Abigail began to make discreet inquiries of her sisters. But there was little they could relate. Royall had moved from the Cranch home in Braintree to Boston.

Johnny left France on May 12, 1785, bound for home. One week later John, Abigail, and Nabby, accompanied by their two servants from Braintree, set out for England. As they said good-bye to their French servants who had gathered to see them off, Abigail impulsively gave her little songbird to the weeping Pauline. With a last lingering look back at their lovely spring garden, just coming into bloom, they were off.

As they traveled, they read aloud from Thomas Jefferson's newly published book, *Notes on the State of Virginia,* which Jefferson had given to them as a farewell gift. John declared its passages denouncing slavery "worth diamonds."[10] Jefferson sent a letter also, telling the Adamses that their departure had left him "in the dumps."[11]

As soon as they arrived in London Abigail decided that she preferred England to France. But France had left its mark on her. An increased sophistication in her dress, in her manners, and in the household furnishings she purchased would be evident for the rest of her life.

She had developed a greater confidence in herself, and she was even more certain now that her belief in the democratic policies of her own country, where virtue and modesty were still revered, was well founded.

In London the family settled into a hotel in Picadilly until Abigail could find a house for them. John immediately delivered his credentials to the foreign minister.

Both John and Abigail understood well that Congress had given John a difficult assignment. To fight for position in London on behalf of the young republic was an unenviable task. England was in no mood to make concessions to her former colonists. Also, John knew that he could expect to be the target of English Tories and of exiled American loyalists. This practical philosopher quickly realized that he had little chance of success in the main objects of his embassy. But he would try.

Now he set about preparing for his formal presentation to King George III, scheduled for June 1. He spent much time composing a speech which he hoped would reconcile the two nations. When he had read it aloud to Abigail and was certain that she approved, he committed it to memory.

Together John and Abigail shopped for the proper clothes for the occasion. John was coached on the accepted etiquette of approaching and addressing the king.

When the day arrived, it proved to be an emotional one for John. He was conscious of the fact that he was simply a provincial lawyer and farmer about to face the king of the most powerful nation in the world. Yet, he realized, it was the farmer who represented victory, and the king defeat. So he was delighted when the king received him with unexpected respect and civility and the offer of friendship.

As John began the obligatory round of official calls, Abigail and Nabby went to hear Handel's *Messiah* at Westminster Abbey. "It was sublime beyond description," Abigail wrote to Jefferson.[12]

Soon it was the ladies' turn to be presented at court. Abigail directed her dressmaker to make her a gown that was "elegant, but plain as I could possibly appear, with decency." She would have no "foil or tincel about me," she insisted.

Her dress was of white silk trimmed with white crepe, lilac ribbon, and mock point lace over a hoop of "enormous extent." Ruffled cuffs, a lace cap with two white plumes, a lace handkerchief, and two pearl pins for her hair completed her "rigging," as she called it.

On the day of the reception, Abigail and Nabby spent the entire morning dressing. "My head is drest for St. James and in my opinion looks very tasty," Abigail wrote to Mary while waiting for Nabby's hair to be arranged.[13]

Finally, as the two stepped gingerly into their carriage to be driven the few blocks to the palace, their hoops barely cleared the doors and the feathers in their hair brushed the ceiling. Both mother and daughter felt ridiculous.

At the palace they were ushered into a vast reception hall where more than two hundred people were gathered for an audience with the king and queen. When the king, queen, and the princesses entered, they slowly made their way around the room, making polite conversation with each guest. Abigail and Nabby waited four hours for their turn.

When the king reached Abigail, he asked her if she had taken a walk that day. She wanted to reply that she had been too busy dressing, but resisted the temptation and simply said, "No Sire." She and Nabby returned home exhausted.[14]

Writing to John Quincy, Abigail reflected that she must be a fool to stand for four hours only to be spoken to by royalty. Yet, she told him, "I had vanity enough to come a way quite self satisfied. I saw many who were vastly richer drest . . . but I will venture to say that I saw none neater or more elegant."[15]

Nabby, too, wrote scornfully to her brother of the "ridiculous" ceremony. She rather liked the king, she told him, but found the queen haughty and proud. The Prince of Wales looked "stuffed."

The experience, though, helped Abigail to overcome her shyness in public life and provided her with a wonderful tale for friends and family back home.

Early in July the Adamses moved into a handsome and spacious house in Grosvenor Square, near Hyde Park, and John sent for the furniture from his house at The Hague.

Their windows looked out on a beautifully landscaped circle in the center of the square, lighted at night by dozens of lamps. The house faced the town house of Lord North,* so Abigail could joke in a letter to a friend that "We have not taken a side with Lord North, but are still opposite to him."[16]

Their home soon became the meeting place for all the Americans in London, among them the artists John Singleton Copley, John

* The former British prime minister.

Trumbull, Benjamin West, and Mather Brown. The young Trumbull had just completed a painting of the Battle of Bunker Hill, and was planning to paint other dramatic episodes in the history of America. His *Signing of the Declaration of Independence* would become the most famous of these.

John took a special liking to the very young Mather Brown, and consented to sit for him. He was so pleased with the result that Abigail and Nabby allowed him to paint their portraits as well. Again John felt that Brown had captured their likenesses exactly.

Abigail loved London more and more. She particularly loved the theater here, and attended numerous plays by William Shakespeare which she had been reading over and over since she was a child. She made warm friendships among a group of Englishmen who had supported American independence. And she had an opportunity to meet her old heroine, Catherine Macaulay.

The Battle of Bunker Hill, showing the death of the Adamses's dear friend Dr. Joseph Warren. Painted by John Trumbull in London about 1785.

∽

But she found diplomatic receptions uninteresting. The gambling and card playing that were favorite pastimes here were, to her, a terrible waste of time and unfit for ladies. When she was trapped at a card table one evening, though, to her astonishment she won four games in a row.

"Tho I sometimes like to mix in the gay world, . . . I have much reason to be grateful to my parents that my early education gave me not an habitual taste for what is termed fashionable life," she informed Mary.[17]

Sunday quickly became her favorite day of the week. The family would drive to a church six miles outside of London to hear Dr. Richard Price preach. Abigail found the topics this descendant of Puritans and outspoken supporter of the colonial cause chose for his sermons "instructive."

Living in London was causing great financial stress. John and Abigail could not give the expected diplomatic dinner for the other ministers because Congress simply would not pay for it, nor did they have personal funds to spend. They were counting every penny and shilling in an effort to avoid bankruptcy. The fear of debt haunted them.

When Abigail tried to take over the shopping herself in an effort to cut costs, she became the butt of jokes in the newspapers. The London press ridiculed her for her frugality, cruelly comparing her to a farmer's wife "going in an old chaise to market with a little fresh butter." Now she began to long for America, where frugality was considered a virtue. The experience left her with a distrust of the press which she never abandoned.

Finally, she and John decided that they had no choice but to give a dinner for the foreign ministers, regardless of the cost. At just that time they had an unexpected stroke of good fortune. A ship arrived from Boston by way of the West Indies, bringing a giant codfish from the New England waters and a 114-pound turtle from the Indies. These were presented to the Adamses as a gift from the captain of the ship.

Now John was able to preside over a table at which were seated all the ambassadors of the great powers of Europe. He proudly served them a classic New England dinner. Since protocol dictated that only men were invited, mother and daughter visited the Copleys that evening, where they worried that everything was going smoothly.

I t was September before Abigail finally learned of John Quincy's safe arrival in America. He had left France four months before and, in fact, had celebrated his eighteenth birthday on board the ship. The family was at breakfast one morning when a packet of letters from Braintree relatives and friends was deliverd to them.

"Up we all jumped," Abigail wrote to John Quincy, "your sister siezed hold of a letter and cried, "My brother, my brother! . . . The chocolate grew cold, the teapot was forgotten, and the bread and butter went down [stairs] uneaten, yet nobody felt the loss of breakfast."[18]

N abby, with none of her mother's social obligations, was often bored and unhappy. She missed her brother and wished he were there to offer advice. By now she had learned from family members at home that Royall Tyler was gossiping about all the Adamses, particularly Nabby. Royall had shared their personal letters to him with his friends in Boston, and boasted that Nabby was pursuing him, writing to him regularly despite the fact that he was not responding. Aunts Mary and Elizabeth had written that when he got hold of a packet of letters from Nabby to various members of the family he refused to deliver them and hid them away in his room. He had even opened one to her cousin and confidante, Betsy Cranch.

Nabby was devastated. Royall had violated her trust. She had tolerated his neglect over the past year, but she could not tolerate his attack on her reputation.

Throughout this period Colonel William Smith, John's secretary, was a constant visitor at the Adams house. Handsome, polite, attentive, he had fallen in love with Nabby almost as soon as he met her. Nabby, too, found herself attracted to him. She was in a turmoil.

Abigail, sensing what was happening, took it upon herself to warn Colonel Smith that Nabby was engaged. "Honour, Honour, is at stake," she told him.[19]

She and John decided to send Smith to Prussia for several weeks to observe military demonstrations there. It must not seem as though William Smith were the cause of a rift between Nabby and Royall Tyler.

While Colonel Smith was gone Nabby wrote to Royall breaking their engagement. She returned his letters and the miniature he had given her. She asked friends and family not to mention him to her again.

The colonel, meanwhile, stayed in Europe far longer than John had intended. When he completed his duties in Prussia he traveled widely, stopping in Paris to visit Thomas Jefferson. His absence left John overburdened with paperwork and without a secretary. John survived by pressing Nabby into service.

Colonel Smith returned at the beginning of December. His three-week journey had turned into an absence of more than four months, but his charm quickly restored him to Ambassador Adams's good graces. Nabby, overjoyed to see him, suddenly realized how much she had missed him.

Soon Abigail noticed a subtle change in her daughter. Nabby joined in conversations now instead of sitting quietly by and just listening. Her shy smiles delighted her mother. Nabby's wounds from Royall Tyler were slowly healing.

Near the end of December William Smith asked Abigail for permission to marry her daughter. He needed Abigail's support, he explained, before he could find the courage to approach her husband. By February 1786 William and Nabby were officially engaged, and had set a June date for their wedding. While Abigail thought it a little hasty, she philosophized that

Nabby Adams on the eve of her marriage to Colonel William S. Smith, in London, 1786. From an engraving of the painting by John Singleton Copley.

~

"a Heart agitated with the remains of a former passion is most susceptable of a new one."[20] But she was pleased with the choice. "Your niece is engaged to a gentleman worthy of her; one, whom you will be proud to own as a nephew," Abigail wrote to Mary.[21] At the time it seemed like a fairy-tale match: the lovely daughter of the ambassador to the Court of St. James and his lady, and a dashing, high-ranking military officer, former adjutant to George Washington and secretary to the American legation in London. It promised a "happily ever after" life.

~ CHAPTER XVII ~
"the three-fold cord"

Early in 1786, at John's urging, Thomas Jefferson came to London. John felt that England might be ready to negotiate a commercial treaty with America. The wealth of the new nation depended on the growth of foreign markets.

Abigail was elated that Mr. Jefferson had come. She welcomed him into their home as a member of the family. They spent many hours in stimulating conversation, went to the theater in Drury Lane together, and visited the studios of the artists John Trumbull and Mather Brown. Abigail even convinced Mr. Jefferson to have his portrait painted by Brown.

But soon after Jefferson arrived he and John realized that they had been too optimistic. They were kept waiting endlessly, and were treated rudely. When they were finally granted an audience with George III at Buckingham Palace, the king, in full view of surrounding courtiers, abruptly turned his back on the author of the Declaration of Independence without saying a word. Jefferson never forgot this insult.

After his return to Paris, Mr. Jefferson remained a comfort and a source of joy to Abigail. They continued to correspond and to shop for each other. Abigail bought shirts and table linens for him. Jefferson sent shoes, silk fabric for dresses, and decorative tableware from France.

By the fall of 1786 Abigail was so hungry for news of home that she invited every American ship captain in port to dinner. She wanted to hear the latest information about the United States. The news was disheartening. Economic storm clouds hung low over the country. The United States was in a depression, commerce was at a standstill, bankruptcies were on the rise, and farmers were losing their land. Interest on the public debt was piling up at home, while the nation's credit was evaporating abroad.

The worst news was from Massachusetts. An alarming uprising, known as Shays's Rebellion, had flared up there. Impoverished back-country farmers, many of them revolutionary war veterans, were losing their farms through mortgage foreclosures and tax delinquencies. In November, under the leadership of Daniel Shays, they took up their muskets and rebelled.

Abigail was horrified. She was beginning to fear that while America had won the war, it was in danger of losing the peace. How could Americans turn against one another?

"For what have we been contending against the tyranny of Britain if we are to become the sacrifice of a lawless banditti?" she asked Mary.[1] And to Uncle Tufts she wrote: "How totally ignorant are our countrymen of the consequences of their wild schemes. . . . God save the people."[2]

In a letter to Thomas Jefferson she denounced the Massachusetts rebels as "Ignorant, wrestless, desperadoes, without conscience or principals."[3] Abigail was not pleased with Jefferson's reply: "The spirit of resistance to government is so valuable on certain occasions, that I wish it always kept alive. It will often be exercised when wrong, but better so than not to be exercised at all. I like a little rebellion now and then."[4]

Abigail disagreed. "An unprincipled mob," she felt, was the "worst of all Tyrannies."[5] Her New England Puritan upbringing had surfaced once again. And when she learned, shortly after, that Congress had voted to maintain a regular army, she broke down and wept.

This was a difficult period for Abigail. Her three sons were now at Harvard, and her only daughter was about to marry and leave her home. She knew that Nabby would start her own family quickly, and the everyday intimacy of their mother-daughter relationship would change.

From Abigail's sisters came reassurances that her sons were doing well. Tommy was the solid, practical one, while Charles was more social. He was really *too* handsome, Mary observed. He would soon steal the heart of every girl he met. John Quincy, Elizabeth told her, had thrown himself into his studies with great determination. He "searches out knowledge as if it was his Meat, & Drink & considered it as more precious than choice Gold."[6]

*Nabby wrote to her brother John Quincy that
this picture of Abigail Adams, painted in London in 1786,
was "a good likeness of Momma." Artist unidentified.*

~

Abigail sensed, though, that Johnny was having some difficulty settling down to the life of a student after his years in Europe. He had initially been turned down by Harvard for the advanced standing for which he had applied because he had not read "certain" books. After extensive tutoring from Uncle Shaw, he was accepted into the upper junior class in the spring of 1786. Now he complained to his mother that his teachers were too young and inexperienced for their positions. She responded by reminding him that his teachers were to be respected regardless of his opinion.

"Reflect that you have had greater opportunities of seeing the world," she admonished him. He must not look down on his peers. She went on to remind him "that you have never wanted a Book but that it has been supplied you, that your whole time has been spent in the company of men of Literature & science. How unpardonable would it have been in you, to have been a Blockhead."[7]

Now, perhaps more than ever before, Abigail was dependent on her sisters. They remained her closest friends. They wrote to one another constantly. The three had formed early what Elizabeth called the "three-fold cord." As children they had played, prayed, and learned together. As young adults they had meddled in one another's courtships and marriages. They had shared "recipes" for raising children, and had cared for one another's offspring. They were a support system without which they couldn't have functioned. Loyalty and genuine affection overcame any tensions that might arise.

It was Mary's and Elizabeth's support that had allowed Abigail to remain home alone while John was away. Later they made it possible for her to follow her husband to Europe. Mary looked after their home and gardens, as well as John's mother. Elizabeth cared for their sons until they were in college. Then Mary, who lived closer to Cambridge and had her own son at Harvard, took over.

Now Abigail reflected gratefully on the good home, the love, and the "prudent care" her sons had had with Elizabeth. Her home became a haven for them. Their aunt kept after them to do their best, praised them constantly, and encouraged them to "stretch their wings." She had cut down outgrown jackets and breeches of one boy for the other, darned their socks, patched knees and elbows, and turned frayed collars and cuffs, and she had made them both new winter coats. Young Tommy, Elizabeth had assured her absent sister, was showered with hugs and kisses. Elizabeth's pride when Charles was accepted at Harvard was unmistakable. And when John Quincy left for Harvard after a brief stay with her, she wrote to Abigail of how "gloomy" her house was with him gone. Johnny, for his part, remained deeply attached to her for the rest of her life.

Mary sent puddings and pies to school with the boys, and frequently slipped extra pocket money to Charles.

While Abigail and John paid Elizabeth for taking care of their sons, and provided some financial assistance to both sisters when they could, Abigail knew that money could never repay their kindness and love. She frequently sent fabric from London for her sons' and nephews' clothes, and for her sisters and their daughters she sent luxuries they could neither obtain nor afford in Boston: silks, fashionable shoes, bonnets, and ribbons.

A hint of the banter and teasing that went on among the sisters appears in a letter from Abigail to Elizabeth that accompanied a beautiful piece of silk: "I was deliberating some time whether it should be virgin white or sky blue," Abigail quipped. "Upon the whole, I concluded that you had more pretensions to the sky than to the appelation annexed to the white."

Since it was illegal to export silk, Abigail urged her sister to keep the gift a secret, meanwhile picturing "how pretty you will look in it."[8]

She hastened to assure her sisters that her own style of dress in England was no different from that worn in Braintree. She wore only calico, chintz, and muslin, with a double gauze handkerchief, and an apron. She was immune, she told them, to the temptations of Paris and London.

Mary, Abigail knew, looked forward to her letters. She was eager to hear about Europe—its fashions, politics, and interesting sights. She read parts of Abigail's letters aloud to relatives and friends, and this sharing became a much anticipated village event. But parts of the letters were private. Abigail yearned to be back in Mary's kitchen, talking to her face-to-face, rather than through letters.

Nabby and William Smith were married quietly on Sunday, June 12, 1786. Since only the clergy of the Church of England could perform a marriage ceremony, Abigail and John requested, and were granted, special permission by the archbishop of Canterbury for a marriage ceremony outside the church. They asked Jonathon Shipley, the only bishop to support the colonies during the Revolutionary War, to officiate. Among the very few invited guests were John Singleton Copley and his wife and daughter.

The night before the wedding Abigail dreamed about Royall Tyler. It was one of the few dreams she ever recorded. She knew that both Mary and Uncle Tufts were relieved that the affair with Tyler was over. But now, unable to sleep, Abigail recalled how she had "trembled" for the fate of her only daughter before coming to England, and she worried that Nabby might be making a mistake.

She wrote to Mary, "Some evil spirit sent Mr. Tyler to visit me in a dream. I really have felt for him."[9]

To a friend she wrote: "I wish the gentleman well. . . . . He has good qualities, indeed he has but he ever was his own enemy."[10]

Tyler, for his part, left Boston soon after Nabby's marriage and settled in New York. There, unpredictably, he wrote a play destined to earn him a place in American cultural history. *The Contrast,* performed in New York in 1787, was the first play staged in this country written by an American on an American topic. Tyler's reputation as a playwright soared. In time he married and moved to Vermont, where he became a judge and continued to write plays and short stories.

Two and a half weeks after Nabby and William were married they moved into a rented house just a mile and a half from Grosvenor Square. They continued to dine with Abigail and John every day. Still, Abigail missed the closeness she and Nabby had developed when John was away.

John, too, felt the separation keenly. Nabby and her husband had been gone just twenty-four hours when John, who normally worked in his library from after breakfast until one o'clock in the afternoon, startled Abigail by knocking on her door at 11:00 a.m., hat and cane in hand, and announcing, "Well, I have been to see them."

"Could you not have stayed in the house until the usual hour of departure?" Abigail asked.

"No, I could not. I wanted to go before Breakfast," was his reply.

In August, John decided that Abigail should accompany him on a business trip to the Netherlands. They spent five weeks touring and visiting friends there. Abigail was charmed by the country—the dikes lined with willow trees, the flat meadows, the canals, the windmills, and the neatness of the Dutch ladies.

147

*William Stephens Smith,
a graduate of Princeton
University, had served
valiantly under General
George Washington during
the revolutionary war.
He was secretary to
John Adams in London
when he met and married
Nabby Adams. Portrait by
Mather Brown, 1786.*

She was particularly impressed with the respect, attention, civility, and politeness of the Dutch people. They were, she thought, a contented, happy people who kept their country clean and neat. Their houses all seemed freshly painted, and even the milk pails were painted inside and out.

In Delft Abigail bought tiles to take home to Braintree. Leyden she pronounced the cleanest city she had ever seen. Her visit to the church in Leyden where the Pilgrims had worshipped when they fled from persecution was a moving experience for her.

On their return to London news reached John of a national convention in America being organized to revise the Articles of Confederation or, perhaps, to write an entirely new constitution for the United States. Congress was finding it increasingly more difficult to govern a country at peace than one at war. But the members understood that they needed a better way of governing themselves. The theory of government so

*John Adams thought
this portrait of Nabby Adams
caught his daughter's blend
of "drollery and modesty."
Painted by Mather Brown
in London in 1785.*

~

eloquently put forth in the Declaration of Independence must be given form in a constitution. This would be a revolution in itself, but a peaceful and lasting one.

John Adams, removed from the efforts of Congress by three thousand miles, would nevertheless put his imprint on the new constitution. His original draft of the Massachusetts Constitution, written eight years before, would be used as a model. John believed that a strong executive was essential to a stable government, and that a powerful central government with authority over state governments would be needed. Now he resolved to write a treatise on the nature of government. He set aside all other business and went to work.

He bought every book available on different European governments, both ancient and modern, and attempted to compare them. He wrote quickly, feeling a sense of urgency that his book be in the hands of the delegates when they met in Philadelphia the following May. The result was *A Defence of the Constitutions of Government of the United States of America*, published in London early in 1787, and reprinted in the United States. Two more volumes would follow. *Defence*, the first extensive examination by an American on the nature of government, became one of his most famous works, but also one of his least popular. After reading the manuscript, Abigail warned John that he would be accused of advocating monarchy. He disagreed, but she would turn out to be right.

While John wrote feverishly in his upstairs library, the door locked to anyone but Abigail, she fretted over the long hours he was working and the consequences to his health. But she knew she couldn't hope to slow him down.

Finally, she left him to his work and went off with the newlyweds to the beautiful resort town of Bath for Christmas. A showplace of Georgian architecture and site of ancient Roman baths, the town had become a fashionable spa for London's wealthy. Abigail, Nabby, and William thoroughly enjoyed the winter holiday festivities there, engaging in a round of balls, concerts, plays, and parties. Later, though, Abigail described Bath as "one constant Scene of dissipation and Gambling from Monday till Saturday Night," and on the trip back to London she reflected on the question, "What is the Chief end of Man?" Every "rational Being," she believed, must have some purpose in life beyond mere pleasure for pleasure's sake. People must look for happiness "in their own Hearts," not in outside amusements, she philosophized.[11]

I n the spring of 1787 Thomas Jefferson asked Abigail if she would take charge of his eight-year-old daughter, Polly, who was on her way from Virginia to join her father and older sister in France. Polly would arrive in London, and Jefferson hoped that Abigail would look after her until he or a servant could come for her. Abigail was delighted to oblige.

Polly, who had been living with her aunt in Virginia, arrived in late June. She was accompanied by a slave girl named Sally Hemings, just a few years older than she. Polly had been unhappy about leaving the security of the home where she knew she was much loved, and frightened about crossing the ocean alone. But her father had insisted she must come to him.

On board ship Polly, a sweet little girl with a sunny disposition, had become attached to the kindhearted captain who watched over her. Now she cried at being separated from him. But Abigail's warmth soon won her over, and the two became very fond of each other. Abigail described her as the favorite of everyone in the household. Abigail took her shopping for clothes and to a nearby amusement park. "Books are her delight," she wrote to Polly's father, "and I have furnished her out a little library, and she reads to me by the hour with great distinctness, and comments on what she reads with much propriety."[12] It was a painful parting for them both when Polly had to leave for Paris.

Fortunately, Abigail had another child on whom she could lavish attention and love. In April Nabby had given birth to a little boy who "his Grandmama thinks is as fine a Boy as any in the Kingdom," Abigail wrote to Jefferson.[13] The baby was named William after his father. Grandmama was only forty-two.

That spring, though, just after the birth of little William, Abigail had been ill. She was in bed for three weeks, and had to be bled* to relieve a "swimming" in her head. Her greatest distress came from being forced to miss seven out of a series of twelve scientific lectures to which she had subscribed.

Writing to her young niece Lucy Cranch, Abigail compared the five lectures she did attend to "going into a beautiful country which we never saw before, a country to which few females are permitted to visit or inspect." She lamented the fact that science was a subject normally closed to women in America. While she agreed that "the study of the Household" was an appropriate subject for women, "Surely as Rational beings their reason may properly receive the highest possible cultivation." No one could say, she continued, that a wife and mother would become "less capable or willing to superintend the domestic economy of her family for having wandered beyond the limits of the dressing room & the kitchen." Indeed, knowledge would make her an even more pleasing companion to her husband. Improvements in the education of women, she argued, would lead to richer lives.[14]

---

* In the eighteenth century, bloodletting (with an unsterile instrument) was recommended for everything from headaches to yellow fever.

I n July Abigail's heart was in Massachusetts. John Quincy was graduating from Harvard, and Abigail sorely wanted to be there. "Neither time or Distance have . . . diminished the . . . affection which I bear you—you are ever upon my heart and mind," his lonely mother wrote to him.[15] Johnny distinguished himself as a class orator and member of the newly founded Phi Beta Kappa Society. His cousin Billy Cranch graduated with him, and Mary Cranch, as was the custom, furnished all the food and drink for the commencement party, including a huge plum cake made of twenty-eight pounds of flour.

July brought sad news from home as well. Abigail's brother, William Smith, had died of "black jaundice" in a remote town far from home. He was only forty-one. His life had been unproductive and unhappy, and Abigail wept at the thought that neither her parents, her sisters, nor Billy's wife had been able to help him.

By the summer of 1787 both Abigail and John were longing for home. Now John wrote to Congress requesting that his commission as minister to England, which would expire in the spring of 1788, not be renewed.

At just about this time Cotton Tufts wrote to Abigail to say that a spacious house and farm had come up for sale in Braintree. Abigail knew the house and remembered particularly its lovely garden with its fine selection of fruit trees.

For some time she had been uneasy at the thought of returning to their tiny cottage. John's books alone would overflow it, not to mention all the furniture they had purchased in Europe. She responded to Uncle Tufts immediately, instructing him to offer six hundred dollars. He did so, and the house was theirs. They began to plan in earnest for their return to America.

A s the second volume of John's *Defence* went off to the printer's, Abigail and John decided to see some more of the English countryside. With Nabby and little William in tow (Colonel Smith was on a mission to Portugal), they toured southern and western England. In Southampton, where it had recently become the fashion to bathe in the ocean, they "tried the experiment." A bath attendant provided mother and daughter with an oilcloth cap, a flannel gown, and warm socks. Thus outfitted, they ventured into the ocean. It was an exhilarating experience.

They visited Weymouth and Braintree, England, as well, then continued on through several towns where they met numerous members of Richard Cranch's family. They went on to Oxford University and then to Blenheim Castle, and were back in Grosvenor Square by the middle of August.

The beginning of the year 1788 found the Adamses and the Smiths making firm plans to return to America. While John made one last trip to Holland, Abigail had their personal belongings packed and crated for shipment home. She sent detailed instructions to Cotton Tufts about how their new house was to be painted. In the sitting room she would like windows cut through to the garden, and he must make certain that the locks for the doors were brass. She was looking forward, she wrote to Thomas Jefferson, to a life of making butter and cheese, raising poultry, and looking after her garden. This had "more charms for my fancy, than residing at the Court of St. James's where I seldom meet with characters so inofensive as my Hens and chickings, or minds so well improved as my garden."[16]

Braintree and Boston would be changed, she knew. Old, loved faces would be gone. Eight members of her family and many close friends had died while she was in Europe. Yet she longed for home—for her sons, for her sisters and their families, for John's mother, her uncles, for Penn's Hill looking out over the bay, the sight of her tiny cottage, the stone fences that divided the fields about Braintree, the birds of New England.

John, too, was certain that he would once again take up the life of a farmer. He had always dealt too openly and candidly with his countrymen to be popular, and so could never become a candidate for public office. He remained throughout his life maddeningly outspoken in both public and private situations.

Abigail's only sadness was at parting with Nabby and her adored baby grandson. The Smiths would be sailing on a different ship, bound for William's home in New York.* John and Abigail would sail to Boston.

"I have frequently been called in the course of my life to very painful separations. But this is the first time that I have suffered a separation from her, and it is more painful, as she has always been my closest companion

---

* The Smiths sailed from Falmouth on April 5 and landed in New York on May 13.

and associate," Abigail wrote to Margaret Smith, Nabby's mother-in-law, shortly after they had said their wrenching good-byes.[17]

To Nabby she wrote, "How is my dear sweet boy? I think of him by day and dream of him by night."[18]

At the beginning of May, as the *Lucretia*'s keel cut through the water carrying the ambassador and his lady home, Abigail's husband chatted with the sailors, quizzed the captain, and poked into every corner of the ship. Abigail, for her part, reflected quietly that her life in Europe had been a rich educational experience. She was grateful that, though past forty, she could continue to grow in mind and spirit. But, she thought ruefully, she and John had both grown fatter in body as well.

Perhaps most important, she realized that although they were disappointed that John had been unable to bring home the coveted treaty with Great Britain, they were bringing home something far more precious—an even greater love and respect for each other. The years they had spent in London had strengthened the bonds between them. And for Abigail, her time in Europe "has only more attached me to America."[19]

~ CHAPTER XVIII ~
"You, I must and will have"

On June 17, 1788, after the stormiest spring the sailors aboard the *Lucretia* could recall, John and Abigail Adams sailed into Boston Harbor. As soon as the ship was sighted, a signal was given from the lighthouse and cannons in the fort fired a volley. Thousands cheered from the dock, and church bells pealed until sundown. Ambassador and Mrs. Adams were returning home to a hero's welcome.

John and Abigail were taken in Governor John Hancock's carriage to his mansion, where they were invited to remain until their house was ready. Charles and Tommy came from Haverhill, and Johnny from Newburyport, where he was studying law, for a joyous reunion.

When Hancock offered to escort them to Braintree in style, John and Abigail declined. They wanted no show or parade. First John, then Abigail accompanied by her sons, slipped out of Boston quietly and traveled to the Cranches, in nearby Milton, where they remained until their furniture could be unloaded and delivered to their new home.

Abigail was horrified at the state of the house. None of the repairs that she had so meticulously detailed to Uncle Tufts had been completed, and the house, which she remembered as a mansion, appeared far smaller than she had pictured it. After their enormous and elegant homes at Auteuil and Grosvenor Square, this house, with its low ceilings and tiny rooms, looked to her like a "wren's nest."

"Be sure you wear no feathers and let Col. Smith come without heels to his shoes, or he will not be able to walk upright," she wrote to Nabby.[1]

To her dismay, much of the furniture, shipped from Europe at great expense, arrived damaged. They lived in a state of confusion and

155

The "Old House" that John and Abigail purchased in September 1787,
while they were still in London, and returned to in 1788.
Abigail was "sadly disappointed" by its size,
and called it "a wren's nest." Sketch by E. Malcom in 1798.

∽

disorder for several weeks, with a "swarm" of carpenters, masons, and painters constantly about. While Abigail oversaw the workers inside, John supervised the building of stone walls, digging of ditches, and clearing of the fields. But he impulsively went off and bought six cows even before they had a decent barn.

Abigail didn't ignore the outside either. Gardening was always her delight, and she had brought two plants from England: a cutting each of the red rose of Lancaster and the white rose of York. These she planted in the front yard. Soon after, she planted three lilac shrubs on either side of the path leading from the gate to the front door.*

In spite of the problems, it was a joy to be home again amid the bustle of sisters, nieces, nephews, and her own three sons, now tall young men looking down at their parents. Abigail couldn't hide her pride in John

---

* Her roses and lilacs still bloom today.

Abigail's lilacs at the "Old House" as they look today. Abigail told Thomas Jefferson that gardening held many more charms for her than the people she met at the Court of St. James.

~

Quincy's brilliance, in Tommy, the cutup of the family with "a spice of fun in his composition," and Charles, who "wins the heart as usual and is the most gentleman of them all."[2]

Nabby was now living in Jamaica, Long Island, just outside of New York City, with a widowed mother-in-law and William's nine brothers and sisters. Here Nabby was beginning to see her husband in a new light. Back in his mother's home, he had once again become the pampered and spoiled younger son in a large and domineering family. Nabby felt like an outsider. But her parents cautioned her to show her mother-in-law "dutiful filial respect, affection, and attention."[3]

John, relishing the serenity of their new home in Braintree, away from the bustle of Europe, named the house "Peacefield." But he was moody and restless. He had been abroad for ten years, and now he was distressed at not being able to provide for his family financially. There was talk of his assuming a role in the emerging government, but it seemed to him that he wasn't held very high in the esteem of his countrymen. He was sure that in his long absence he had been forgotten. In fact, he was far more popular than he realized.

Abigail spent sleepless nights worrying about his frame of mind and their precarious financial situation. Renovations to the house were far more costly than they had anticipated. Yet they had to be completed. There was no adequate kitchen, no library for John's extensive collection of books, and no dairy for their cows. And she felt even more keenly the absence of Nabby when she learned that her daughter was expecting another baby.

Soon Abigail began to hear rumors that her husband was being considered for the vice-presidency. There was no question that George Washington would be president. In fact, he would be elected unanimously.* The first elections for president and vice-president of the new nation were scheduled for November.

While John protested that he would prefer to remain on his farm, and that he was too honest to be popular, Abigail knew that he would remain in politics. Letters from friends in Congress were already arriving in Braintree urging him to accept. These shrewdly appealed to his patriotism, his vanity, and to his sense of duty.

In November Abigail traveled to New York alone to be with Nabby at the birth of her baby, but John Adams Smith arrived before his grandmama. Grandpapa remained in Braintree. He feared that his presence in New York might make it appear that he was seeking the office.

New York was now the nation's capital and, therefore, the center of political gossip, so Abigail would have an opportunity to speak to numerous members of Congress. But she promised John that she would hear all and say little. She sent encouraging news. John Jay rode out to Jamaica to talk to her, and Alexander Hamilton indicated that Virginians would support John Adams for vice-president.

Abigail remained with the Smiths for six weeks. She liked Nabby's in-laws, describing her mother-in-law as "charming" and fond of Nabby. Of William's siblings, she particularly liked seventeen-year-old Sally, who, she told Mary, had "a fine figure & a pretty Face, [and was] unaffected and artless in her manners, modest and composed." But she worried about John Quincy's health, about her own mother-in-law who had recently had an accident, and about whether she would be back home in time for Betsy Cranch's wedding.[4]

---

* He was the only president ever to be so honored.

To Abigail's concerns about her eldest son, Mary replied that Johnny was studying so hard that they hardly saw him. "When we turn into books he will visit us," she commented wryly. As for Abigail's husband, Mary informed her sister that he had bought fifteen heifers to add to his dairy herd. "Mr. Adams will cover his farms with living creatures unless something is done soon to distract him," she wrote.[5]

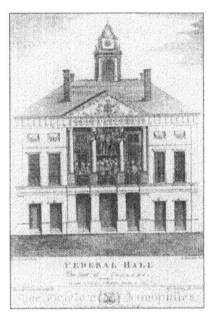

Federal Hall, in New York City, where John Adams was officially recognized as the first vice-president of the United States

∼

Shortly after the first of the new year, Abigail brought Nabby, William, and their two little sons to Braintree for a visit. They made the two-hundred-mile journey in a horse-drawn sleigh.

Unofficial word that John had been elected vice-president of the United States reached Braintree early in March, but it wasn't until April 12, 1789, that he received official notification.

Now they decided that Abigail had had enough traveling for one winter. John would go to New York without her. Before he left she saw to it that he had several new suits, new silk stockings, and a new wig, among other things, so he would fit in among the sophisticated New Yorkers. Once again, Abigail would have to face separation from John and then from her family. Once again, she would have to pack and move by herself.

As John journeyed from Braintree to New York, the inhabitants in every town and village along the way turned out to cheer him. Bells tolled in Boston and he was feted at the governor's mansion. When he arrived in New York he was met by an official reception committee and escorted to the home of his old friend John Jay.

John Adams was officially recognized as vice-president of the United States at the recently redecorated Federal Hall a few days before the arrival in New York of George Washington. No one was certain how to act in the new circumstances. There were no set forms, no precedents. John delivered a speech to the Senate, then attended a quiet dinner in his honor at the home of John Jay.

April 30, Inauguration Day, was in startling contrast. Tumultuous crowds cheered as John Adams formally greeted George Washington. After the oath of office was administered, the American flag was raised, ships in the harbor gave a thirteen-gun salute, and city bells rang. The presidency of the United States was born. The man who had led the nation through the agony of revolution to independence was now its first president. Many wept unashamedly. Thomas Jefferson, recently returned from France, was named secretary of state. John Jay was appointed chief justice of the supreme court, and Alexander Hamilton became secretary of the treasury.

As the question of how to address the officers of the government was debated hotly in the Senate, Benjamin Franklin suggested that the office of vice-president should carry the title "His Superfluous Excellency."

John soon found that Benjamin Franklin was right. The vice-presidency was a limited and inconsequential post. He had not "the smallest degree of power to do any good either in the executive, legislative, [or] judicial departments" and was "a mere mechanical tool to wind up a clock," John wrote to James Lovell.[6] Officially, he was in power as president of the Senate. But protocol dictated that he could not join in debate, and could cast a vote only to break a tie.

Abigail, at home without her husband, faced all the problems of their farm. She now had to oversee the work outside as well as inside. She felt overwhelmed.

John, for his part, living temporarily at the Jays' home, was impatient to have her with him. She must forget the problems of the farm and come to New York at once, he told her. He missed her. They must find a house in New York and set up housekeeping there. But Congress had not yet voted a salary for the vice-president, and they were virtually without money.

Finally, John rented a house in Richmond Hill, just outside the city, that was cheaper than smaller houses within the city. But it was unfurnished. Abigail would have to send beds, tables, linens, and silverware from home. She could borrow money for the trip or she must sell the horses, oxen, sheep, cows, "any and everything rather than delay," John instructed her.[7]

"If no one will take the place, leave it to the birds of the air and beasts of the field, but at all events break up that establishment and that household," he continued in another letter, "but you, I must and will have."[8]

Now Abigail canceled a planned trip to Haverhill to visit her sister Elizabeth, and somehow managed to arrange for the care of the farm, pay her debts, and supervise the crating of furniture to ship to New York. But it upset her to have to sell the oxen at half their worth. And what would they use for furniture when they returned to Braintree during congressional recesses? she agonized.

On June 19, 1789, one year and one day after her return from England, Abigail set out for New York to join her husband. Her son Charles, her thirteen-year-old niece Louisa, and a maid accompanied her. Charles had recently gained a reputation for keeping bad company at school, so his parents had decided that he would miss his Harvard commencement and accompany Abigail to New York. Brother Johnny would pick up his diploma for him.

The four traveled through Providence and Newport, Rhode Island, where they boarded a packet bound for New York. As they sailed from Buzzards Bay into Long Island Sound, they were buffeted by Atlantic Ocean storms that subjected them to five days of unrelenting winds and angry seas. Abigail admitted to being terrified—and seasick. Once more she resolved never again to "embark upon the water."[9]

In 1789 New York City was confined to the southern tip of Manhattan Island. Richmond Hill was about one mile north. The house that John had rented there was situated high on a hill overlooking the Hudson River and "the Jerseys." It was surrounded by greenery.

As soon as Abigail drove up the long, sloping hill and along the winding, tree-lined drive to the house, and saw Nabby waiting at the doorway to embrace her, her spirits soared. John had invited Nabby and her family to live there with them.

Abigail barely had time to change her clothes before a stream of visitors began to arrive to pay their respects to the vice-president's lady. The morning after her arrival, Abigail and Nabby went to pay their respects to Martha Washington. The president was ill and confined to his room, but Mrs. Washington received them "with great ease and politeness," Abigail told Mary. "She is plain in her dress, but that plainness is the best of every article. . . . Her manners are modest and unassuming, dignified and feminine."[10]

Several days later, when Washington had recuperated enough to "receive" Abigail, she was as pleased with him as she was with his wife. She described him as "a singular example of modesty and diffidence. He has a dignity which forbids Familiarity mixed with an easy affibility which creates Love and Reverence."[11] The Adamses and the Washingtons visited each other frequently, and Abigail and Martha became good friends. Genuine respect and admiration developed between them.

Abigail was happier now than she had been in years. She loved the house, the grounds, the large garden, the view, and particularly, the "lovely variety" of birds that serenaded her every morning. And she loved to play with her oldest grandson, whom she adored and delighted in calling "William Magpye."

Thomas added to her happiness as well. He had recently graduated from Harvard, and had come to Richmond Hill. His cheerfulness and high spirits were a tonic to his parents.

But Abigail found that if she weren't careful all her time could be spent making and receiving calls. Etiquette demanded that visits be made and returned. But, she learned, it was not necessary to actually see the person visited. One simply left a calling card. So she devised a plan. She would make all her visits after 6:00 P.M., when most women were not at home. In this way she could make fifteen or twenty calls in a short period of time. Since it was expected that as the vice-president's lady she would be at home to callers at all times, she made a rule to receive no visitors on Sunday. That day was reserved for her family.

Now she began to worry that, living as she was as the wife of the vice-president, she might change in subtle ways. She begged Mary to warn her if she noticed any change in her attitude toward her friends and family. She missed them all.

Telling Mary that parts of her letter had made her "melancholy," Abigail asked, "Are you in any difficulties unknown to me?" Then, concerned that her sister might be in a trying financial situation, she arranged to send her "my own pocket money. . . . Do not talk of oblagations. Reverse the matter & then ask yourself if you would not do as much for me?"[12] Encouraging Mary to look on the brighter side of life, Abigail told her: "Cheer up my good Sister. A merry Heart does good like a medicine."[13]

When Congress adjourned at the end of September, that body had established the executive departments, laid the groundwork for a federal judicial system, and approved the Bill of Rights. Now John Adams was tired and ready to go home to Braintree for a rest. But his wife did not feel strong enough to cope with packing and moving her household once again—and for a very limited stay. Congress would reconvene at the beginning of the new year. So John went by himself and stayed with his mother. He returned in December with the butter Abigail had asked for. It was too expensive in New York. She had also asked Uncle Tufts to find a "sley" for her, "for to go to market in winter, living two miles from it."[14]

While John was gone Nabby's baby had smallpox, and Louisa was inoculated from him. Colonel Smith was off grouse shooting on Long Island.

The beginning of the year 1790 and early spring were bitterly cold and damp. Abigail's rheumatism flared up, and she ran a very high fever. Charles was ill, as were all the servants. And Abigail was worried about her daughter. Nabby was pregnant again, and Colonel Smith seemed unable to deal with the realities of life. He could not find a decent job, and he was unwilling to assume responsibilities. The Smiths had moved to a tiny house where Nabby would spend the last few months of her pregnancy.

Even George Washington was seriously ill, and for several days his life was in danger. Abigail feared that his death would have disastrous consequences. It was Washington's prestige that was holding the country together. Abigail and John both understood that John, who would succeed Washington as president should the latter die in office, had no such power. Happily, Washington recovered.

When Abigail recuperated she spent much time reading, and she was delighted by Noah Webster's new simplified "Americanized" system of spelling. She sent off a stream of instructions to Uncle Tufts concerning their Braintree farm. She wished he could visit them in New York, she told him. She knew he would love it. Uncle Tufts continued to be "Friend, Guardian and parent" to Abigail. She and the entire family looked to him for advice and assistance.

In March, Elizabeth, just a few years younger than her sister, gave birth to a nine-pound baby girl whom she named Abigail Adams Shaw. "If some good angel would permit me to look into futurity, and I could behold my daughter like my sister, virtuous and good, adorning every station she may be called to," Elizabeth wrote, she would be supremely happy.[15]

In July John and Abigail attended a dinner with George Washington, Thomas Jefferson, and Alexander Hamilton. There Abigail learned that a bargain had been struck to move the federal government to Philadelphia for ten years, and then to a permanent site on the Potomac River.

"It will be a grievous thing to me to be obliged to leave this delicious Spot, your Sister and the children, your Brother and other connections. Yet for the sake of peace, harmony and justice I am Submissive," Abigail wrote to Johnny.[16] In September John rode to Philadelphia, rented a house outside the city, and returned to move his family.

Once again Abigail watched as her much traveled furniture was crated for shipping, then steeled herself to bid a painful good-bye to her children and grandchildren. Charles was hoping to open a law office in New York and would live with Nabby and her family. Abigail's only consolation was that eighteen-year-old Thomas would accompany his parents to Philadelphia. It had been decided that he would be apprenticed to a lawyer there. The decision pleased his father, but Abigail felt that her son would have been happier in business than in law.

It would be particularly difficult for Abigail to part with her daughter. In August Nabby had given birth to a third son, Thomas Hollis. Shortly after, Colonel Smith had sailed unexpectedly for England. His sudden decision, he explained, was prompted by a desire to collect some debts owed to his family. Abigail worried about Nabby even more now. Nabby had three small children, the baby appeared sickly, and her financial situation was precarious.

"I feel low-spirited and Heartless," Abigail lamented to Mary. She was going among a "new set of company, to form new acquaintances, to make and receive a hundred ceremonious visits," which she was certain would not afford her any pleasure, and she must endure an endless round of official social functions. She lived "upon the Hope that I shall come and see you next summer."[17]

But just as they were about to set out for Philadelphia, Abigail came down with an extremely high fever which made her delirious for five days. Nabby was with her constantly, doing her best to nurse her mother back to health. It was a month before Abigail was strong enough to travel. When they left they took with them Nabby's second son, John. The baby, Thomas, was recuperating. He had been "very near dying with the Small Pox."[18] Abigail seemed to have one or the other of Nabby's children with her constantly.

The jolting coach trip to Philadelphia was made in small stages, in the hope of preserving Abigail's strength. Since they traveled only twenty miles a day, it took five days to reach the city. Once again, they were forced to move into an incomplete house. Called "Bush Hill," the house had not been inhabited for four years, and was in a sorry state. A few days after they moved in, Louisa took sick, and then Thomas came down with what Abigail called "acute rheumatism" (probably rheumatic fever). He was paralyzed and ran a high fever for eighteen days. His mother never left his bedside.

In the midst of all this, ladies and gentlemen anxious to show their respect "were visiting us every day from 12 to 3 oclock in the midst of Rooms heepd up with Boxes, trunks, cases,&c." Now Abigail wanted her family near her: "Notwithstanding I have been such a Mover, I feel in every New place more & more the want of my own near & dear connexions. . . . Pray let my son J.Q.A. know that his Brother is sick, that we should be glad to have him come here."[19] Charles had already arrived to help.

Throughout this time of turmoil and upheaval, Abigail had an additional worry. John Quincy, now twenty-three, had been admitted to the Massachusetts bar, had set up an office in the front room of a house his parents still owned in Boston, and was impatiently waiting for clients there. He was depressed and lonely, he told his mother. And, he had fallen in love with blonde, blue-eyed Mary Frazier, a bright and beautiful young girl from the nearby town of Newburyport. Johnny had written to his sister about Mary several months before.

When Abigail learned of this she immediately wrote to her son to remind him that he was still financially dependent on his parents and therefore in no position to marry: "A too early Marriage will involve you in troubles that may render you & yours unhappy the remainder of your Life." It was unfair to any woman, she continued, to win her affections with no prospect of supporting her adequately in marriage. Half-jokingly, she did concede that there might be one benefit from his marriage—a wife might correct his sloppy dress.[20]

Abigail reinforced her position by reminding her son of his sister's plight. William Smith was not able to support his wife and children, and Nabby was growing more and more disillusioned.

John Quincy eventually promised that he would not see Mary again. He would remain a bachelor, he assured his mother, until he was no longer dependent on his parents' financial support. But five years later, when his brother Charles was about to marry, he reflected that the sacrifice of Mary Frazier had been too great.

Abigail was deeply troubled, too, about Nabby's situation and constantly tried to cheer her despondent daughter. Nabby, never an outgoing person, was having a difficult time, and Abigail did her best to offer loving advice and comfort. She wrote to her often of little Johnny's amusing antics, describing how Nabby's little boy chased his grandpapa around the room for an hour at a time with a willow stick. She reminded Nabby of her own years of loneliness when John was away from home, and tried to offer the strength to her daughter that she had received from her parents:

> Why do you say that you feel alone on the world? I used to think that I felt so too; but, when I lost my mother, and afterwards my father, that "alone" appeared to me in a much more formidable light. It was like cutting away the main pillars of a building; and, though no friend can supply the absence of a good husband, yet, whilst our parents live, we cannot feel unprotected. To them we can apply for advice and direction, sure that it will be given with affection and tenderness.[21]

Now, as Thomas recuperated and slowly regained his strength, Abigail's spirits revived. Soon she plunged into Philadelphia social life, which was even more extensive than it had been in New York. Calls, theater, teas, balls, and receptions could take up six afternoons and evenings each week. She was exhausted, but her optimism for the new government soared. By early 1791 all the states had ratified the Constitution, and the economy of the new country was growing.

When Congress adjourned early in May, Abigail and John set out for Braintree, stopping in New York on the way to see Nabby. There Abigail took ill with malarial fever, which she called "intermittent fever." Abigail had first contracted this disease the summer they lived in New York, and she would suffer recurrent attacks almost every year. Like yellow fever, malaria was caused by mosquitoes, but was much less dangerous. It was rarely fatal, although it could never really be cured. It attacked its victims at intervals of months or years with chills, fever, and aches.

Now Abigail was so weak that she was unable to walk unaided, and she spent a quiet summer recuperating in Braintree. She was gladdened when Nabby came for a visit.

In October the Adamses returned to Philadelphia. This time, in order to avoid the commute to the suburbs, they found a smaller house in the center of the city. But it was more expensive. John called it a democratic house at a princely rent. But even more guests came to call now that it was conveniently located, and Abigail paid a steep price.

The additional entertaining thrust upon her caused many problems. She held a "levee" (an open house) every Monday evening, and gave a formal dinner every Wednesday. All day Tuesday was spent preparing for Wednesday, and all day Thursday was devoted to cleaning up. The kitchen in the house had no oven, and Abigail, who loved to bake and did all her own baking, was compelled to bake pastries in the ashes of the kitchen fireplace.

"I feel that day a happy one that I can say I have no engagement but to my Family," she wrote to Mary.[22]

Abigail was much concerned about her sister. Richard Cranch had been dangerously ill when Abigail and John had left home. Now she wrote to Dr. Tufts to send Mary five cords of wood "on my account," cautioning him, "Do not let her know from what quarter it comes." Mary might be sensitive about accepting the gift.[23]

There were happy times, too. Abigail renewed her friendship with Martha Washington. The two women continued to enjoy each other's company. At a dinner party at the Washington's home one evening, the president picked some sugarplums from a cake on the dining room table for Abigail to take home to little Johnny.

Soon Abigail was ill again. This time she was forced to remain in bed for six weeks. She was racked with pain and fever, and her eyes were so sensitive that she could neither read, write, nor sew by candlelight. The bloodlettings she was subjected to made her even weaker. In an age when medicine was little more than a collection of country remedies, ancient superstitions, and a few recent barbarous "scientific" innovations, it's a wonder she survived at all. Yet throughout this period her interest in the well-being of her family, her friends, and her servants never lessened. Her letters to Mary were filled with references to them—of instances of care and concern.

~ CHAPTER XIX ~
"a jewel of great price"

O
nly a few weeks after Washington's inauguration in 1789, the curtain had risen on the first act of the French Revolution. Few non-American events have left a deeper scar on American political and social life.

John Adams reacted to the French Revolution by writing a long series of anonymous newspaper articles in 1790 and 1791. Entitled "Discourses on Davila," they defended his view that political freedom could be preserved only by a balanced government that effectively controlled the natural rivalry of men for wealth and power. The quest of the French people for equality, he felt, would bring only terror, mass violence, and, eventually, the loss of the freedom they sought. He would ultimately be proved right.

Abigail, for her part, feared that the French revolutionaries might abolish Christianity. She worried about the social and moral implications of this for the United States. Her own deep religious faith had caused her to reflect that a neglect of religion was at the heart of most social and political problems.

Thomas Jefferson, on the other hand, viewed the French Revolution as a praiseworthy effort to follow the American example of 1776. It was this difference of opinion that eventually caused a rift between these two old friends. It would take years to heal the wounds.

By the beginning of 1791, Abigail and John were acutely aware of the partisan debates swirling around them in Philadelphia. The issues involved the reaction to the French Revolution. But they involved much more.

Secretary of the Treasury Alexander Hamilton was the architect of a bold plan to strengthen the federal government. As advocates of a strong central government, both Abigail and John supported Hamilton's plan, and were shocked at the opposition it generated. But they had no enthusiasm for Hamilton's plan to create a national bank, modeled after the Bank of England.

Thomas Jefferson, too, opposed a federally chartered bank. He argued that the power to establish such an institution had not been given to Congress, and he urged President Washington to veto the legislation. In spite of this, Washington signed the bill on February 25, 1791.

By now two distinct political parties were forming: Republicans, headed by Thomas Jefferson; and Federalists, comprising Hamilton's supporters. Republicans, or Democratic-Republicans as they called themselves, advocated a weak central government, insisting that the best government was the one that governed least. The bulk of the power should remain in the hands of the states. Basically pro-French, they believed that it was to America's advantage to support the liberal ideals of the French Revolution.

The Federalists advocated rule by the upper classes, whom they considered the "best people." They put little trust in the common man. In direct opposition to the Republicans, they endorsed a strong central government which would maintain law and order and protect the lives and the estates of the wealthy. They were passionately pro-British.

It was in this atmosphere that, during the spring of 1792, speculation about the coming federal elections in November were running rampant, and Abigail and John had a critical decision to make. George Washington wanted to step down from the presidency, but had been persuaded to seek another term. Clearly, he would be reelected. The vice-presidency was another story. The Republicans wanted to have one of their party in office.

Now John, who claimed he wanted to retire to the quiet of the farm that Abigail called his "Hobby Horse," had to fight for reelection to a job he despised. To be defeated when Washington was reelected would be humiliating.

John and Abigail interpreted the election as a test of the fate of their country. Like most Americans, they were uncomfortable with the notion of party conflict.* He and Abigail equated opposition to John's reelection with attacks on the very fabric of the nation. Abigail considered her husband a statesman, with only the interests of his country at heart.

---

* The idea of loyal opposition had not yet developed in America.

John had always been a lonely independent who prided himself on standing above party, yet all his writings placed him firmly in the camp of the Federalists. Five years before, in England, he had advocated governments composed of three separate branches: a strong executive, whom he called a "first magistrate"; an independent judiciary; and a legislative branch divided into an upper and a lower house. Later, when John suggested that George Washington be called "his Majesty," he became the butt of jokes and was dubbed "his Rotundity" by the press.

By the time Congress adjourned in late April of 1792, Abigail was still very weak but fearful of remaining in Philadelphia during the summer because of its unhealthy climate. Yellow fever had replaced smallpox as the most dreaded disease of the late eighteenth century. They had no idea what caused it. They knew only that it appeared in the summer and ended with the first sign of cold weather.*

Abigail and John traveled northward slowly, stopping in New York on the way to see Charles. Nabby was not there. Her baby son Thomas had died, and she and her two older sons had accompanied Colonel Smith to England on another of his speculative ventures. "You may be sure that this is a heavy stroke to me. . . . but my Family are destined to be scattered I think," Abigail wrote to Mary.[1]

When Abigail and John arrived home they found that the North Precinct of Braintree had recently been incorporated as a separate town and renamed in honor of Abigail's grandfather John Quincy. Abigail was delighted to be home and to see her family and friends, all of whom came to visit, bringing with them tokens of affection for the "Duchess of Braintree"—an apple or cranberry pie, a bottle of homemade wine. Elizabeth came from Haverhill with baby Abigail, and Mary visited almost every day. John Quincy came often from Boston for his mother's good food. And Abigail was happy to see for herself the complete recovery that Richard Cranch had made.

When the time came for John to return to Philadelphia, Abigail was still not strong enough to make the three-hundred-mile journey or to risk another winter in the damp air of the city. They decided that she would remain at home in Quincy. When John left in November she experienced once again that deep loneliness she had known when he first went to

---

* They later learned that yellow fever was carried by mosquitoes.

Europe. It was heightened now by the fact that, for the first time since her marriage, none of her children lived with her.

Before he left, John had put together a pile of books to take with him to Philadelphia, then went off without them. The sight of the forgotten books on the table only served to further intensify her loneliness.

Even before John had gotten one-third of the way to Philadelphia, Abigail was writing to him and worrying about his health: "I hope [your servant] Brisler minds to have a fire in your Bedroom and that your sheets are well aird and your Bed well cloathd."[2]

One month later she joked, "I have the advantage of you, I have Louisa for a bedfellow but she is cold comfort for the one I have lost."[3]

It would be five years before Abigail would feel strong enough to join her husband in the nation's capital. Still the tenderness and love between them continued to grow. When John wrote that he was as impatient to see her as he had been twenty years before, Abigail replied: "Years subdue the ardour of passion but in lieu thereof a Friendship and affection deep rooted subsists which defies the Ravages of Time, and will survive whilst the vital Flame exists. Our attachments . . . increase I believe with our Years."[4]

In December 1792, on the eve of election, Abigail wrote to her husband: "tomorrow will determine whether their Government shall stand four years longer—or Not."[5] Actually, by then there was little doubt that John Adams would be elected, and when that did occur his wife decided that the country did, indeed, know where its best interests lay.

Abigail and John continued the pattern of his spending the winters in Philadelphia without her, then returning to Quincy when Congress adjourned. They rationalized that they were preserving Abigail's health. In reality, there was another reason. At the end of John's first term as vice-president, they were two thousand dollars in debt. When John lived alone in Philadelphia they were able to stay out of debt and even to save some of his meager salary to put toward improvements on the Quincy farm. George Washington had a salary five times that of the vice-president, and he, too, had trouble making ends meet.

They resumed the practice they had begun during John's years in the Continental Congress of writing letters to each other analyzing the political situation. John described the debates in Congress and sent Abigail the Philadelphia and New York newspapers with detailed accounts of government proceedings. Abigail reported local political opinion as well as her own views of political events. Their ideas were often similar, and when they wrote the same thing to each other in letters that crossed in the mail Abigail called it "the Tellegraph of the mind."[6]

Her letters contained more than just politics. She considered them a kind of conversation with her absent husband. "I want to sit down and converse with you every evening," she wrote. "I sit here alone and brood over probabilities and conjectures." And she kept him informed of the day-to-day happenings on the farm: A newborn lamb was sick with the mumps and couldn't eat, she told him, so she had its throat rubbed every day with "goose oil."[7]

Once again Abigail found herself sole manager of all their holdings. She had responsibility for running their old farm at Penn's Hill as well as Peacefield. In the spring of 1794 she negotiated for the purchase of yet another farm, and bought more cows and equipment for a dairy. And there was the never-ending problem of finding workers. She tried to take comfort from the fact that her husband was necessary "to the welfare and protection of a country which I love and a people who will one day do justice to your memory."[8]

John told her her letters kept him alive. They were "a rich treasure" that gave him more entertainment than all the speeches he heard in the Senate.

John Adams, painted by Charles Wilson Peale, 1794. Abigail understood that her husband was necessary "to the welfare and protection of a country which I love and a people who will one day do justice to your memory."

⁓

John's mother, living now with his brother Peter just three hundred yards up the road from Peacefield, often walked there to visit with Abigail. She came even in deep snow, anxious to keep her daughter-in-law company while John was away. Susanna took great pride in her son's accomplishments, and read all the newspaper accounts. She and Abigail were always good friends.

When Abigail decided she needed her furniture back home in Quincy, John had it crated and shipped. It had been stored in Philadelphia since her departure. But as the already damaged furniture was being unloaded at the Quincy town wharf it began to rain, soaking the upholstery and spotting the wood. To Abigail, it told the sad story of their seemingly endless wanderings.

Early in 1794 John Quincy, bored with the practice of law, had begun to respond to the political situation by writing a series of letters to the newspapers defending the administration's position on France. His letters were read from Boston to Philadelphia. Suddenly, at the age of twenty-six, John Quincy became a leading citizen of Boston, and he caught the eye of George Washington. By the end of May, President Washington had nominated John Quincy Adams to be minister to the Netherlands. The Senate agreed unanimously.

His mother's prediction that "the Time will come when this Young Man will be sought for as a Jewel of great price"[9] had come true. But she reminded her husband that their sons still needed their father's advice: "You will not teach them what to think, but how to think, and they will then know how to act."[10]

When John Quincy left for Philadelphia to prepare for his mission, he carried a note from his mother to Martha Washington "acknowledging the honor done him by the unsolicited appointment," and ending by telling her friend that "At a very early period of Life I devoted him to the publick, . . . and I have the satisfaction to say to you, Madam, perhaps with the fond partiality of a parent, that I do not know in any one Instance of his conduct either at home or abroad, [that] he has given me any occasion of regret."[11]

Johnny invited his brother Thomas to accompany him to Holland as his secretary. Tommy, though reluctant to leave the law practice he had recently begun to establish in Philadelphia, heeded his parents' advice that

Thomas Boylston Adams at the age of twenty-three, when he was serving as secretary to his brother John Quincy, who had been appointed minister to the Netherlands. Abigail had this miniature made into a bracelet as a reminder of him while he was gone. Oil on ivory, by Parker.

as a young man of twenty-two he would benefit immeasurably from an opportunity to see Europe. By November the two brothers were in Holland, viewing the disruption of Europe caused by the French Revolution. Their mother, at home alone in Quincy, lay awake nights worrying about her sons abroad in "this Whirligig of a World."

But she could still write to John Quincy, "I know you too well to believe or even wish you to look back or shrink from your duty however arduous or dangerous the task assign'd you. You will prove yourself the Genuine Scion of the Stock from whence you sprang."[12]

The summer of 1794 was a serene and happy one for Abigail. John was home in Quincy and he relieved his wife of many of her duties on the farm. Family and friends continued to visit, and Abigail regained her strength. Just the nearness of her husband cheered her. Then, shortly after John returned to Philadelphia in the fall, Elizabeth's husband, John Shaw, died suddenly, leaving his wife a near-penniless widow with three young children. Abigail was distraught. How different the lives of the sisters were, she mused. How much more fortunate she was. An accident of marriage had sent them on diverse paths.

174

Charles Adams, at twenty-seven, two years after his marriage to Sally Smith. Charles captured the hearts of all. Oil on ivory, artist unknown. From an article by Harriet Taylot Upton, "The Household of John Quincy Adams," in Wide Awake, an illustrated magazine, November 1888.

Now she did her best to help "my dear Eliza," going to Haverhill to be with her, offering financial assistance, then bringing her sister's teenage daughter Betsey home with her. Elizabeth found Betsey "difficult" and thought she needed a "new mother" for a while.

While Abigail was still reeling from the death of her brother-in-law, she had wonderful news from New York City. Nabby, back from England and living now in Eastchester, twenty miles north of the city, had given birth to a little girl, Caroline Amelia, in February 1795. Early in the spring, as soon as the roads were passable, a delighted Grandmama traveled south to visit.

Abigail saw Charles, also, and the young lady he would soon marry. Charles had fallen in love with Nabby's sister-in-law, Sarah (Sally) Smith when Charles lived with the Smith family in Jamaica. Abigail had been taken with Sally when she first met her six years before. Nabby, too, approved of the match: "after all the Hair Breadth scrapes and iminent dangers he has run, he is at last Safe Landed," she wrote of her brother Charles to John Quincy and Thomas in Holland.[13] Everyone loved Sally. But John Adams thought that at twenty-five Charles was still too young to marry. Despite his objections, the couple was married in August.

175

~ CHAPTER XX ~
"Splendid Misery"

L
ate in 1792 France had declared herself a republic, and the guillotine was set up. King Louis XVI was beheaded in 1793, Christianity was abolished (as Abigail had predicted), and the head-rolling Reign of Terror began. Soon England was drawn into the conflict. War was declared between Britain and France. Ominously, the French-American alliance of 1778 was still in effect. John and Abigail were fearful that the Republican party's pro-French activities would spur the British to declare war on the United States.

But President Washington had boldly issued a Neutrality Proclamation in 1793 and had warned Americans to remain impartial. Then, in an attempt to resolve the crisis, in 1794 he appointed John Jay as a special envoy to London to negotiate a treaty with England. The treaty that Jay effected was finally ratified in 1795 and did avert war, but it contained few concessions from the British ministry and angered the Jeffersonian Republicans.

John Jay's popularity plummeted with the treaty. When a weary and disillusioned George Washington indicated that he would retire to Mount Vernon in 1797, at the end of his second term of office, it was apparent that Jay would not be a contender for the presidency.

By January of 1796 John Adams realized that he had a major decision to make. With his friend John Jay out of the running, there were reliable rumors that the Federalists would endorse John Adams for president. His countrymen knew that, although lacking in tact, John Adams was learned and upright. The stout, indomitable little man would do what he thought was right regardless of party or what was said in the press. He was a man of stern principles who did his duty with stubborn devotion.

The Republicans would support Thomas Jefferson.

John reminded Abigail of the consequences: "Either We must enter upon Ardours more trying than any ever yet experienced; or retire to Quincy, Farmers for Life."[1]

His wife understood what he meant. If John were not elected he could not return to the bar. Although only sixty-one, age was taking its toll. Palsy made his hands tremble and he wrote with increasing difficulty. He was beginning to lose his teeth, so when he arose to address the judge or jury his speech might not be clear. And he had been away from the law for twenty years.

Abigail replied in her usual manner: "My ambition will extend no further than Reigning in the Heart of my Husband," she told him. "That is my throne, and there I aspire to be absolute."[2]

She found no comfort or pleasure in contemplating her role as first lady. Yet "in a Matter of such Momentous concern," she would not influence her husband. She did have one strong feeling: "As to holding an office of Vice President there I will give my opinion. Resign, retire. I would be second unto no Man but Washington."[3]

Abigail understood her husband all too well. He would never relinquish the presidency to the man who had been his friend, but was now a bitter rival. The presidency, she knew, would be "a most unpleasant seat, full of thorns, briars, thistles. . . . But the Hand of Providence ought to be attended to and what is designed, cheerfully submitted to." It would be a difficult job, but there would be compensations: it would be a "flattering and Glorious Reward."[4]

As their letters to each other continued to sail back and forth between Quincy and Philadelphia, Abigail anguished about whether she could be as ideal a first lady as Martha Washington had been. And could she curb her outspokenness? "I must impose a silence upon myself when I long to talk," she said a bit wistfully.[5]

John's characteristic reply was: "A woman *can* be silent when she will."[6]

In September, soon after Abigail had seen to it that the cider was poured into dozens of sturdy barrels and stored in the cellar, George Washington's farewell address to the nation appeared in the Boston newspapers. Washington did not deliver it orally. Abigail had mixed emotions.

"The die is cast! All America is or ought to be in mourning," she wrote to Thomas in Holland.[7] Two months later she wrote, "We shall not look upon his like again." Washington, she was certain, would be seen in time as "the first of heroes and greatest of benefactors to mankind."[8] But her future now hung in the balance.

By mid-December Thomas Jefferson was ready to concede the presidency to John Adams. He instructed his friend James Madison that in the event of a tie vote, which seemed possible, Madison was to request, on Jefferson's behalf, that John Adams be preferred. Mr. Adams, Jefferson said, had always been his senior, and had always "ranked" him in public life, both in France and America.

Alexander Hamilton, secretary of the treasury in George Washington's cabinet. Abigail didn't trust him. "I have ever kept my Eye upon him," she told her husband.

~

Abigail, writing to John about Mr. Jefferson, said of him: "Though wrong in politics . . . I do not think him an insincere or a corruptible man. My friendship for him has ever been unshakable."[9]

She felt quite differently about Alexander Hamilton, and she didn't hesitate to say so. She warned her husband that Hamilton was a dangerous man, scheming to keep both John Adams and Thomas Jefferson out of the presidency. She was certain that there was conspiracy afoot behind the scenes. Hamilton, Abigail told John, was as "ambitious as Julius Caesar, a subtle intriguer," who had a "thirst for fame. . . . I have ever kept my Eye upon him," she declared.[10]

It was hard for Abigail and John to be separated at such a time, but their letters were the link that bound them together. As Quincy was gripped in a cold that froze the ink in her pen, Abigail told her husband that the cold chilled her bones but "not the warmth of my affection for him for whom my heart beats with unabated ardour through all the changes and vicissitudes of life, in the still calm of Peacefield, and the turbulent scenes in which he is about to engage."[11]

178

John, for his part, worried about the great expenses they would incur if he became president. An acceptable house would cost twenty-seven hundred dollars a year to rent, and they must furnish it. Horses, too, were very expensive. Abigail replied with her usual good sense:

My dearest friend, as you have been called in Providence into the chair of government, you did not accept it without knowing that it had its torments, its trials, its dangers and perplexities. Look stead-fastly at them, arm yourself with patience and forbearance and be not dismayed, and may God and the people support you. Having put your hand to the plow, you must not look back.[12]

In the meantime, as Abigail waited for the results of the election, she wrote to John of an incident that had recently occurred in Quincy. She described how she had sent James, a black servant boy, at his own request, to an evening school to learn reading, writing, and ciphering. When a respectable neighbor, the father of two other boys in the school, came to her to report the serious objections of some "others" to James's presence, Abigail asked, "Pray, has the boy misbehaved?"

"Oh, no," was the reply.

"Well, then, why are there objections? And why haven't the others come too?"

When the ill-at-ease neighbor couldn't answer, Abigail pressed her advantage: "This," she declared, "is attacking the principle of liberty and equality upon the only grounds upon which it ought to be supported, an equality of Rights. The Boy is a Freeman as much as any of the young Men, and merely because his Face is Black, is he to be denied instruction? How is he to be qualified to procure a livelihood? . . . I have not thought it any disgrace to take him into my parlour and teach him both to read and write." Tell the "others," she said, "I hope we shall all go to Heaven together." No further complaints were made.[13]

On February 8, 1797, John Adams, as vice-president of the country and therefore president of the Senate, opened the ballots of the electoral college and announced the results to Congress. He had received seventy-one votes. Thomas Jefferson had received sixty-eight. Thus, Adams was elected president by a narrow margin and

Jefferson, as runner-up, became vice-president. Hamilton's treachery had not accomplished his purpose, but it had caused a situation in which the president and the vice-president were of opposing parties. Just a month before, John had observed to Abigail that it would be a "dangerous crisis in public affairs if the President and Vice President should be in opposite boxes."[14] Now it had come to pass.

Never anticipating that the president and the vice-president might represent antagonistic points of view, the framers of the Constitution had provided simply that the man who received the most votes would become president, and the one who received the second highest number of votes would be vice-president.*

Abigail tried to put her emotions into words: "My feelings are not those of pride or ostentation. . . . They are solemnized by a sense of the obligations, the important Trusts and Numerous duties connected with it."[15]

Several days later she pledged her support to her husband: "I am my dearest Friend allways willing to be a fellow Labourer with You in all those Relations and departments to which my abilities are competent, and I hope to acquire every requisite degree of Taciturnity which my Station calls for, tho . . . truly . . . it will be putting a force upon Nature." It would be hard for her to curb her tongue, but she would try.

Fearful of risking Abigail's health with a wintry trip to Philadelphia for the inauguration, John and Abigail decided that she would remain in Quincy. She would make arrangements for the care of their farms while she waited for warmer weather.

On March 4, 1797, Abigail was home alone in Quincy. In Congress Hall in Philadelphia John Adams took the oath of office as the second president of the United States. The chamber was packed, and many in the audience wept unashamedly as power was transferred peacefully from one head of state to another.† Not a single member of John's family was present.

In Philadelphia, John yearned for Abigail's "invaluable" support and company as ardently as he had when they had been young and separated by an ocean. "I must go to you or you must come to me. I cannot live without you till October," he wrote less than a week after his inauguration.[17]

He continued with a barrage of letters: "I never wanted your advice and assistance more in my life," he wrote less than a week later.[18] He

* This possibility was changed in 1804 by the Twelfth Amendment to the Constitution.
† This was a new process then, but one we take for granted today.

longed to hear her brisk step and her voice directing the servants. She would bring order out of chaos.[19] "The times are critical and dangerous, and I must have you here to assist me," he pleaded. "I can do nothing without you."[20]

At the end of April John pleaded once again for Abigail to come to him. Until then she had been nursing her eighty-nine-year-old mother-in-law and a young niece and would not leave. Word had not reached him yet that both had recently passed away. Abigail had done all she could. Now she was free. "I want no courting to come. I am ready and willing to follow my husband wherever he chooses."[21] She left home on April 27.

Just three days out of Quincy, traveling through "Sutbury" and "Woster" in rain and mud with a party of thirteen, including "my Family of Domesticks" and her niece Louisa, she wrote to Mary that while she knew that John needed her, "My Thoughts are continually like Noah's Dove, returning to the Ark I have left."[22]

On the way to Philadelphia Abigail stopped in Eastchester to see Nabby and two-year-old little Caroline, whose bright red hair delighted her grandmother but mortified her mother. Caroline was Abigail's only joy. Nabby and her daughter were living alone on an isolated farm with no one to talk to. "The col. gone a journey, I know not where, I could not converse with her. I saw her Heart too full," Abigail lamented to Mary. She remained at Nabby's for a day and a half, depressed and unable to eat, then continued on to New York to visit Charles, Sally, and their new baby, Susanna Boylston. There Abigail received a constant stream of visitors who came to pay their respects to the new first lady.[23]

Two days later the party set out for the final leg of their journey to Philadelphia. Twenty-five miles outside of the city Abigail was delighted to see John's carriage approaching. He had driven out to meet her. He handed her into his carriage, abandoning the others, and they continued the trip together. Just over the Pennsylvania border, they had a lavish dinner that he had ordered, then spent the night there. The next day they ambled along the banks of the Delaware River, enjoying the soft spring air, then made the remainder of the trip through "the Jersies" on "the worst Roads I ever travelld," with "furroughs of 2 feet in depth."[24] But as they approached Philadelphia at sunset, John told his wife that he felt a renewal of courage and hope. With her at his side he could face whatever was in store for him and the nation.

In The president's mansion Abigail suddenly felt threatened by John's "elevated station." The presidency held so many difficulties and dangers that it appeared to her "as a slippery precipice, surounded on all sides by rocks, shoals, and quicksands."[25] But she would do her best.

Just three days after their arrival in Philadelphia, "from 12 to half past two I received visits, 32 Ladies and near as many Gentlemen." The next day "Strangers &c making near one Hundred asked permission to visit me, so that from half past 12 till near 4, I was rising up & sitting down. Mr. Adams will never be too big to have his friends."[26]

Her only leisure time was from 5:00 A.M. to 8:00 A.M.. Those early morning hours were her own, and she treasured them. She prayed, she read, she wrote letters, or she simply savored the slow rising of the sun in the east and the peaceful quiet of the early morning before her household came to life.

After breakfast at eight with John and Louisa, she did her chores for the day. She planned menus, ordered food, and attended to hundreds of details connected with running a complicated household. At eleven she dressed for the day, then received company from twelve until two or three. Lunch (or dinner) was an elaborate meal at which they often entertained thirty or forty guests—members of Congress, the Cabinet, foreign dignitaries. After dinner she "rode out" until seven, visiting, shopping, or occasionally simply enjoying the countryside around Philadelphia.

Abigail often acted as a "sounding board" for John, listening to the problems he faced in governing the nation and offering moral support and sometimes advice. Frequently, she wrote semi-official letters explaining or reinforcing some point made by the president. Those who knew the influence she exerted on her husband took pains to try to enlist her support.

In addition to her role as "minister without portfolio," and running a large and complicated household, she tended to her husband's health and, through letters to Mary and Uncle Tufts, managed the Quincy farms. She asked Mary to get dill from her table drawer in the parlor and give it to their neighbor to make her cheese a little tastier, then have the cheese sent to her. And would Mary please send her new crepe cap which she had forgotten, as well as a piece of canvas that Mary would find in her "Bathing machine." She would like the steps and the floor in the kitchen painted, and her garden attended to.

Her letters to Mary were filled also with the politics of the day and the goings-on in Congress. "My Letters to you are first thoughts, without correction," she told her.[27] She often sent Mary a letter she had received and asked her to see to having it printed in the Boston newspapers in the hope of counteracting some of the "lies, falsehoods, calumny, and bitterness" directed at her husband's administration by the press. And she told Mary that she couldn't get through a week without a letter from her.[28]

Her interest in and concern for all her nieces and nephews were apparent in all her letters to Mary. She gave them financial support as well as love, bought them books and clothes, and frequently slipped them extra money. She kept up a steady correspondence with them.

She was solicitous, too, of all her servants and their children. She provided well for them and cared for them when they were sick. "Let the Friends of my domesticks know that they are all well," she instructed Mary shortly after they had arrived in Philadelphia.[29]

Describing her role as first lady, Abigail wrote to Mary, "Mrs. [Cotton] Tufts once stiled my situation, splendid misery. She was not far from Truth."[30]

The one bright spot in the otherwise dreary month of June was the arrival from England of a crate containing a portrait of John Quincy, painted by Copley. It was one of the painter's finest accomplishments. Everyone thought it captured Abigail's son perfectly, and she was delighted

John Quincy Adams at age twenty-nine. Mrs. Copley, wife of the artist, sent this portrait to Abigail as a surprise gift from England. Abigail was delighted when people commented on how much the son resembled the mother, but the painting intensified her longing for him. Oil by John Singleton Copley, 1796.

∽

Louisa Catherine Johnson, who married John Quincy Adams in London in 1797. Abigail asked for a miniature of her new daughter-in-law and a lock of her hair, telling her son, "whom you call yours shall be mine also." Oil by Edward Savage, about 1801.

~

when people commented on how much John Quincy resembled his mother. But it only served to intensify her longing for her "dear absent son."[31]

When Congress rose in early July, Abigail and John made the long, hot, dusty journey back to Quincy. They would escape from the "Bake House" that was Philadelphia, and would avoid the capital's yellow fever. Abigail wrote ahead to Mary asking her to prepare the house for their arrival. If there were indications that they would be met on the road to Quincy by a reception committee of townspeople, would Mary have wine and punch ready to refresh them? She could draw wine from the casks in the cellar. "Punch must be made by Gallons." Would Mary be at the house to greet them when they arrived, and have a table set in the dining parlor?

As always, once home, both Abigail and John felt a sense of renewal on the farm and enjoyed the close companionship of relatives and friends.

Then, as the summer drew to a close, they received word that John Quincy had married the talented and beautiful Louisa Catherine Johnson, daughter of an American father and a British mother, in London on July 26, 1797. In a letter to his parents, Thomas described his new sister as sweet tempered, "a most lovely woman." Louisa was twenty-two; John Quincy was thirty.[32]

When she had first become suspicious that John Quincy might be falling in love, Abigail had warned him of the danger of marrying a wife accustomed to the luxury of European life and, therefore, likely to be dissatisfied with the comparatively simple style of life in America.

"You have Years sufficient to judge for Yourself, and whom you call yours shall be mine also," she assured him, "only weigh well, consider maturely of the most important action of your Life."[33]

Her son, perhaps remembering his parents' objections to his earlier romance with Mary Frazier, had replied that if he waited until all conditions were right, he would be single forever. "Prudence is a sorry match maker," he told his mother. His choice was "irrevocably made."[34]

Six months later he tried to allay his mother's fears. He was grateful for her concerns, he told her, but while he could not say that there were no grounds for them, "the Lady . . . has goodness of heart & gentleness of disposition as well as spirit and discretion . . . and I hope you will find her . . . such a daughter as you would wish for your son."[35] Louisa would strive always to be worthy of John Quincy's description and to win the respect and affection of his parents.

Now Abigail wrote asking for a miniature of her new daughter-in-law and a lock of her hair. Ultimately the two women would grow to love and admire each other.

John Quincy's joy in his marriage was in sharp contrast to the sorrow of Nabby's plight. When Abigail arrived at her daughter's home on her way back to Philadelphia, she found an anxious and troubled young woman "with not a single creature within 20 miles of her to speak a word to, or shorten the long solitary winter Evening." Nabby's two sons were spending the winter with their great-aunt Elizabeth, remarried now to the Reverend Stephen Peabody and living in Atkinson, New Hampshire. Abigail believed that Elizabeth would be a good influence on her grandsons. She worried that the boys had learned bad habits from their father and his brothers, and she hoped her sister could break those habits. She was also fearful that, should their father return, he might "take it into his Head to take them away."[36]

A bigail begged Nabby to go to Philadelphia with her, but Nabby was afraid to leave, concerned that her husband might return and not find her.

At the end of January Nabby was still alone in Eastchester, waiting and hoping for her husband to come home. Smith finally returned at the beginning of February.

"I have been more distresst for her than I have been ready to own," Abigail confided to Mary.[37]

L etters to Mary continued to be Abigail's lifeline. She was wise and kind. Abigail loved her and relied on her. "One of Sister Cranch's Letters is worth half a dozen others," John told Abigail. She had found him standing at the fire "very gravely reading" a letter from Mary. Abigail was furious. She "scolded" very hard.[38] John promptly promised that he would not open any more letters addressed to her, and would "be satisfied with such parts as I am willing to communicate."[39]

Soon Abigail cunningly suggested that Mary enclose letters from Dr. Tufts to Abigail in her own letters, in order to ensure that John did not read them. "The Dr. and I have some business transactions which are between ourselves," she explained.[40] Abigail knew that John wanted her uncle to buy more land for him. Abigail wanted him to invest their savings in stocks. She was looking ahead to their future, when the interest on the stocks might provide a small income for them.

~ CHAPTER XXI ~
"If man is Lord,
woman is Lordess"

One of John Adams's first tasks when he returned to Philadelphia in the fall of 1797 had been to appoint three ministers to France in an attempt to resolve existing differences between the United States and France. When the men reached Paris they expected to meet Charles Maurice de Talleyrand, the crafty French foreign minister. Instead, they were secretly approached by three go-betweens, referred to only as X, Y, and Z, who demanded a large bribe for the privilege of merely talking to Talleyrand. The terms were unacceptable to the American envoys.

It was the following March before dispatches from the ministers finally arrived in Philadelphia. These indicated that war with France seemed inevitable. Abigail expressed concern to Mary that her husband was overwhelmed, "contemplating what can be done at this critical period, *knowing what he thinks ought to be done,* yet not cetain whether the people are sufficiently determined to second the government. . . . All Good people ought to pray Heartily for him and for our Country."[1]

Concerned also that a declaration of war would bring a sharp rise in prices, she immediately ordered 50 pounds of coffee and 150 pounds of brown sugar.

When the dispatches from France were published in the newspapers, public opinion rallied in support of the President. Although war hysteria swept the country, neither John nor Congress was ready to actually declare war. Instead, they concentrated on strengthening the United States' military defenses. The Navy Department was created, and the three-ship navy expanded. John was particularly anxious to create a strong navy, what he called "wooden walls," to defend the country's coastline and protect its shipping. The slogan of the country became, "Millions for defense, but not one cent for tribute."

In France, Talleyrand realized that he had been outwitted and let it be known that if the American government sent a new minister, he would be received with proper respect. Suddenly, to his great surprise, for a brief, dizzying period John Adams became a hero. Instead of being attacked in the press as they had been, he and Abigail were cheered wherever they went.

But John Adams's popularity was short lived. It wasn't long before public criticism of Federalist policies was reaching unprecedented heights. Abigail was particularly upset by one description in the newspaper of her husband as "old, querulous, bald, blind, crippled, toothless Adams." And when President Adams promoted his young diplomat son to the post of minister to Prussia, the Republican press immediately cried nepotism. As she writhed under the "wicked and base, violent . . . abuse" leveled at the president, Abigail termed the editors of the newspapers "criminal," and compared them to the devil.[2]

Criticism of the government and its officers could be borne, she agreed, and a free press was the support of free government. But there must be some defense against lies and deliberate misrepresentations. The people must have access to the truth. The right of a free press, she contended, carried with it a responsibility to truth and decency. "Nothing will have an Effect until Congress pass a Sedition Bill," she wrote to Mary.[3]

Indeed, the verbal violence in the press was unrestrained. Editors assailed John Adams's anti-French policy in vicious terms. Now the Federalists drove through Congress a sheaf of laws designed to silence them. The Sedition Act provided that anyone who impeded the policies of the government or falsely defamed its officials, including the president, would be liable to a heavy fine and imprisonment. The measure was severe, but the Federalists believed it was justified.

The Republicans considered it an attempt by the Federalists to silence the opposition, a direct slap at freedom of speech and freedom of the press. Thomas Jefferson viewed it as an experiment to see how Americans would react to a violation of the Constitution.

The laws ultimately proved enormously unpopular and either lapsed or were repealed by 1801. But they gave the Republicans a critical issue to use against John Adams in the next election.

In July Congress finally declared the French treaty of 1778 void, but they stopped short of declaring war. Now Abigail and John were free to make their annual trek back to Quincy and the cool ocean breezes that Abigail longed for.

Before they left, Abigail wrote to her nephew William Shaw, who was about to graduate from Harvard, expressing disappointment that she could not attend his commencement exercises. As a gift, Abigail sent him a handsome white waistcoat. John had invited the young man to be his secretary for the summer, and now Abigail sent William instructions to arrange the "book room" at Peacefield with "strict order and method." He must file every letter and paper alphabetically in the places designed for them so there would be no difficulty in locating them. As a surprise for John, Abigail had secretly arranged to have an addition built on to the house of a library-office with an outside entrance. John would be delighted.

The trip home was extremely hot and tiring. All along the way they were met by enthusiastic crowds of people eager to see them and to show their respect and admiration. Abigail would have preferred to "slide along . . . unnoticed and without parade."[4] By the time they reached Quincy she was seriously ill.

John Adams's study about 1800

~

Doctors summoned from Boston diagnosed it as a combination of dysentery, intermittent fever, and diabetes. There was fear that she would not live. Nabby and Louisa Smith nursed her, and John, distraught, neglected all his duties to hover at her bedside. It was eleven weeks before she was able to leave her bedroom, and months before she regained her strength.

Her agonizingly slow recuperation may well have been the result of anxiety. She knew that Tommy had been on his way home from Europe for several months, and there had been no word from him. She feared that his ship had gone down at sea. Charles, too, was a source of anxiety, but of a different nature. He had been acting strangely lately and was beginning to show signs of poor judgment and emotional instability. And he was alarmingly silent concerning money John Quincy had left with him to invest. Nabby's husband was a constant source of disappointment and distress. His salary "will not feed his Dogs, and his Dogs must be fed if his children starve," John lamented.[5]

When John and Abigail learned that an epidemic of yellow fever in Philadelphia during the summer had carried off hundreds of people, leaving fifty children as orphans, and many others destitute, they immediately sent five hundred dollars to be distributed anonymously among the neediest.

Toward the middle of November, an anguished John Adams finally set out for the capital without his wife. She must not again endanger "a life that is dear to me beyond all expression."[6] Unwilling to believe that there were some members of his cabinet who were disloyal to him and would take his absence as an opportunity to scuttle his ship of state, John had chosen to remain at home with Abigail until he was certain that she was recovered.

Louisa Smith, now twenty-one, went with him to Philadelphia to act as his hostess. William Shaw would continue as his secretary. Nabby, torn between her concern for her mother and what she saw as her duty to her husband, at first chose to remain in Quincy. But when Abigail realized Nabby's dilemma, she sent her flying after her father in order to ride as far as Eastchester with him. Once again, Abigail faced the prospect of a cold winter alone.

She would be "but a half way politician this winter," she joked with her husband. But she did insist that he keep her informed of all political developments in the capital. She knew that John was still clinging to his desire to avoid war with France. He felt strongly that America should not allow itself to be drawn into a foreign war that would divert its energy from domestic issues that were crucial for the new nation. She was amused when John wrote that there were many in Philadelphia who lamented her absence. They believed she was the only person from whom her stubborn husband would take advice. One Federalist called her "as complete a politician as any Lady in the old French Court."[7]

On his way to Philadelphia, John stopped in New York to see Charles. It was a depressing visit. Charles was obviously ill. Sally confided to her father-in-law that she was alarmed at her husband's physical and emotional state. He was often away from home and frequently returned drunk. He had neglected his law practice, and his creditors were beginning to threaten him. Speculation in the stock market had recently ruined thousands like him. But Charles agonized over the fact that he had betrayed his brother's trust. John Quincy had left money with Charles to invest for him. Charles had used some of that money, he explained to his father, to try to save Nabby's husband from debtors prison. John was distraught, and at a loss to know what to do.

"Happy Washington! happy to be Childless! My Children give me more Pain than all my Enemies," John cried out to Abigail.[8]

"I do not consider GW at all a happier man because he has not children. If he has none to give him pain, he has none to give him pleasure," Abigail sharply rebuked her husband.[9]

Thomas landed safely in New York on January 10, 1799, and hurried to Philadelphia to see his father and to deliver critical reports from France. He arrived just as guests were beginning to leave one of the president's Tuesday night receptions. Tears streamed down John's face as he greeted his youngest son for the first time in almost five years.

Abigail waited impatiently for Tommy in Quincy. When he arrived in February, she was as pleased with him as his father had been. Thomas remained at home until April, when he left to resume the practice of law in Philadelphia. His mother had urged him to remain at home and go into business, but this quiet, good-natured but independent young man was determined to live on his own, out from under his mother's watchful protectiveness. He spent much of his time with Quakers, and preferred their simple dress to the more fashionable ornate styles. He wore his hair short, and refused to wear a wig.

A
t the beginning of April, the president returned to Quincy and remained there until October. Once again he refused to heed the advice of his friends in Congress that he remain in the capital. He was certain that nothing would be done without his advice and direction. And he was determined to be with Abigail.

When he arrived home, work was already under way on a new barn that he and Abigail had planned. Soon they began thinking about an addition to the house that would substantially enlarge it. Peacefield would be transformed from a comfortable seven-room farmhouse into a mansion fit for a president and his lady.

D
uring the summer, Abigail bought a book as a gift for her niece, Elizabeth's daughter Abby. Before she sent it off she read it, only to discover that its wording implied that women had a subordinate role in the world. She sent a warning note to her sister along with the book: "I will never consent to have our sex considered in an inferior point of light. Let each planet shine in their own orbit. God and nature designed it so—if man is Lord, woman is Lordess—that is what I contend for."[10]

Abigail had felt well all summer and decided that she could spend the winter in Philadelphia with John. She knew that this would be the last time the government would meet there. The capital was scheduled to move to the new federal city of Washington before the start of the next session. John left early in October. Abigail would follow at the end of the month.

When John stopped in Eastchester he was pleased to find that Nabby and Caroline were fine. Colonel Smith had accepted a commission in the newly organized army and was training troops at a camp in New Jersey. Sally Adams and her two daughters were staying with Nabby. Charles had disappeared. Now Sally told her father-in-law the full story of her husband's terrible disintegration.

"I pitied her, I grieved, I mourned," a heartbroken John wrote to Abigail. "I renounce him."[11] He felt powerless to help his son. He was filled with rage and humiliation.

When Abigail arrived in Eastchester to pick up Nabby and Caroline, who would accompany her to Philadelphia, Sally and the girls were still there. Like a proud grandma, Abigail boasted to Mary that three-year-old

Susan was very bright, and would "stand all day to hear you read stories." "She tells me all her Letters and would read in a month if she had a good school." Bright-eyed Abbe walked alone at nine months. But, Abigail sighed, they made her heart ache as she wondered what would become of them.

Abigail worried, too, about John Quincy and Louisa, knowing they were both deathly ill in Europe.

"Who of us pass through the world with our paths strewn with flowers, without encountering the thorns?" she asked.[12]

On their way south, Abigail, Nabby, and Caroline stopped in Plainfield, New Jersey, to visit Colonel Smith at his encampment. There Abigail reviewed the troops. "I acted . . . as your proxy," she told John.[13]

Feeling better now than she had in a long time, and happy to have her daughter and granddaughter with her, Abigail was looking forward to her stay in Philadelphia. Thomas had relented and had consented to live with his parents for the winter. Abigail had promised that he could come and go as he pleased.

When they arrived Abigail was immediately caught up in the social life of Philadelphia. The city had become the country's fashion capital, and she sent home detailed descriptions of the latest styles. She asked Mary to send her her "white Lutestring Gown & coat which is trimd with silver," and a plain muslin gown embroidered with silk that belonged to Nabby. If Mary would send them with the next person coming to Philadelphia from Boston, Abigail would give him "as many good dinners as they will Eat." She would also appreciate some red broadcloth, since cloaks of this material were "all the mode, trim'd with white furs." But she decided that her age and position entitled her to try to change those styles she didn't like.[14]

Some of the ladies, she complained, didn't dress warmly enough— silk was preferable to muslin in winter—and some of the new fashions were indecent: the necklines were too low and the sleeves too short. Criticizing those women who wore these daring fashions, she told Mary: "Not content with the *show which* nature bestows, they borrow from art, and litterally look like Nursing Mothers." They rouged their cheeks "Red as a Brick hearth," and everyone, young and old, had begun to wear her hair in curls.[15]

As attention began to focus on the coming presidential election, it became more and more probable that John might lose. Defeat, Abigail worried, would be more than he could bear. She believed that a president, once elected, should remain in office until he chose to retire or he betrayed the public trust. She feared that the election of a Republican might cause the government to topple: "What ungrateful Beings must we be in America, if we permit party animosities, and private ambition to overturn the goodly fabrick of our National Government."[16]

In December, when John delivered his annual speech to Congress, its calm message seemed to promote a spirit of moderation. It was received "with more applause & approbation than any speech which the President has ever before deliverd," Abigail announced proudly to Mary.[17]

A few days later, John Adams had the unhappy task of reporting to Congress the death of George Washington on December 14, 1799. House and Senate members went at once to the presidential mansion to express condolences. Abigail received them.

The funeral procession along the unpaved streets to the church the following week was in mud so thick it sucked off some of the men's shoes. The service lasted from eleven in the morning until four in the afternoon. Abigail arrived home from church exhausted, but had to preside at a formal presidential dinner for thirty people that evening.

For a brief period Washington's death seemed to draw the nation together. But Alexander Hamilton was still agitating for war and speaking out against the peace commission that John planned to send to France.

By spring, attacks on both the Federalists and the Republicans grew even more bitter than they had been. Abigail and John were slandered unmercifully. There was enough abuse and scandal, Abigail told Mary, to "ruin & corrupt the minds and morals of the best people in the world." Commenting on the forthcoming elections, she said she was sure that New York would be "the balance in the scaile, scale, skaill, scaill (is it right now? it does not look so)."[18]

As her stay in Philadelphia drew to a close, Abigail was saddened at the prospect of leaving. She had grown to love this city with its orderly brick-paved streets, elegant town houses, and abundant trees. And she was apprehensive about going to Washington, little more than a village in the wilderness.

"There is something always melancholy, in the Idea of leaving a place for the last time. It is like burying a Friend," she lamented to Mary.[19]

In the spring she sat for her portrait by the painter Gilbert Stuart. Stuart commented that he wished he could have painted Mrs. Adams when she was young: "I should have had a perfect Venus," he said.

"So he would," John agreed.

Abigail left Philadelphia on May 19, 1800. John went in the opposite direction. He would inspect the "Federal City."

As always, Abigail stopped in New York on her way home. There she found only unhappiness. Colonel Smith's regiment had been disbanded, so once again he was out of work and unable to provide for his family. Nabby was gloomy and depressed.

Charles, at home now but ashamed of his condition and sinking rapidly, was pathetically

When Abigail Adams sat for this portrait in 1801, the painter, Gilbert Stuart, said he wished he could have painted her when she was young. "I should have had a perfect Venus," he said.

happy to see his mother. Abigail was heartbroken to see this special child, her beloved middle son who had been the "darling of the neighborhood" and of his father's companions in Europe, this handsome and charming young man who won the hearts of all who met him, sunk now in misery and despair. When she left New York she took his little Susan home with her.

"Vice and destruction have swallowed him up," she mourned. "Trials of various kinds seem to be reserved for our gray Hairs, for our declining years," she wrote to Mary. But, she continued, "Shall I receive good and not evil? I will not forget the blessings which sweeten life."[20]

Abigail arrived back in Quincy on the last day of May and found that the addition to their house was progressing nicely. Now she would be able to supervise the last stages of building herself.

Peacefield, the name John Adams gave to the "Old House," after it had been enlarged from a comfortable farmhouse to an elegant mansion fit for a president and his lady. The name, he said, commemorated the "Peace and Tranquility which I have enjoyed in this Residence."

~

There was a much larger kitchen and a huge drawing room on the first floor, and she moved her finest European furniture and the family portraits into this room. While the drawing room was cool and bright in summertime, she soon discovered that its fireplace was not always effective against the cold of winter. John's study was upstairs.

Abigail spent the summer preoccupied with the house and the children—Nabby and Caroline were there in addition to little Susan. But the coming elections were never out of her mind. She was terrified that the election of a new president with views that differed from John's would be a disaster for the country. Hamilton (Abigail called him the "Little General") was openly working to keep John out of office. He wanted a candidate whom he could control. Abigail was convinced that Hamilton was dividing the Federalists and undermining the present administration. She was sure this would contribute to the election of Thomas Jefferson.

J ohn arrived back in Quincy early in July. He needed the restorative magic of his farm, not only for his always precarious health, but also for the calm of Quincy away from the confusion of the capital. It gave him a better perspective on the problems facing him and his country. But he was not completely removed from politics. He was in constant communication with others in the capital, and there were many Massachusetts politicians who came to Quincy seeking or offering advice.

As the summer of 1800 ended, Abigail decided that it was time for John Quincy to come home from Europe. He had been gone for six years, and she missed him. And she had not met his wife. She was certain, too, that a Republican president would recall him. It would be best for his career. He could serve his country better at home than abroad, she explained. She analyzed the situation shrewdly: "Services rendered to a Country in a diplomatic line can be known only to a few. If they are important and become conspicuous they rather excite envy than gratitude."[21]

Perhaps it was more than patriotism, though, that spurred Abigail to encourage her oldest son to come home. Life at this time was painful for her. As she stood by helplessly witnessing her "dearest friend's" political career disintegrate, her son Charles's terrible decline, and the bleak circumstances of Nabby's life unfold, she needed the comfort of John Quincy's presence.

But John Quincy was not ready to come home. It would be proper to wait to be recalled, rather than resign, he countered gently. He liked being in Europe. He was just beginning to feel that his presence there was important.

J ohn Adams left Quincy early in October. He was on his way to the new capital in Washington. At first they had thought that Abigail would remain at home until after the elections. She would join John in Washington only if he were reelected. Then John decided he had to have his wife with him. She agreed to follow later. Mary was ill and Abigail wouldn't leave until she was certain her sister was out of danger.

While she was still at home, Abigail received a letter from John, written on his first night in the new Executive Mansion. He described his journey, then wrote: "Before I end my letter, I pray heaven to bestow the best of blessings on this house, and on all that shall hereafter inhabit it. May none but honest and wise men ever rule under this roof!"[1]*

---

* One hundred forty-five years later, President Franklin D. Roosevelt had these words carved into the marble mantel of the State Dining Room.

Abigail's trip to Washington was not a happy one. When she stopped in New York to see Charles, she found him at the home of a friend, desperately ill and unhappy. He was beset by a racking cough, a liver infection, and dropsy.* The doctors had given up hope, and his distraught mother recognized that he didn't have long to live. She sensed that this would be the last time she would see her son. His father, passing through New York on his way south earlier in the month, had not stopped to see him.

Charles died three weeks later, on November 30, with only his wife and her mother at his bedside. He was thirty years old.

"I know, my much loved Sister," Abigail cried out to Mary, "that you will mingle in my sorrow and weep with me over the Grave of a poor unhappy child who cannot now add an other pang to those which have pierced my Heart for several years past. . . . He was no mans Enemy but his own—He was beloved, in spight of his Errors, and all spoke with grief and sorrow for his habits."[23]

Abigail kept Charles's daughter Susan with her and continued to raise her as her own. Sally and Abbe, after a few months with her parents, came to live with them also.

As the despondent band of travelers continued on their journey south, they took a wrong turn outside of Baltimore and lost their way in the woods. They wandered for more than two hours, trying different paths, breaking branches off trees when they were unable to pass. There was not a village in sight and nothing but woods for miles and miles. The exhausted group arrived in Washington a day later than they had planned.

Abigail found "The Presidents House" twice as large as the meeting house in Quincy, and "built for ages to come." It was beautifully situated, facing the Potomac River, with a lovely view of Alexandria. The surrounding countryside was romantic and wild. Nearby Georgetown, though, was "the very dirtiest Hole I ever saw."[24]

The house itself was unfinished and unfurnished, damp and cold, and certainly not ready for occupancy. For this meticulous housewife who made an art of organizing a household, the unfinished state of the house and the lack of servants to staff it were most distressing.

* An excessive accumulation of fluids in the body that usually causes heart failure.

*Abigail and her party finally saw this view of Washington, or Federal City,
after having taken a wrong turn outside of Baltimore and been lost
in the woods for more than two hours.*

She settled in quickly and tried not to complain. But she soon found that the dampness aggravated her rheumatism and she didn't feel as well as she had the winter before.

"I patch up, but it is hard work," she said.[25] She kept thirteen fires going in the fireplaces in an attempt to offset the damp and the cold, but they weren't always enough. She strung a clothesline across the main conference room to dry the wash. In its present condition, she found the large room good for little else.[26] She cautioned Nabby, the one person to whom she did complain, to "keep all this to yourself." Nabby must tell everyone who asked how her mother liked Washington that the "situation is beautiful, which is true."[27]

Washington was clearly part of the South, and the atmosphere there was very different from Philadelphia. Abigail couldn't get used to the slow pace of life. "The universal character of the inhabitants is want of punctuality," she complained to Uncle Tufts.[28]

199

What upset Abigail most was the widespread use of slave labor in Washington. She had always had strong feelings about racial discrimination, and now she didn't like what she was seeing. Slavery, she contended, was evil. She objected particularly to the sense of superiority that it instilled in all white people. She was shocked by the extent to which southerners depended on slavery. How could they reconcile human bondage with the ideology of freedom that Americans had fought for?

A bigail didn't have long to remain in the President's House. John Adams was defeated in his bid for reelection. Thomas Jefferson would be the next president of the United States. But the Republicans won a very close victory. In spite of the Alien and Sedition Acts, John's resistance to maintaining a standing army, Hamilton's treachery, and a disloyal cabinet, John Adams had done remarkably well.

Furthermore, immediately after the election it was learned that on October 30 a peace treaty had been signed in Paris. John Adams had avoided a war with France. But he had wrecked his career as a politician, for he had alienated some Federalists and split his party, and the other members of his party couldn't forgive him for it.

Abigail strung a clothesline across the main conference room in the President's House. She found the room good for little else. Here she and her granddaughter Susan watch as a servant hangs the wash to dry. Painting by Gordon Phillips, 1966.

~

Now both he and Abigail felt that John was being turned out of office by an ungrateful country. Their grief over the death of Charles only served to intensify their feelings of disgrace and despair.

John Quincy, learning the news at his post in Berlin, offered some measure of consolation when he wrote to his father that he was a shining example "of a statesman who made the sacrifice of his own interest and influence to the real and unquestionable benefit of his country. . . . You have . . . given the most decisive proof that in your administration you were not the man of any party but of the whole nation," he told him.[29]

As they pondered their future, John and Abigail wondered what effect a quiet life of retirement would have on them. Abigail was concerned that their finances would be limited, and her husband would be unable to "indulge himself in those improvements upon his farm" which he might enjoy and which would "contribute to his health." As for herself, she told her son Thomas, she would be far happier at Quincy. "Neither my habits, or my education or inclinations have led me to an expensive style of living. . . . If I did not rise with dignity, I can at least fall with ease, which is the more difficult task."[30]

A few days before the inauguration of Thomas Jefferson, Abigail and John invited him to the President's House. As always, Abigail went in to dinner on Mr. Jefferson's arm. The pleasure they found in each other's company had not diminished. Abigail held no resentment toward him. Nor did her husband. They disagreed with Jefferson politically, but continued to respect him, and considered him a friend.

Jefferson made a point of visiting again to say good-bye to Abigail before she left for Quincy.

Abigail was anxious now to return home. In spite of the danger of the five-hundred-mile trip along icy roads and across frozen streams, she left at the beginning of February. John would follow later.

Her niece Louisa, frightened by the "horrid" roads and "shocking wilderness," begged her to turn back. How could she travel without a gentleman to protect her? she worried. Her aunt told her she was too independent to want a gentleman always at her side. While it might have been "very agreeable" to have one along, Abigail explained, she was "accustomed to get through many a trying scene and combat many difficulties alone."[31]

And there were difficulties. When they reached the Susquehanna River between Baltimore and Philadelphia they found that it was frozen, but not solidly enough to bear the weight of their entire party. So they sent the horses across one at a time, then hired some men to push the empty carriage across. Finally, Abigail and her companions were dragged across in a boat fitted with runners. Just as they reached the opposite side, the ice gave way and the men fell into water over their boots. They had made it just in time. Within hours warmer weather thawed the ice and made the river unsafe to cross.

In Philadelphia, Abigail stopped to see Thomas. Once again, she tried, unsuccessfully, to convince him to come back to Quincy.

I n Washington, John Adams had problems of a different nature. For a long time he had been advocating the need to reorganize the circuit courts and expand the judicial system. Now, when Congress finally passed the Judiciary Act on February 13, John seized the opportunity to fill the newly created offices with political friends and family members whom he considered worthy, and he appointed John Marshall chief justice of the Supreme Court.* It was the "one act" of John's life that Thomas Jefferson considered "personally unkind." Jefferson felt he should have been left free to make his own choices. It would be many years before the wound was healed.

John Adams left Washington before dawn on the morning of Jefferson's inauguration. The cause of his abrupt and early departure is uncertain. On the day he arrived home two weeks later, "a violent gale of wind" hit Quincy. Then it poured for ten straight days. John called it an old-fashioned storm that made him hope that "nature is returning to her old good-nature and good-humor," and was substituting a storm in the elements for revolutions in the political world.[32]

Together John and Abigail rejoiced in the knowledge that they would never again have to endure a prolonged separation. Their days of serving their country had come to an end. But for the rest of her life Abigail referred to her husband as "the President."

Abigail presided over her large, complex household with her usual efficiency. She mothered, instructed, guided, and fed with renewed energy. To those who were absent she wrote letters full of advice and encouragement. When she wrote to thank her son-in-law for his present of raspberry bushes and a pot of strawberry vines, she included a message for Nabby: "Tell her I have commenced my operation of dairywoman; and she might see me, at five o'clock in the morning skimming my milk."[33]

* These have come to be known as the "midnight appointments."

～ CHAPTER XXII ～
"young shoots and branches"

On September 4, 1801, the ship carrying John Quincy and Louisa Catherine Adams and their five-month-old son George Washington home from Berlin docked in Philadelphia. It was seven years since John Quincy had sailed for Europe. He stopped briefly in New York to see his sister, then went directly to Quincy for a reunion with his parents. Louisa and the baby went to see her parents in Washington, where they were now living. She came to Quincy a few weeks later.

John and Abigail were elated to have them home, but for Louisa Catherine it was a difficult and overwhelming experience. An extremely shy and reserved young woman, she felt that had she "stepped into Noah's Ark," she "could [not] have been more utterly astonished." The bustling household, country manners, Indian puddings and boiled potatoes all made her feel that she was in a strange land. Abigail's original concern that Louisa had been raised in Europe and would have difficulty adjusting to the simple New England way of life seemed justified.

Added to this, Louisa Smith was so jealous of the new Louisa and of Abigail's thoughtful attempt to welcome her daughter-in-law with special foods on the evening of their arrival, that she refused to eat, and ran from the dinner table crying.

"I was literally and without knowing it a *fine* lady," Louisa Catherine noted ruefully years later. Her mother-in-law thought she was helpless. But "the Old Gentleman took a fancy to me," Louisa said, and she and her father-in-law became fast friends.

Abigail treated her daughter-in-law "in the kindest manner," offering her advice and instruction, but the more Louisa tried to please her, the more insecure and tongue-tied she became. Her shyness was misinterpreted as pride.[1]

John Quincy went back to the practice of law, but in 1803, when he was thirty-six, he was elected a senator from Massachusetts. His mother was proud but heartbroken when he left for Washington, taking with him his wife and two sons. The infant, John, had been born on July 4.

John Quincy sent his mother long, detailed letters about politics, and Louisa's gossipy accounts of social life in Washington delighted her. Meanwhile, Abigail looked after John Quincy's farm just as Mary Cranch and Cotton Tufts had done for her. Two years later, when John Quincy decided to leave his sons in his mother's charge while he and Louisa were in Washington for the congressional session, the grandparents were delighted. Not so Louisa, who hated to leave them behind.

Abigail particularly loved little John, who, at two and a half, considered his grandmamma his special playmate. He objected when she wrote letters because then he had to be quiet and wait for her.

As her senator son's prestige continued to grow, Abigail still felt compelled to offer advice. She appealed to Louisa to help her improve John Quincy's health and his appearance: "I wish you would not let him go to Congress without a cracker in his jacket," she urged her daughter-in-law. "The space between Breakfast and dinner" was far too long.[2]

While her son's "genius" entitled him to admiration, Louisa must see to it that "the cut of his coat, the strangeness of his wigs, or color of his neckcloth" were not criticized. "If we live in the world and mean to serve ourselves and it, we must conform to its customs, its habits and in some measure its fashion."[3]

She criticized her son's "stiffness," his "reserve" and "coldness" in company. She warned him to be careful of what he said. She lectured him: "I hope you never appear in the Senate with a Beard two days old, or otherways make, what is called a shabby appearance." He must not "give occasion to the World to ask what kind of Mother he had? or to charge upon a Wife negligence and inattention when she is guiltless."[4]

John Quincy calmly accepted his mother's interference in his life as an adult. He loved her and he respected her. And he had learned well the lesson of duty to parents. While he became the patriarch to his own wife and children, he remained always a son to Abigail.⁵

Thomas, still a bachelor with an unsatisfactory law practice in Philadelphia, finally agreed to come home when his parents promised him complete independence. By the time he arrived, in December of 1803, his mother had fully recovered from a fall she had taken down a flight of stairs the previous June. He found her as busy and active as ever.

In the summer of 1805, at the age of thirty-three, Thomas married Ann Harrod and brought her to live in his parents' home. Abigail and Nancy, as Ann was always called, liked each other immensely, and Abigail was delighted to have them living with her. Nancy fit into the household easily. There was never any of the tension between them that existed between Abigail and Louisa Catherine. Thomas settled down to a quiet career as a judge and, in time, he and Nancy had seven children. Thomas had none of John Quincy's energy or talent, but he was always "dutiful and affectionate," and a comfort to his parents.

The summer of Thomas and Nancy's marriage was one of the happiest Abigail had known. Nabby and the children visited in August, and Abigail and John were surrounded by children and grandchildren. John, particularly, responded to his grandchildren, and to the host of other youngsters who seemed always to be there. His Puritan stiffness dissolved with them, and he took pleasure in all their antics. Abigail, more formal in her "rich silks and laces," considered herself responsible for their training and discipline. But she loved them equally, and they, in turn, adored her. She simply couldn't let herself go the way her husband did.

She continued to cook and to bake in spite of the often chilly kitchen and the ice-cold water: "I really believe that I can do it better than any of my family," she explained.⁶

Spring of 1806 brought a new crisis. Nabby's husband became involved in a daring scheme to free the people of South America from Spanish rule. The colonel had even involved his eighteen-year-old son, William. When Abigail learned of it, she called it a "don Quixot expedition."

The adventure turned into a disaster. Somehow, young William escaped, but Colonel Smith landed in prison in New York, awaiting trial. Nabby went to live on the prison grounds in order to be near him. Smith was tried and acquitted at the end of the summer, but his reputation was ruined and he couldn't get a job. He had no way of supporting his family. Abigail worried constantly about them. Finally, when Colonel Smith went to upstate New York, where he planned to build a house on land owned by his brother, Nabby agreed to come to Quincy with Caroline until the house was finished.

The summer of 1807 was more hectic than usual. Thomas and Nancy still lived with Abigail and John, and now they had an infant daughter, Elizabeth. Nabby and Caroline were still there. John Quincy and his family came every Sunday. Nabby's sons, William and John, came for visits, as did Sally Adams and Abbe. Susan was home from school for the summer. In August Louisa had had a third son, Charles Francis. And Louisa Smith was a permanent member of the family.

On the Sunday before Louisa and John Quincy were to leave for their annual trip to Washington, the entire family gathered for dinner. Abigail had all but one grandchild (John Smith) around her dining-room table. It was a joyous occasion she wouldn't soon forget.

Abigail loved to have tea with her
sisters in this mahogany-paneled sitting room . . .

When news arrived that Colonel Smith had finally established himself on a small farm in Lebanon, New York, south of Lake Oneida, and wanted his family to join him there, Abigail was devastated. What would Nabby and Caroline do in that isolated wilderness? She begged Nabby to remain in Quincy. When Nabby insisted that she must follow her husband, Abigail realized that her daughter was doing exactly what she would have done. But she would miss Nabby and Caroline desperately. Caroline, at twelve, was turning into a lovely young lady, and was her grandmother's delight.

Despite her preoccupation with her family, Abigail never lost interest in the world outside Quincy. She read several newspapers regularly and looked forward eagerly to John Quincy's letters from Washington. By the fall of 1808, when she found herself supporting James Madison, Thomas Jefferson's handpicked successor for president, she realized that her political views had gradually changed. She was becoming a Republican.

. . . and to entertain her children and grandchildren around the dining-room table for festive family dinners.

~

Over the last few years she had come to recognize that the two parties were very much alike. Furthermore, she was distressed by the Federalists' extreme pro-English policies which, she believed, threatened American neutrality and independence.

When Madison was elected president, he immediately nominated John Quincy Adams as ambassador to Russia. John Quincy, who had resigned from Congress and was practicing law in Boston, promptly accepted the post. His parents watched with heavy hearts as he prepared to leave for St. Petersburg.

Abigail feared that she would never see him again. This son had been her "support," she told her sister Elizabeth.[7] It was like "takeing our last leave of him."[8] His "tenderness and affection" made him particularly dear to her.

John Adams recognized the significance of the post. Russia was a tremendous power whose future influence could not yet be foreseen. To promote friendship and understanding with her was essential.

John Quincy, Louisa, and their infant son Charles Francis, accompanied by Louisa's sister Caroline Johnson and Nabby's son William Smith, who would be John Quincy's private secretary, left from Mr. Gray's Wharf in Charlestown on Saturday, August 5, 1809. Young George and John were left behind in the care of their grandparents. Abigail was not at the dock to see them off.

"My dear Children," she wrote, "I would not come to Town today because I knew I should only add to yours and my own agony. My Heart is with you. My prayers and blessing attend you. The Dear Children you have left, will be dearer to me for the absence of their parents."[9]

On Thanksgiving Day, as she looked at the grandchildren gathered around her table, Abigail counted the empty places. She hoped the youngsters who were there would enjoy their plum puddings, but she prayed silently that she would be able to hide from them her worries about some of their absent parents. She consoled herself that the "young shoots and branches remained," two from each family, the "promising successors of their dear parents."[10]

Now Abigail read all she could about Russia, she began a correspondence with Louisa's mother, Catherine Johnson, and she cared for her grandchildren. Ten-year-old George reminded her of his father at the same age. He was just as stubborn. John, small for his age, made up for his size in energy and affection. Abigail, writing to his mother, told her how he "claps me round the neck and says o! how I do Love you Grandmamma."[11]

The winter of 1809–1810 was the coldest in New England memory. The water in the bedroom washbasins froze every night, and Abigail could barely keep the ink flowing freely enough to write letters. It pointed up even more how bitterly cold it must be in Russia. When letters from both John Quincy and Louisa complained about the severe cold they were experiencing, how they hated living in St. Petersburg, and about John Quincy's inadequate salary, Abigail immediately concluded that they wanted to come home. Remembering her own feelings in Europe, she ached for her daughter-in-law.

But she knew her son. He would never request permission to leave his post. She would have to do it for him. So she wrote to President Madison. Madison responded, granting John Quincy permission to return if he requested it. And the president offered him a seat on the Supreme Court.

By now John Quincy had settled into more comfortable living quarters, and he saw fresh opportunities for serving his country at the czar's court. Further, Louisa was expecting another baby and they could not subject her to the six-thousand-mile voyage home. His sense of duty was as strong as his parents' had been.

~ CHAPTER XXIII ~
"What have I not lost"

"**W**hat a wreck does age and sickness make of the human frame!" Abigail cried out during the summer of 1811, as she watched her elder sister wasting away from consumption. It would indeed be a year filled with agony for Abigail. Now, as she moved back and forth between her own home and Mary's, trying desperately to nurse her sister and to keep her spirits up, she had alarming news about her daughter. Nabby had discovered a tumor in her breast, and suspected it might be cancerous. Abigail, who had not seen Nabby in three years, so great was the distance between Quincy and Lebanon, begged her to come to Boston to seek medical advice. Nabby, fearful that surgery would be the only solution, was reluctant. The prospect of the excruciating pain was terrifying.*

Finally Nabby did come, accompanied in an open carriage through the heat and dust of July by her son John and her daughter Caroline. Abigail's joy at their reunion was clouded by her fear of what lay ahead.

There were many consultations. Doctors in Boston recommended hemlock pills. Dr. Tufts advised against them. Finally, Nabby wrote to her father's dear friend in Philadelphia, Dr. Benjamin Rush, carefully describing all her symptoms. He urged immediate surgery as the only possibility of saving her life.

After much soul-searching, Nabby submitted to having her entire breast removed early in October. She remained conscious during the twenty-five minutes that the surgery lasted. Dressing the wound took another hour. When the doctors had finished, they pronounced her cured. Her husband arrived a few days later.

One month afterward, Nabby still could not use her arm, nor could she

---

* Anesthesia did not come into common use until later in the nineteenth century.

210

feed or dress herself. It was three months before she had the strength to leave the house.

Within days of Nabby's surgery, both Mary and Richard Cranch died. Throughout the summer Mary had continued to sink slowly and steadily, all the while clinging tenaciously to life. She remained calm and lucid. Then, suddenly, Richard suffered a stroke and died quickly. Mary, seemingly unwilling to live on after her husband was gone, gave up the struggle to survive, and died peacefully in her sleep the next day. They were buried together on the same day. Abigail was inconsolable. "The threefold silken cord is broken," she mourned to her sister Elizabeth.[1]

Nabby slowly regained her strength under her mother's care. Her husband and son returned home, while she and Caroline stayed on until the following summer.

In the midst of all the sadness and turmoil, John went outside in the dark one evening in November to view a comet, stumbled and fell on a sharp stick, and tore the skin off his leg. It produced a long, nasty wound that forced him to remain off his feet with his leg "horizontal on the sofa" for two months. The doctor came every day to treat it. Now Abigail had to care for him, too. It was a cold and gloomy winter.

"My Bosom has indeed been lacerated by wound upon wound," Abigail wrote to her daughter-in-law Louisa Catherine, in Russia. "I can scarcely trust my pen to describe them."[2]

She poured out her heart to John Quincy, also. But she would submit with "resignation to the all wise all merciful Sovereign of the Universe," she assured her son.[3]

By the end of the year Abigail herself was sick. Finally, she decided that she must send George and John, John Quincy and Louisa's sons, to her sister Elizabeth's in New Hampshire. She simply didn't have the strength to give them the care they needed. The Reverend Peabody would instruct them, and Elizabeth would give them love and affection.

1 812 was the year of James Madison's reelection, and the year of the outbreak of war with England. Both John and Abigail were happy with President Madison, and they believed strongly that war with Britain was necessary to preserve independence. Many New Englanders disagreed with them.

1812 brought devastating personal losses. In July, Thomas's infant daughter died in the room where John Adams had been born. "Why was I preserved three quarters of a century, and that rose cropped in the bud?" an anguished grandfather cried out.[4]

Then a letter arrived from Russia: Louisa and John Quincy's baby daughter, just one year and one month old, who looked like Grandma Adams, "very handsome, with the finest pair of black eyes you ever saw," had died in September. John Quincy had mourned the loss of his brother's infant. Now he grieved for his own.[5]

Abigail wept, then rode to New Hampshire in a snowstorm to comfort George and John. In an effort to help Louisa come to terms with her loss, she wrote to her of her own grief forty years before over the loss of Susanna. It was a subject she had never discussed.

As death claimed more and more family members and friends, Abigail clung to those precious few remaining. Now she wrote to Hannah Green, who had been her earliest friend when they were still teenagers and she had signed herself Diana: "As our Lamp of Life is nearly burnt out, I feel a sympathy drawing me nearer & nearer to those dear surviving Friends who began the race with me."[6]

And she wrote to Mercy Warren. Their friendship had collapsed when Mercy's book, *History of the Revolution,* was published in 1805. In it Mercy had criticized John Adams's presidency and his policies. John and Abigail had been enraged. Now Abigail began a correspondence with her eighty-year-old friend. Mercy was delighted to respond.

It was at about this time that Abigail began anew her old friendship with Thomas Jefferson. Eight years before, in 1804, when she had read in the newspaper of the death of Maria Jefferson Eppes, the little "Polly" whom she had loved and cared for in London, she broke the nearly three and a half years of silence between them. She could no longer still her pen, she told her old friend. "The powerful feelings of my heart have burst through the restraint, and called upon me to shed the tear of sorrow" over the loss of his beloved daughter. Her own anguish over the death of Charles was still fresh in her mind. She had "tasted the bitter cup." She could understand Jefferson's agony.[7]

Jefferson responded with gratitude and with an appeal to their former affection and friendship. But he could not resist mentioning some of their old political disagreements. Abigail replied courteously, but, with clear and burning logic, refuted his "sentiments," point by point, showing just how deep and unhealed the old wound was. She considered his conduct as "a personal injury," she told him, then concluded: "Faithful are the wounds of a Friend. . . . I bear no malice I cherish no enmity. I would not retaliate if I could." But she left him in no doubt as to how she felt.[8]

The exchange of letters had continued for five months. A correspondence that Abigail had begun simply as an expression of sympathy over the death of his daughter had turned into a confrontation of political principles. That had not been her intent. In October she declared the correspondence closed. Jefferson had always occupied a "little corner" of her heart from which it was difficult to dislodge him. Yet, caught in a situation that forced her to choose between allegiance to her family and affection for a friend, her loyalty to her husband came first.

John knew nothing of the correspondence until it had ended.

Now, eight years later, time had dimmed the memory of their differences, and when their good friend Dr. Benjamin Rush appealed to both John Adams and Thomas Jefferson to end their silence, John made the first move. His old friend responded immediately. They agreed that only future generations could judge who was right, but they ought not to die before they had explained themselves to each other. So began an extraordinary correspondence that continued until the end of their lives.

Abigail joined in this renewal of friendship. She and Thomas Jefferson had always responded warmly to each other as human beings. They shared the same values. In the end, their feelings of mutual respect and admiration overcame the political wounds.

The specter of death seemed to be lurking everywhere. By the end of 1812 Nabby was once again suffering from "rheumatism" in her limbs and her back. As her health continued to decline, she finally came to realize that her ailment was not rheumatism. Her reprieve had been short-lived. The cancer had reappeared and was spreading throughout her body. She continued to suffer severe pain. Once again, she and her children were alone on their remote farm. Nabby, proud that her husband had recently been elected to Congress from their district in New York, had encouraged him to go to Washington to attend the congressional session. The colonel had already written guardedly to his mother-in-law of Nabby's desire to be with her mother. But Nabby was so weak, Caroline reported to her grandmother, she could scarcely walk across the room.

Abigail, who felt too old and weak herself to make the three-hundred-mile journey, despaired of ever seeing her daughter again. But Nabby, aware that she was dying, was determined to die in her parents' home. With her children John and Caroline, she made the agonizing journey to Quincy in slow stages in a bumpy carriage.

When she arrived at the end of July, she was carried from her carriage to bed. Abigail, Caroline, Susan Adams, and Louisa Smith all did their best to keep her comfortable. Nabby died on August 15, a few days after her husband reached her bedside. She had just turned forty-eight. John called his daughter a "monument to Suffering and to Patience."[9]

Abigail had never known such anguish. This was a burden she couldn't bear. Nabby had been her "closest companion."

"The wound which has lacerated my Bosom cannot be healed," she wrote to John Quincy. "The broken Heart may be bound up; and religion teach submission and silence . . . but it cannot cure it. The unbidden sigh will rise, and the bitter tear flow long after the Tomb is closed."[10] Even her faith in God didn't have the power to sustain her this time.

"I have lost, O what have I not lost in . . . my only daughter," she cried.[11] It was a loss from which she would never recover. But Nabby left her mother a treasure. She left her daughter Caroline, so much like Nabby, and always a favorite of Abigail's. Caroline continued to live with her grandmother until her own marriage two years later.

CHAPTER XXIV

"Dearest Friend"

In the spring of 1813, shortly before Nabby's death, John Quincy had begun to think seriously of returning home from Russia. It was at just this time that he was appointed one of three commissioners to negotiate an end to the war with Great Britain. James Monroe, then secretary of state, wrote to John and Abigail in the hope that they would encourage their son to accept the appointment.

Abigail rose to the occasion. She promptly responded to Monroe by reminding him of her own past sacrifices for her country. She recognized the importance of her son's role in history, she told him. Much as she had "daily hoped" to embrace him once again, she knew full well her duty, and would "fully and willingly" yield her son to his country. It was "no small satisfaction" to her that John Quincy had earned the confidence of the president.[1]

Life continued at Quincy. Abigail worked hard without a thought to her age or her health. It was only by her constant guidance that things could be made to run smoothly in her large and complicated household. She had to watch every penny. The farm provided very little income. It was the interest on the securities Abigail had quietly purchased over the years through Dr. Tufts that kept them going financially.

A large number of extended family lived at the Adams homestead. The procession of children, grandchildren and eventually great-grandchildren, in-laws, and relatives was never-ending. Visitors were always welcome. To have his grandchildren all around him was John Adams's final idea of happiness, even when they got into his bedroom and mixed up all the papers on his writing table.

John relished the role of overindulgent grandfather, although Abigail scolded him for spoiling the children with candy and fruit. But she, too, could say that they took great delight in living over again in their offspring.

John worried about her, and complained that "she makes me tremble by her uncontrollable attachment to the superintendance of her household."[2] Yet the household revolved around her husband, who frequently insisted on having things his way.

When she felt well enough, Abigail enjoyed having villagers call on Sunday evenings. When friends expressed concern over the many duties she took upon herself, she replied: "I would rather have too much [to do] than too little. Life stagnates without action. I could never bear to merely vegetate."[3] And she instructed her grandchildren not to waste their youth: "It is a treasure you can possess but once," she told them.[4]

Abigail had always felt strongly that women were intellectually equal to men. She had educated her husband to the fact that women could possess first-rate minds and strong personalities worthy of respect. But she felt their place was in the home. She took pride in her female role. Years before, she had told John Quincy that "However brilliant a woman's talents may be, she ought never to shine at the expence of her Husband."[5]

She had been so successful in convincing her husband of the importance of the female role that now he wrote to John Quincy suggesting that the nation ought to adopt a symbolic name that enshrined womanly rather than manly qualities. "Why should we not introduce Matria, instead of Patria?" John asked his son. "Mankind in general love their Mothers, I believe, rather more tenderly than their fathers, & perhaps have more reason for it."[6]

Now Abigail, still concerned about the separate but equal roles of the sexes, told her sister Elizabeth that "no man ever prospered in the world without the consent and cooperation of his wife. It behooves us, who are parents or grandparents, to give our daughters and granddaughters . . . such an education as shall qualify them for the useful and domestic duties of life, that they should learn the proper use and improvement of time, since time was given for use, not waste." Every American wife must know how to "order and regulate her family," she insisted. "For this purpose, the all-wise Creator made woman an help-meet for man."[7]

Abigail and John both read much, and when John's eyesight began to fail, Abigail read aloud by the fire. When he rose at 5:00 A.M. in order to read by the early morning light, Abigail worried that "The President" would catch cold in the chill of the drafty house.

She continued to keep her family together through her ceaseless letter writing. Letter writing, she had told Nabby years before, was a "habit, the pleasure of which increases with practise, but becomes urksome by neglect."[8]

Louisa Catherine, writing to her mother-in-law, wondered how Abigail could write to so many in one family, yet never appear at a loss for subject. It even astonished Abigail at times. "At the age of seventy," she conceded, "I feel more interest in all that's done beneath the circuit of the sun than some others do at, what shall I say, 35 or 40?"[9]

As their fiftieth wedding anniversary approached, their "day of jubile," Abigail told her sister that she had had "few rubs" in her marriage, but there had been some difficulties in her long life. There were times, she told her, when she had "insisted upon my own way, and my own opinion, and sometimes yealded silently!" If she had her youth, and the opportunity to choose again, "my first choice would be the same."[10]

But, she cautioned her granddaughter Caroline on the eve of her marriage to Peter De Windt, "Look out well, for the die once cast, there is no retreat until death."[11]

When Caroline married it created an irreparable void in her life. Caroline had been the "prop" of her age, her "Solace," her "Comfort." But Abigail was pleased with Caroline's choice, and was relieved to know that her beloved granddaughter was "happily settled in life." Caroline and Peter were married in her grandparents' home on Sunday evening, September 11, 1814. Abigail made the wedding supper.

Now, sensing that she might die before her husband, Abigail prepared her will. She tried to be "even-handed" with her sons. To her nieces and granddaughters she gave money and distributed her jewelry and clothes. She expressed contentment with her life: "I ought to rise satisfied from the feast."[12] But she was not satisfied with the reflection she saw in the mirror, "a striking emblem of yellow autumn and the falling leaf." Her hair was "frosted," her eyesight failing, and her memory like a "sieve."[13]

On April 10, 1815, without any warning, Elizabeth Shaw Peabody died in her sleep. Abigail was inconsolable. Grief "had broken her down," she wrote to John Quincy. She told Elizabeth's husband, Stephen Peabody, that only by his own agony could he judge hers. She questioned why she, the older, had been spared.

Then, just eight days later, on April 18, she gathered all her fortitude and put her grandsons George and John on the *New Packet*, bound for England. They would join their father, John Quincy, and mother there.

The war with England had ended. When John Quincy had signed the treaty referred to as the "Peace of Christmas Eve" at Ghent, Belgium, in 1814, it was to his mother that he had written before anyone else. But peace with England did not bring him home to her. He was named minister to the Court of St. James, as his father had been thirty years before. Now, knowing that he would be in Europe for at least another year, he and Louisa wanted their sons with them.

Abigail and John sent their grandsons off with admonitions to be modest, respectful, and good, to write to their grandparents faithfully, and always to carry a pencil in their pockets to make notes on anything unusual that they saw or heard. It was reminiscent of the instructions given to their father so many years before.

At the end of the year, Cotton Tufts died after a brief illness. John and Abigail felt more alone than ever. Uncle Tufts had been their "most ancient, venerable, and most beloved friend." He had been part of the fabric of their lives. He was their adviser, mainstay to Abigail during John's long absences, faithful steward when they were in England, and reliable executor of a thousand small and large commissions. They would miss him.

A few months later Colonel William Smith died with his daughter Caroline at his bedside. John wrote to John Quincy, "Be to his virtues ever kind, to his faults a little blind. The world will never know all the good or all the evil he has done."[14]

After Thomas finally moved his large family to Penn's Hill, Abigail and John were left in the Old House with only Louisa Smith. She had truly become a daughter to them, and was now a faithful nurse as well. They were often lonely. For Abigail, who loved to be with people and missed the bustle of a large household, it was almost as painful as the arthritis and rheumatism that racked her body.

Then, on November 20, 1816, the newspapers reported that John Quincy Adams had been recalled to America to serve as secretary of state under President James Monroe. His nomination was confirmed with only one dissenting vote. Not since George Washington, his proud mother told him, had anyone been chosen for public office with "more universal approbation."[15]

"The voice of the nation calls you home. The government calls you home—and your parents unite in the call. To this summons you must not, you cannot refuse your assent," she pleaded.[16]

The ship carrying John Quincy and his family home to America docked in New York on August 6, 1817, almost eight years after they had left for St. Petersburg. On August 15 Louisa was able to write to her mother-in-law that they had collected their luggage, hired a carriage, and were about to set out for Quincy. Abigail calculated their travel time and probable arrival.

It was Louisa Smith who first spotted their carriage approaching on a hot sunny morning two weeks later. As she cried out excitedly, Abigail ran to the door. Young John jumped out almost before the horses had come to a stop and threw himself into his grandmother's arms. Sixteen-year-old George, at five feet, seven and a half inches, already half an inch taller than his father, followed "half crazy," calling out, "O, Grandmother! O, Grandmother!" Charles, too young when he left Quincy to remember his grandparents, hung back shyly. This day was his tenth birthday.

George was admitted to Harvard soon after, and John and Charles were enrolled in the Boston Latin School. John Quincy and Louisa stayed for a few weeks, then left for Washington in September. Once again, Abigail was in charge of her grandsons.

On their first day in school, John and Charles were back in Quincy by evening, the pretext a forgotten book. But if Grandmamma would allow them to stay with her a few more days, they would return to school and study very hard. Then, the first weekend, they were back again. The boys insisted on coming home from Boston every weekend. Their grandmother loved having them too much to stop them.

Louisa Catherine continued to make her mother-in-law a sharer in her life. She had done it from Russia, then from London, and now she wrote

When Abigail Adams died in this bedroom on October 28, 1818,
John said a part of him died, too. He knew he had lost his dearest friend.

∼

regularly from Washington. The two women had effected a warm and deep friendship through their letters to each other. A continent apart, they had been able to express to each other their true feelings and remove the barriers that had originally existed. They were much alike in their strong wills, their intelligence, and their candor.

Early in October of the following year, less than a month before her seventy-fourth birthday, Abigail developed typhoid fever. It had been an unusually hot summer, spreading disease among many of the inhabitants of the town of Quincy. Abigail was one of its victims. Recognizing that her illness might prove fatal, she nonetheless fought bravely to recover and continued to direct her household from her bed. Her niece Lucy Cranch Greenleaf arrived to help Louisa Smith nurse their aunt. John hovered at her bedside.

On October 28 Abigail suddenly lost her strength. She told John she knew that she was dying. Then she murmured to Lucy that she had been "a mother to me," closed her eyes, and fell asleep. She died quietly in her sleep.

John, gazing down at her, said simply, "I wish I could lay down beside her and die too." For a moment his palsied frame shook uncontrollably. Then he turned to Louisa and led the distraught woman into another room to comfort her.

As the news spread throughout the neighborhood, the house filled with friends and relatives who simply wanted to be there. The outpouring of grief was overwhelming. Soon all of Quincy was dressed in black or wearing crepe on their sleeves in tribute to this great but simple lady.

The funeral took place three days later. John leaned on his great staff to walk the half mile to the church behind the body of his wife, a walk they had taken together so many times. Among the pallbearers were the governor of Massachusetts and the president of Harvard College.

John Quincy, writing to his brother Thomas, said of his mother that "Her life gave the lie to every libel on her sex that was ever written." He always delighted in returning to his mother's house, for there "I felt as if the joys and charms of childhood returned to make me happy."[17] But it was John Quincy's wife, Louisa, who best captured her mother-in-law when she described her as the "guiding planet around which all revolved, performing their separate duties only by the impulse of her magnetic power."[18]

For John Adams, "The dear Partner of my Life for fifty-four Years and for many Years more as a Lover," was gone.[19] A part of him, he said, died with her.

She had been "the delight of [his] heart, the sweetener of all his toils, the comforter of all his sorrows, the sharer and heightener of all his joys. . . . In all his struggles and in all his sorrows, [her] affectionate participation and cheering encouragement . . . had been his never failing support."[20] She had truly been his dearest friend.

Reference Notes

The extensive use of reference notes will, I hope, provide for those interested in further details an opportunity to read some of the letters in their entirety.

The Book of Abigail and John and *New Letters of Abigail Adams* (cited fully in the Bibliography) are both readily available, and provide an extraordinary glimpse into the relationships that existed between Abigail and John, and between Abigail and her older sister Mary.

In these notes, as per scholarly custom, the full citation for each source is provided when it is first encountered. Thereafter, an abbreviated version is used. The abbreviations used are listed below.

Abbreviations of source titles

AAD	Abigail Adams' Diary of her Voyage from Boston to Deal, England
AFC	Adams Family Correspondence
A-JL	Adams-Jefferson Letters
AP	Adams Papers
APm	Adams Papers microfilm
AAS	American Antiquarian Society
BoA&J	Book of Abigail and John
DAJA	Diary and Autobiography of John Adams
J&CMA	Journal and Correpondence of Miss Adams
LJA	Letters of John Adams
LMA	Letters of Mrs. Adams
MHS	Massachusetts Historical Society
NL	New Letters of Abigail Adams
NYHS	New York Historical Society
Works	The Works of John Adams

Abbreviations of people's names

AA	Abigail Adams
CT	Cotton Tufts
ESS/ESP	Elizabeth Smith Shaw/Elizabeth Shaw Peabody (sister)
HQLS	Hannah Quincy Lincoln Storer (cousin)
HSG	Hannah Storer Green (friend)
JA	John Adams
JL	James Lovell
JQA	John Quincy Adams
JT	John Thaxter
LC	Lucy Cranch
LCA	Louisa Catherine Adams
MC	Mary Smith Cranch
MOW	Mercy Otis Warren
TBA	Thomas Boylston Adams
TJ	Thomas Jefferson
WSS	William Stephens Smith

Chapter I
"a very incorrect writer"

1. Abigail Adams to John Quincy Adams, December 30, 1804, *Adams Papers*, 403.
2. *Diary and Autobiography of John Adams*, 2:72.
3. AA to Caroline Smith, Februry 2, 1809, *Journal and Correspondence of Miss Adams*, ed. Caroline Smith de Windt, 1:216.
4. AA to Elizabeth Smith Shaw Peabody, June 10, 1801 (actually 1808), Shaw Family Papers, Library of Congress.
5. AA to Isaac Smith, February 7, 1762, Smith-Carter Papers, Massachusetts Historical Society.
6. AA to Hannah Quincy Lincoln, October 5, 1761, *Letters of Mrs. Adams*, 6.
7. AA to Isaac Smith, February 7, 1762, Smith-Carter Papers, MHS.

Chapter II
"Ballast is what I want"

1. *DAJA*, 1:108.
2. Ibid., 194.
3. Ibid., 234.
4. Ibid., 3:257–258.
5. Ibid., 1:55.
6. October–December 1758. *John Adams' Earliest Diary*, 73.

Chapter III
"You may take me"

1. John Adams to AA, October 4, 1762, *Book of Abigail and John*, 17.
2. AA to JA, April 20, 1764, Ibid., 37.
3. AA to JA, September 12, 1763, Ibid., 21.
4. JA to AA, February 14, 1763, Ibid., 18.
5. Memorandum on a copy of Deacon John Adams's will, July 10, 1761, *Adams Papers*, Wills and Deeds.
6. AA to JA, October 22, 1775, *Adams Family Correspondence*, 1:310.
7. AA to JA, April 12, 1764, *BoA&J*, 28–30.
8. AA to JA, April 16, 1764, *AFC*, 1:33.
9. JA to AA, April 14, 1764, Ibid., 29–30.
10. AA to JA, April 30, 1764, *BoA&J*, 41.
11. JA to AA, April 11, 1764, Ibid., 26.
12. JA to AA, April 12, 1764, Ibid., 27.
13. JA to AA, April 13, 1764, Ibid., 31.
14. AA to JA, April 20, 1764, Ibid., 38.
15. JA to AA, May 7, 1764, Ibid., 40.
16. AA to JA, May 9, 1764, Ibid., 43.
17. JA to AA, September 30, 1764, Ibid., 44.
18. AA to JA, October 13, 1764, *APm*.
19. AA to JA, October 4, 1764, *BoA&J*, 46.

Chapter IV
"the weaker sex"

1. *The Works of John Adams*, 2: Appendix A:521–525.
2. AA to Hannah Storer Green, July 14, 1765, *AFC*, 1:59.
3. Quoted in Bancroft, 3:77–78.

4. *DAJA*, October 10, 1765, 1:265 n. 1.

5. Ibid., December 20, 1765, 1:265 n. 1.

6. Ibid., December 25, 1765, 1:274; 3:282.

7. AA to Mary Cranch, July 15, 1766, *AFC*, 1:53–55.

8. AA to MC, October 6, 1766, Ibid., 55–56.

9. Reverend James Fordyce, D.D., *Sermons to Young Women*, in 2 vols. (London, 1767).

Chapter V
"I should ... have been a rover"

1. AA to JA, September 14, 1767, AFC, 1:62 n. 3.

2. *DAJA*, January 30, 1768, 1:337–338.

3. AA to Isaac Smith, Jr., January 4, 1770, AFC, 1:67–68.

4. AA to Isaac Smith, Jr., April 20, 1771, Ibid., 76.

5. *DAJA*, 3:294–295.

6. Ibid.

Chapter VI
"The flame is kindled"

1. *DAJA*, 2:7.

2. AA to JA, December 30, 1773, *AFC*, 1:90.

3. AA to Mercy Otis Warren, December 5, 1773, Ibid., 88–89.

4. Quoted in Bancroft, 3:455–6.

5. *DAJA*, December 17, 1773, 2:85–86.

6. AA to MOW, July 16, 1773, *AFC*, 1:84.

Chapter VII
"Partner in all the Joys and Sorrows"

1. Quoted in *BoA&J*, 55.

2. *DAJA*, 3:307.

3. *Works*, June 25, 1774, 9:339.

4. JA to AA, July 1, 1774, *BoA&J*, 59.

5. JA to AA, July 2, 1774, *Family Letters*, 8–9.

6. AA to JA, August 19, 1774, *BoA&J*, 67–68.

7. AA to JA, August 15, 1774, *Familiar Letters of John Adams*, 23–24.

8. AA to JA, August 19, 1774, *BoA&J*, 67–68.
9. Ibid.
10. AA to JA, September 17, 1774, Ibid., 71–73.
11. JA to AA, August 28, 1774, Ibid., 68–70.
12. JA to AA, July 7, 1774, Ibid., 62–63.
13. JA to AA, June 29, 1774, Ibid., 56–58.
14. AA to JA, September 16, 1774, Ibid., 73–74.
15. AA to JA, October 16, 1774, *BoA&J*, 79–81.
16. JQA to JA, October 16, 1774, *AFC*, 1:167.
17. AA to JA, September 16, 1774, *BoA&J*, 73–74.
18. JA to AA, April 28, 1776, *AFC*, 1:398–401.
19. JA to AA, September 8, 1774, *BoA&J*, 70–71.
20. JA to AA, October 9, 1774, Ibid., 78–79.
21. *DAJA*, 2:402.

Chapter VIII
"I want some sentimental Effusions of the Heart"

1. AA to MOW, February 3, 1774, AFC, 1:184.
2. AA to JA, May 4, 1775, *BoA&J*, 83–84.
3. AA to JA, May 24, 1775, Ibid., 84–85.
4. AA to JA, June 16, 1775, Ibid., 86–88.
5. AA to JA, July 5, 1775, *LMA*, 1:47–50.
6. AA to JA, July 16, 1775, Ibid., 50–57.
7. AA to JA, June 25, 1775, Ibid., 43–47.
8. AA to JA, June 22, 1775, Ibid., 41–43.
9. JA to Polly Palmer, July 5, 1776, *AFC*, 2:34.
10. JA to AA, May 2, 1775, Ibid., 82–83.
11. Quoted in Scheer and Rankin, 61.
12. AA to JA, June 18, 1775, *BoA&J*, 90–91.
13. JA to AA, July 7, 1775, Ibid., 96.
14. *Memoirs of JQA*, ed. Charles Francis Adams, 1:545.
15. AA to JA, July 12, 1775, *BoA&J*, 97–99.
16. AA to JA, July 5, 1775, *AFC*, 1:247.
17. JA to AA, July 7, 1775, *BoA&J*, 95–97.
18. AA to JA, September 23, 1776, *AFC*, 2:133.
19. AA to JA, July 12, 1775, *BoA&J*, 97.
20. AA to JA, July 16, 1775, Ibid., 99–104.
21. AA to JA, June 25, 1775, Ibid., 92–94.

Chapter IX
"Mrs. Delegate"

1. JA to AA, July 24, 1775, *BoA&J*, 105–106.
2. AA to JA, July 16, 1775, Ibid., 99–104.
3. AA to JA, November 5, 1775, *LMA*, 76–78.
4. AA to JA, July 25, 1775, Ibid., 57–63.
5. AA to JA, August 8–10, 1775, *BoA&J*, 106–107.
6. AA to JA, September 16-17, 1775. *AFC* I:279-280.
7. AA to JA, September 25, 1775, *BoA&J*, 107.
8. AA to JA, October 22, 1775, *AFC*, 1:309–310.
9. AA to JA, October 1, 1775, BoA&J, 108.
10. AA to JA, October 22, 1775, AFC, 1:309–310.
11. JA to AA, October 23, 1775, Ibid., 1:312.
12. JA to AA, October 19, 1775, *BoA&J*, 110–111.
13. JA to AA, October 1, 1775, Ibid., 108.
14. AA to JA, October 25, 1775, *AFC*, 1:313.

Chapter X
"Remember the Ladies"

1. AA to JA, November 27, 1775. *BoA&J*, 112-114.
2. AA to MOW, January 1776, *AFC*, I:422–423.
3. Conway, ed., *Writings of Thomas Paine*, vol. I., *Common Sense*, 84.
4. AA to JA, February 21, 1776, *AFC*, 1:350.
5. AA to JA, March 2, 1776, Ibid., 1:352.
6. AA to JA, March 16, 1776, *BoA&J*, 117–120.
7. AA to JA, March 31, 1776, Ibid., 120–121.
8. AA to JA, March 16, 1776, Ibid., 117–120.
9. AA to JA, March 31, 1776, Ibid., 120–121.
10. AA to JA, May 14, 1776, *BoA&J*, 127–129.
11. JA to AA, May 27, 1776, Ibid., 130–132.
12. AA to JA, June 17, 1776, *AFC*, 2:14.
13. AA to JA, November 12, 1775, Ibid., 1:324.
14. AA to JA, March 31, 1776, *BoA&J*, 120–121.
15. Ibid.
16. JA to AA, April 14, 1776, Ibid., 121-123.
17. AA to JA, May 7, 1776, Ibid., 126–127.

Chapter XI
"I want a companion a nights"

1. JA to John Winthrop, June 23, 1776, *Correspondence Between John Adams and Prof. John Winthrop*, (MHS, Collections, 5th ser.), 4:308.
2. Thomas Jefferson, *Writings of Thomas Jefferson*, 9:337–8.
3. JA to AA, July 3, 1776, *BoA&J*, 138–140.
4. JA to AA, June 26, 1776, Ibid., 137.
5. AA to JA, July 18, 1776, Ibid., 147–149.
6. AA to JT, August 20, 1776, *AFC*, 2:101.
7. JA to AA, August 28, 1776, Ibid., 111.
8. AA to JA, August 5, 1776, Ibid., 116–117.
9. JA to AA, August 30, 1776, Ibid., 115.
10. AA to JA, August 14, 1776, *BoA&J*, 152–153.
11. AA to JA, August 29, 1776, Ibid., 159–161.
12. AA to JA, July 14, 1776, Ibid., 146.
13. AA to JA, April 17, 1777, Ibid., 171–172.
14. Ibid.
15. Ibid.
16. JA to AA, April 26, 1777, Ibid., 172–173.
17. AA to JA, May 18, 1777, *AFC*, 2:241.
18. AA to JA, June 8, 1777, *BoA&J*, 175–177.
19. AA to JA, June 23, 1777, Ibid., 177–178.
20. AA to JA, July 9, 1777, Ibid., 178.
21. JA to AA, July 10, 1777, Ibid., 178–180.
22. AA to JA, July 10-11, 1777, Ibid., 180–181.
23. JT to JA, July 13, 1777, Ibid., 181.
24. AA to JA, July 16, 1777, Ibid., 181–182.
25. AA to JA, September 30, 1777, *Familiar Letters*, 309–310.
26. JA to AA, July 28, 1777, *BoA&J*, 184.
27. JQA to JA, June 2, 1777, quoted in Koch, 225.
28. JA to JQA, August 11, 1777, *BoA&J*, 188.

Chapter XII
"to rob me of all my happiness"

1. JA to AA, August 11, 1777, *BoA&J*, 187.
2. James Lovell to AA, August 29, 1777, *AFC*, 2:333.
3. AA to JA, September 17, 1777, *BoA&J*, 192–193.
4. AA to JA, October 20, 1777, *AFC*, 2:354.

5. AA to JA, October 25, 1777, *BoA&J*, 195–196.
6. Quoted in *BoA&J*, 201.
7. JA to AA, August 24, 1777, *BoA&J*, 191.
8. AA to JL, December 15, 1777, Ibid., 202–204.
9. MOW to AA, January 2, 1778, *AFC*, 2:376.
10. AA to JT, February 15, 1778, Ibid., 391.
11. AA to JQA, March 8, 1778, *LMA* 1:113–115.
12. JA to AA, February 13, 1778, *BoA&J*, 205.
13. AA to JT, February 15, 1778, *AFC*, 2:390.
14. AA to HQLS, March 1, 1778, Ibid., 397.
15. AA to JT, September 2, 1778, Ibid., 3:84–86.
16. AA to JA, May 18, 1778, *BoA&J*, 211–212.
17. AA to JA, June 18, 1778, *AFC*, 3:46.
18. JA to AA, April 12, 1778, Ibid., 9.

Chapter XIII
"And shall I see his face again?"

1. JA to AA, April 25, 1778, *AFC*, 3:51.
2. AA to JA, June 30, 1778, *BoA&J*, 217–219.
3. AA to Lucy Cranch, April 25, 1787, AP, 369.
4. AA to JA, July 15, 1778, *BoA&J*, 219–221.
5. AA to JA, December 13, 1778, *AFC*, 3:135.
6. AA to JA, October 21, 1778, *BoA&J*, 224–225.
7. JQA to AA, September 27, 1778, Ibid., 223.
8. Ibid.
9. AA to JT, August 19, 1778, *AFC*, 3:78.
10. AA to JL, June 12, 1778, Ibid., 41.
11. JL to AA, April 1, 1778, Ibid., 1.
12. AA to JL, June 24, 1778, Ibid., 48.
13. AA to JA, December 27, 1778, *BoA&J*, 233–235.
14. AA to JA, October 21, 1778, Ibid., 224–225.
15. AA to JA, October 25, 1778, Ibid., 225–226.
16. AA to JA, November 12, 1778, Ibid., 228–229.
17. JA to AA, December 18, 1778, Ibid., 232–233.
18. JQA to AA, February 20, 1779, *AFC*, 3:375.
19. AA to JA, February 13, 1779, *BoA&J*, 235–237.
20. JA to AA, February 13, 1779, Ibid., 237–238.

Chapter XIV
"Who shall give me back Time?"

1. AA to JA, December 10, 1779, *AFC*, 3:242.
2. AA to JQA, January 19, 1780, *BoA&J*, 252–255.
3. JA to AA, November 13, 1779, Ibid., 244–245.
4. AA to JA, November 14, 1779, Ibid., 245.
5. AA to JA, November 13, 1780, Ibid., 274–281.
6. JA to AA, December 11, 1779, Ibid., 245.
7. JA to AA, April–May 1780, Ibid., 255–256.
8. JA to JQA, March 17–22, 1780, *APm*.
9. JA to AA, April–May, 1780, *BoA&J*, 255–256.
10. AA to JQA, January 19, 1780, Ibid., 252–255.
11. AA to JQA, March 20–21, 1780, *APm*.
12. AA to Charles Adams, January 19, 1780, *APm*.
13. AA to JA, July 5, 1780, *BoA&J*, 264.
14. JA to AA, December 2, 1781, Ibid., 299–300.
15. AA to JA, May 1, 1780, Ibid., 257–259.
16. AA to JA, October 8, 1780, Ibid., 273.
17. JA to AA, July 27, 1780, *DAJA*, 442.
18. JA to AA, December 18, 1780, *BoA&J*, 281–282.
19. AA to JQA, January 21, 1781, *AFC*, 4:67–68.
20. AA to JQA, November 20, 1783, *APm*.
21. AA to JA, August 1, 1781, *BoA&J*, 294–296.
22. AA to JA, Septembr 29, 1781, Ibid., 296–298.
23. AA to JL, June 30, 1781, *AFC*, 4:164–165.
24. JL to AA, January 13, 1780, Ibid., 3:257.
25. AA to JL, February 13, 1780, Ibid., 31.
26. AA to JL, March 17, 1781, Ibid., 4:91.
27. AA to JA, December 9, 1781, *BoA&J*, 301–304.
28. JA to AA, October 1782, Ibid., 330–331.
29. JA to AA, December 2, 1781, Ibid., 299–300.
30. AA to JA, April 10, 1782, Ibid., 311–315.
31. AA to JA, June 17, 1782, *AFC*, 4:328.
32. AA to JA, July 17, 1782, *BoA&J*, 318–320.
33. AA to JA, October 25, 1782, *AP*, 358.
34. JA to AA, October 12, 1782, *BoA&J*, 330–331.
35. AA to JA, September 5, 1782, Ibid., 323–324.
36. JA to AA, November 8, 1782, Ibid., 331–332.
37. JA to AA, September 7, 1783, Ibid., 362–364.

38. JA to AA, August 14, 1783, Ibid., 360–362.

39. AA to JA, July 21, 1783, *AP*, 361.

40. AA to JA, October 19, 1783, *BoA&J*, 365–367.

41. AA to JA, December 7–13, 1783, *AP*, 362.

42. AA to JA, December 23, 1782, *BoA&J*, 332–336.

43. AA to JA, December 17, 1783, *AP*, 361.

Chapter XV
"safely landed"

1. AA to JA, December 23, 1782, *BoA&J*, 332–336.

2. Nabby to Betsy Cranch, December 1782, Cranch Family Papers, MHS.

3. AA to JA, December 23, 1782, *BoA&J*, 336.

4. JA to AA, January 22, 1783, Ibid., 338.

5. JA to AA, January 29, 1783, Ibid., 339–340.

6. JA to AA, January 22, 1783, Ibid., 336–339.

7. JA to AA, January 29, 1783, Ibid., 339–340.

8. JA to AA, February 4, 1783, Ibid., 340–341.

9. JA to Nabby, August 13, 1783, Ibid., 359–360.

10. JA to Francis Dana, April 28, 1782, Dana Papers, MHS.

11. AA to JA, November 11, 1783, *BoA&J*, 367–370.

12. JA to JQA, May 14, 1783, Ibid., 349–350.

13. JA to AA, August 14, 1783, Ibid., 360–362.

14. AA to JA, December 15, 1783, Ibid., 370–373.

15. JA to AA, September 7, 1783, Ibid., 362–364.

16. AA to JA, December 15, 1783, Ibid., 370–373.

17. Thomas Jefferson to JA, June 19, 1784, *A-JL*, 16.

18. AA, June 20, 1784, *AAD* in *DAJA*, 3:154–155.

19. AA, July 1, 1784, Ibid., 159–161.

20. AA to ESS, July 10, 1784, *BoA&J*, 381–384.

21. AA, June 24, 1784, *AAD* in *AP*, 3:157–158.

22. AA, July 2, 1784, Ibid., 161–162.

23. AA, July 4, 1784, Ibid., 162–163.

24. AA to ESS, July 10, 1784, *BoA&J*, 381–384.

25. AA, July 17, 1784, *DAJA*, 165–166.

26. AA to MC, July 20, 1784, *BoA&J*, 384–388.

27. Ibid.

28. AA to JA, July 23, 1784, Ibid., 388–390.

29. JA to AA, July 26, 1784, Ibid., 391–392.

30. AA to MC, July 26, 1784, *LMA*, 2:38–39.

31. AA to MC, July 25, 1784, Ibid., 31.
32. AA to MC, July 30, 1784, *BoA&J*, 395.
33. Nabby, August 7, 1784, Ibid., 397–398.
34. AA to MC, December 12, 1784, *LMA*, 2:64.

Chapter XVI
"one of the choice ones of the earth"

1. AA to LC, September 5, 1784, *LMA*, 2:54–55.
2. AA to CT, September 8, 1784, *AP*, 363.
3. AA to MC, December 12, 1784, *LMA*, 2:63.
4. AA to MC, February 20, 1785, Ibid., 81–83.
5. AA to MC, September 5, 1784, Ibid., 188–194.
6. AA to MOW, September 5–December 12, 1784, *AP*, 363.
7. AA to MC, May 8, 1785, AAS.
8. AA to MC, February 20, 1785, Ibid.
9. AA to MC, May 8, 1785, *LMA*, 247–249.
10. JA to TJ, May 22, 1785, *A-JL*, 21.
11. TJ to JA, May 25, 1785, Ibid., 23.
12. AA to TJ, June 6, 1785, Ibid., 28–31.
13. AA to MC, June 24–26, 1785, *LMA*, 251–258.
14. Ibid.
15. AA to JQA, June 26, 1785, *AP*, 364.
16. AA to Dr. Thomas Welsh, July, 1785, *APm*.
17. AA to MC, January 26, 1786, *AP*, 369.
18. AA to JQA, September 6, 1785, *LMA*, 267–269.
19. AA to WSS, September, 1785, *AP*, 365.
20. AA to JQA, February 16, 1786, Ibid., 367.
21. AA to MC, February 26, 1786, AAS.

Chapter XVII
"the three-fold cord"

1. AA to MC, February 25, 1787, *NL*, 317–319.
2. AA to CT, July 20, 1787, NYHS, ms.
3. AA to TJ, January 29, 1787, *A-JL*, 168.
4. TJ to AA, February 22, 1787, Ibid., 173.
5. AA to ESS, April 29, 1787, *AP*, 369.
6. ESS to AA, March 18, 1786, Ibid., 367
7. AA to JQA, July 21, 1786, Ibid., 368.

8. AA to ESS, March 10, 1787, Shaw Family Papers, Library of Congress.
9. AA to MC, June 13, 1786, AAS.
10. AA to Charles Storer, May 22, 1786, *AP*, 368.
11. AA to MC, January 20, 1787, AAS.
12. AA to TJ, July 6, 1787, *A-JL*, 183–184.
13. Ibid.
14. AA to LC, April 25, 1787, *AP*, 369.
15. AA to JQA, November 17, 1787, Ibid., 359.
16. AA to TJ, February 26, 1788, *A-JL*, 227–228.
17. AA to Mrs. Margaret Smith, April 22, 1788, *AP*, 371.
18. AA to Nabby, April 9, 1788, *LMA*, 67–69.
19. AAD, March 30–May 1, 1788, in *DAJA* 3:212–215.

Chapter XVIII
"You, I must and will have"

1. AA to Nabby, July 7, 1788, *J&CMA*.
2. Ibid.
3. JA to Nabby, July 16, 1788, Ibid., 2:87–89.
4. AA to MC, November 24, December 15, 18, 1788, *NL*, 3–7.
5. MC to AA, December 14, 1788, *AP*, 371.
6. JA to JL, July 16, 1789, *AP*, 372.
7. JA to AA, May 5, 1789, *AP*, 119.
8. JA to AA, May 14, 1789, *LJA*, 2:115–116.
9. AA to MC, June 28, 1789, *NL*, 11–14.
10. Ibid.
11. AA to MC, July 12, 1789, Ibid., 14–18.
12. Ibid.
13. AA to MC, August 9, 1789, Ibid., 18–22.
14. AA to CT, November 22, 1789, NYHS.
15. ESS to AA, March 14, 1790, *APm*.
16. AA to JQA, undated [ante July 11, 1790], *AP*, 374.
17. AA to MC, October 3, 1790, *NL*, 59–60.
18. AA to MC, November 7, 1790, Ibid., 64–65.
19. AA to MC, December 12, 1790, Ibid., 65–67.
20. AA to JQA, November 7, 1790, *AP*, 374.
21. AA to Nabby, January 25, 1791, *LMA*, 412–414.
22. AA to MC, December 18, 1791, *NL*, 75.
23. AA to CT, December 18, 1791, *APm*.

Chapter XIX
"a jewel of great price"

1. AA to MC, February 5, 1792, *NL*, 77.
2. AA to JA, November 26, 1792, *AP*, 375.
3. AA to JA, December 29, 1792, Ibid.
4. AA to JA, November 26, 1792, Ibid.
5. AA to JA, December 4, 1792, Ibid.
6. AA to JA, February 13, 1795, Ibid., 379.
7. AA to JA, March 26, 1794, *APm*.
8. AA to JA, May 17, 1794, Ibid.
9. AA to JA, January 5, 1794, Ibid.
10. AA to JA, February 2, 1794, Ibid.
11. AA to Martha Washington, June–July, 1794, *AP*, 377.
12. AA to JQA, September 15, 1795, *APm*.
13. Nabby to JQA, October 26–November 14, 1795, *AP*, 380.

Chapter XX
"Splendid Misery"

1. JA to AA, January 5, 1796, *APm*.
2. AA to JA, February 26, 1794, *APm*.
3. AA to JA, January 21, 1796, *AP*, 381.
4. AA to JA, February 14, 1796, Ibid.
5. AA to JA, February 20, 1796, Ibid.
6. JA to AA, March 1, 1796, Ibid.
7. AA to TBA, September 25, 1796, Ibid., 382.
8. AA to JQA, November 4, 1796, *APm*.
9. AA to JA, January 15, 1797, *APm*.
10. AA to JA, December 31, 1796, *APm*.
11. AA to JA, January 15, 1797, *APm*.
12. AA to JA, January 29, 1797, *APm*.
13. AA to JA, February 13, 1797, *APm*.
14. JA to AA, January 7, 1796, *LJA*, 2:189.
15. AA to JA, February 8, 1797, *LMA*, 2:235.
16. AA to JA, February 19, 1797, *APm*.
17. JA to AA, March 13, 1797, *APm*.
18. JA to AA, March 22, 1797, *APm*.
19. JA to AA, March 27, 1797, *APm*.

20. JA to AA, April 6,7, 1797, *APm*.
21. AA to JA, April 26, 1797, *LMA*, 2:236–237.
22. AA to MC, April 30, 1797, *NL*, 86–87.
23. May 5, 16, 1797, *NL*, 88–91.
24. AA to MC, May 16, 1797, *Ibid.*, 90.
25. AA to Elbridge Gerry, December 31, 1796, MHS, *Proceedings*, Vol. 57 (1923–1924): 499–500.
26. AA to MC, May 16, 1797, *NL*, 89–91.
27. AA to MC, May 26, 1798, Ibid., 182.
28. AA to MC, June 8, 1797, Ibid., 96–98.
29. AA to MC, July 6, 1797, Ibid., 100–102.
30. AA to MC, May 16, 1797, Ibid., 89–91.
31. AA to JQA, June 23–24, 1797, *APm*.
32. AA to MC, December 12, 1797, *NL*, 115–116.
33. AA to JQA, May 25, 1796, *APm*.
34. JQA to AA, August 16, 1796, *AP*, 382.
35. JQA to AA, February 8, 1797, Ibid., 383.
36. AA to MC, December 26, 1797, *NL*, 119–20.
37. AA to MC, February 6, 1798, Ibid., 130–131.
38. AA to MC, November 15, 1797, Ibid., 110–111.
39. AA to MC, December 27, 1797, Ibid., 119–120.
40. AA to MC, March 14, 1798, Ibid., 144–146.

Chapter XXI
"If man is Lord, woman is Lordess"

1. AA to MC, March 13, 1798, *NL*, 142–144.
2. AA to MC, April 26, 1798, Ibid., 164–166.
3. Ibid.
4. AA to MC, July 13, 1798, Ibid., 202–205.
5. JA to AA, January 5, 1799, *APm*.
6. JA to AA, November 28, 1798, *AP*, 119.
7. Fisher Ames, September 24, 1800.
8. JA to AA, December 17, 1798, *AP*, 392.
9. AA to JA, January 12, 1799, Ibid., 393.
10. AA to ESP, June 19, 1799, Smith Papers, Library of Congress.
11. JA to AA, October 6, 1799, *AP*, 120.
12. AA to MC, October 31, 1799, *NL*, 210–212.
13. AA to JA, May 22, 1800, *AP*, 397.

14. AA to MC, December 4, 1799, *NL*, 217–219.

15. AA to MC, March 15, 1800, Ibid., 238–242.

16. AA to WSS, December 25, 1799, Smith–Townsend Papers, MHS.

17. AA to MC, December 11, 1799, *NL*, 219–222.

18. AA to MC, May 5, 1800, Ibid., 250–252.

19. AA to MC, February 27, 1800, Ibid., 234.

20. AA to MC, May 26, 1800, Ibid., 252–253.

21. AA to JQA, September 1, 1800, *AP*, 398.

22. JA to AA, November 2, 1800, *LJA*, 2:113.

23. AA to MC, December 8, 1800, *NL*, 260–262.

24. AA to MC, November 21, 1800, Ibid., 256–260.

25. AA to MC, January 15, 1801, Ibid., 262–264.

26. AA to MC, November 21, 1800, Ibid., 256–260.

27. AA to Nabby, November 21, 1800, *LMA*, 432–435.

28. AA to CT, November 28, 1800, *AP*, 399.

29. JQA to JA, November 25, 1800, *Selected Writings of John and John Quincy Adams*, 253–255.

30. AA to TBA, November 13, 1800, *LMA*, 430–432.

31. AA to William Shaw, February 14, 1801, Shaw Family Papers, Library of Congress.

32. JA to Benjamin Stoddert, March 31, 1801, *Works*, 10:582.

33. AA to WSS, May 3, 1801, *LMA*, 436.

Chapter XXII
"young shoots and branches"

1. LCA, *Adventures of a Nobody*, *AP*, 269, beg. July 1, 1840.

2. AA to LCA, December 8, 1804, *AP*, 403.

3. AA to LCA, January 27, 1805, Ibid., 404.

4. AA to JQA, March 24, 1806, Ibid.

5. See Gelles, 147–149, for a fuller discussion.

6. AA to ESP, December 29, 1811, *APm*.

7. AA to ESP, June 5, 1809, *LMA*, 438–441.

8. AA to CS, August 12, 1809, *AP*, 408.

9. AA to JQA & LCA, August 5, 1809, Ibid.

10. AA to CS, November 30, 1809, *J&CMA*, 1:218.

11. AA to LCA, January 12, 1810, *AP*, 409.

Chapter XXIII
"What have I not lost"

1. AA to ESP, October 21, 1811, *AP*, 412.
2. AA to LCA, November 26, 1811, Ibid.
3. AA to JQA, December 8, 1811, Ibid.
4. JA to Benjamin Rush, July 19, 1812, quoted in Smith, 2:1113.
5. JQA to AA, September 21, 1812, *AP*, 414.
6. AA to HSG, February 20, 1810, Samuel Abbot Green Papers, MHS.
7. AA to TJ, May 20, 1804, *A-JL*, 268–269.
8. AA to TJ, July 1, 1804, Ibid., 271–274.
9. JA to TJ, August 16, 1813, Ibid., 366.
10. AA to JQA, October 22, 1813, *AP*, 416.
11. AA to JQA, September 24, 1813, Ibid.

Chapter XXIV
"Dearest Friend"

1. AA to James Monroe, April 20, 1813.
2. JA to JQA, June 25, 1816, *AP*, 432.
3. AA to ESS, June 5, 1809, *LMA*, 401–403.
4. AA to George Adams, May 25, 1812, *AP*, 413.
5. AA to JQA, May 20, 1796, Ibid., 379.
6. AA to JQA, May 30, 1815, Ibid., 122.
7. AA to ESS, June 5, 1809, *LMA*, 401–403.
8. AA to Nabby, May 8, 1808, *APm*.
9. AA to Harriet Welsh, December 8, 1814, Ibid., 421.
10. AA to ESP, February 10, 1814, Shaw Family Papers, Library of Congress.
11. Ibid.
12. AA to ESP, January 13, 1814, Ibid.
13. Ibid.
14. JA to JQA, June 25, 1816, *AP*, 122.
15. AA to JQA March 17, 1817, Ibid., 436.
16. AA to JQA, March 12, 1817, Ibid.
17. Quoted in Nagel, *Descent From Glory*, 131.
18. Ibid.
19. JA to TJ, October 20, 1818, *A-JL*, 528–529.
20. *Diary of JQA*, quoted in James Truslow Adams, 176.

Bibliography

Manuscript Sources

American Antiquarian Society. Worcester, Massachusetts.
  Abigail Adams Papers.

Library of Congress. Manuscript Division. Washington, D.C.
  Shaw Papers. Microfilm edition.

Massachusetts Historical Society. Boston, Massachusetts.
  Adams Papers. Microfilm edition, 609 reels.
  Cranch Family Papers.
  De Windt Collection.
  Smith–Carter Collection.

Secondary Sources

Adair, Douglas. *Fame and the Founding Fathers*. New York: W. W. Norton and Co., 1974.

Adams, James Truslow. *The Adams Family*. Boston: Little, Brown, and Co., 1930.

Akers, Charles W. *Abigail Adams: An American Woman*. Boston: Little, Brown, and Co., 1980.

Bailyn, Bernard. *Faces of Revolution*. New York: Alfred A. Knopf, 1990.

Bancroft, George. *History of the United States*. Vol. 3. New York: D. Appleton and Co., 1897.

Bober, Natalie S. *Thomas Jefferson: Man on a Mountain*. New York: Atheneum, 1988.

Bowen, Catherine Drinker. *John Adams and the American Revolution*. Boston: Little, Brown, and Co., 1950.

Chinard, Gilbert. *Honest John Adams*. Boston: Little, Brown, and Co., 1933.

Degler, Carl. *At Odds: Women and Family in America from the Revolution to the Present*. New York: Oxford University Press, 1980.

De Pauw, Linda Grant. *Founding Mothers: Women of America in the Revolutionary Era*. Boston: Houghton Mifflin Co., 1975.

East, Robert A. *John Quincy Adams: The Critical Years*. New York: Bookman Associates, Inc., 1962.

Ellis, Joseph J. *Passionate Sage*. New York: W. W. Norton and Co., 1993.

George, Carol V. R., ed. *"Remember the Ladies": New Perspectives on Women in American History*. Syracuse, N.Y.: Syracuse University Press, 1975.

Gelles, Edith B. *Portia: The World of Abigail Adams*. Bloomington and Indianapolis: Indiana University Press, 1992.

Harris, John. *American Rebels*. Boston: Globe Newspaper Co., 1976.

Harris, Wilhelmina S. *Adams National Historic Site*. Washington, D.C.: U.S. Department of the Interior National Park Service, 1983.

Kerber, Linda K. *Women of the Republic*. New York: W. W. Norton and Co., 1980.

Ketcham, Ralph. "The Puritan Ethic in the Revolutionary Era: Abigail Adams and Thomas Jefferson." In *Women in American History*. Syracuse, New York: Syracuse University Press, 1975.

Levin, Phyllis Lee. *Abigail Adams: A Biography*. New York: Ballantine Books, 1987.

Morgan, Edmund S. *The Meaning of Independence*. New York: W. W. Norton and Co., 1978.

Nagel, Paul C. *Adams Women*. New York: Oxford University Press, 1987.

———. *Descent From Glory*. New York: Oxford University Press, 1983.

Norton, Mary Beth. *Liberty's Daughters*. Boston: Little, Brown, and Co., 1980.

Notable American Women, 1607–1950: A Biographical Dictionary. Vol. 1. Cambridge, Mass.: The Belknap Press of Harvard University Press, 1971.

Oliver, Andrew. *Portraits of John and Abigail Adams*. Cambridge, Mass.: The Belknap Press of Harvard University, 1967.

Peterson, Merrill D. *Adams and Jefferson: A Revolutionary Dialogue*. New York: Oxford University Press, 1976.

Russell, Francis. *Adams: An American Dynasty*. New York: American Heritage Publishing Co., 1976.

Scheer, George F., and Hugh F. Rankin. *Rebels and Redcoats*. New York: Da Capo Press, 1987.

Shaw, Peter. *The Character of John Adams*. Chapel Hill, N.C.: University of North Carolina Press, 1976.

Shepherd, Jack. *The Adams Chronicles*. Boston: Little, Brown, and Co., 1975.

Smith, Page. *John Adams*. 2 vols. Garden City, N.Y.: Doubleday and Co., 1962.

Withey, Lynne. *Dearest Friend: A Life of Abigail Adams*. New York: Free Press, 1981.

Periodicals

Illick, Joseph E. "John Quincy Adams: The Maternal Influence." *Journal of Psychohistory* 4 (Autumn 1976): 185–195.

Musto, David F. "The Adams Family." *Proceedings of the Massachusetts Historical Society* 93 (1981): 40–58.

———. "The Youth of John Quincy Adams." *Proceedings of the American Philosophical Society* 113 (August 1969): 269–282.

Shaw, Peter. "All in the Family: A Psychobiography of the Adamses." *The American Scholar* (Autumn 1985).

The Writings of John and Abigail Adams

Adams, Charles Francis, ed. *The Familiar Letters of John Adams and his Wife Abigail Adams, during the Revolution*. Boston: Houghton Mifflin, 1875.

———, ed. *Letters of John Adams Addressed to his Wife*. 2 vols. Boston: Freeman and Bolles, 1841.

———, ed. *Letters of Mrs. Adams, Wife of John Adams*. 2 vols. 2nd ed. Boston: Charles C. Little and James Brown, 1840.

———, ed. *Memoirs of John Quincy Adams*. 2 vols. Philadelphia: J. B. Lippincott and Co., 1874–1877.

———, ed. *The Works of John Adams*. 10 vols. Boston: Charles C. Little and James Brown, 1850.

Butterfield, L. H., ed. *Adams Family Correspondence*. 4 vols. Cambridge, Mass.: Belknap Press of Harvard University Press, 1963–1973.

———, ed. *The Adams Papers*. 5 vols. Cambridge, Mass.: Belknap Press of Harvard University Press, 1962.

———, ed. *Diary and Autobiography of John Adams*. Cambridge, Mass.: Belknap Press of Harvard University, 1962.

———, ed. *John Adams' Earliest Diary*. Cambridge, Mass.: Belknap Press of Harvard University, 1966.

Butterfield, L. H., Marc Friedlaender, and Mary-Jo Kline, eds. *The Book of Abigail and John: Selected Letters of the Adams Family 1762–1784*. Cambridge, Mass.: Harvard University Press, 1975.

Cappon, Lester J., ed. The Adams-Jefferson Letters. Chapel Hill, N.C.: University of North Carolina Press, 1988.

De Windt, Caroline Smith, ed. *Journal and Correspondence of Miss Adams*. 2 vols. New York and London: Wiley and Putnam, 1841.

Koch, Adrienne, and William Peden, eds. *The Selected Writings of John and John Quincy Adams*. New York: Alfred A. Knopf, 1946.

Mitchell, Stewart, ed. *New Letters of Abigail Adams 1788–1801*. Westport, Conn.: Greenwood Press, 1973.

Nevins, Allan, ed. *The Diary of John Quincy Adams 1794–1845*. New York: Longmans, Green, and Co., 1929.

Unpublished Letters of Abigail Adams in the American Antiquarian Society and the New York Historical Society.

Index